To Drink and To Eat

more meals and mischief from a French Kitchen

Introduction

YOU'VE SEEN IT IN YOUR DREAMS... OR MAYBE NEVER GIVEN IT A THOUGHT. IN HONOR OF THE PUBLICATION OF THE FIRST VOLUME BY LION FORGE, WELCOME TO...

Behind the scenes at TDTE*

A RETROSPECTIVE IN IMAGES OF THE INCREDIBLE ADVENTURE OF AN UNCONVENTIONAL BOOK OF GROWING SUCCESS, AS WELL AS AN INSIDER'S LOOK INTO A TYPICAL WORKDAY, AS AUTHORIZED BY ITS GENEROUS CREATOR, GUILLAUME LONG:

*"TO DRINK AND TO EAT" AMONG FRIENDS.

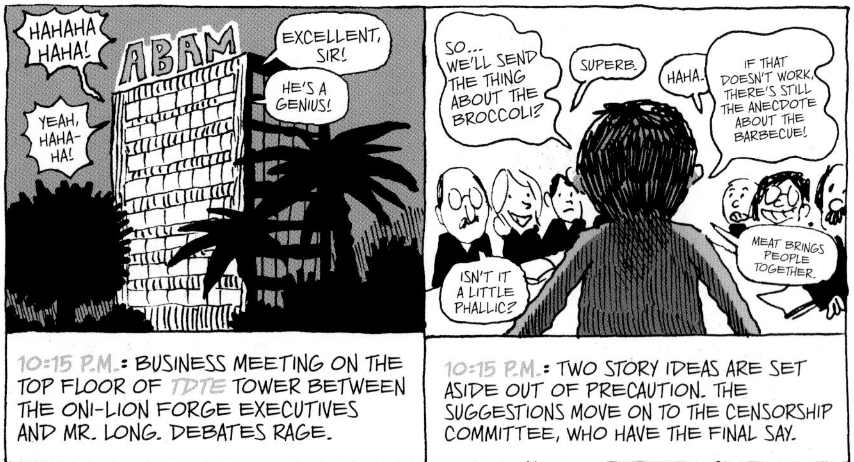
HAHAHA HAHA!
ABAM
EXCELLENT, SIR!
HE'S A GENIUS!
YEAH, HAHA-HA!
10:15 P.M.: BUSINESS MEETING ON THE TOP FLOOR OF TDTE TOWER BETWEEN THE ONI-LION FORGE EXECUTIVES AND MR. LONG. DEBATES RAGE.
SO... WE'LL SEND THE THING ABOUT THE BROCCOLI?
SUPERB.
HAHA.
IF THAT DOESN'T WORK, THERE'S STILL THE ANECDOTE ABOUT THE BARBECUE!
ISN'T IT A LITTLE PHALLIC?
MEAT BRINGS PEOPLE TOGETHER.
10:15 P.M.: TWO STORY IDEAS ARE SET ASIDE OUT OF PRECAUTION. THE SUGGESTIONS MOVE ON TO THE CENSORSHIP COMMITTEE, WHO HAVE THE FINAL SAY.

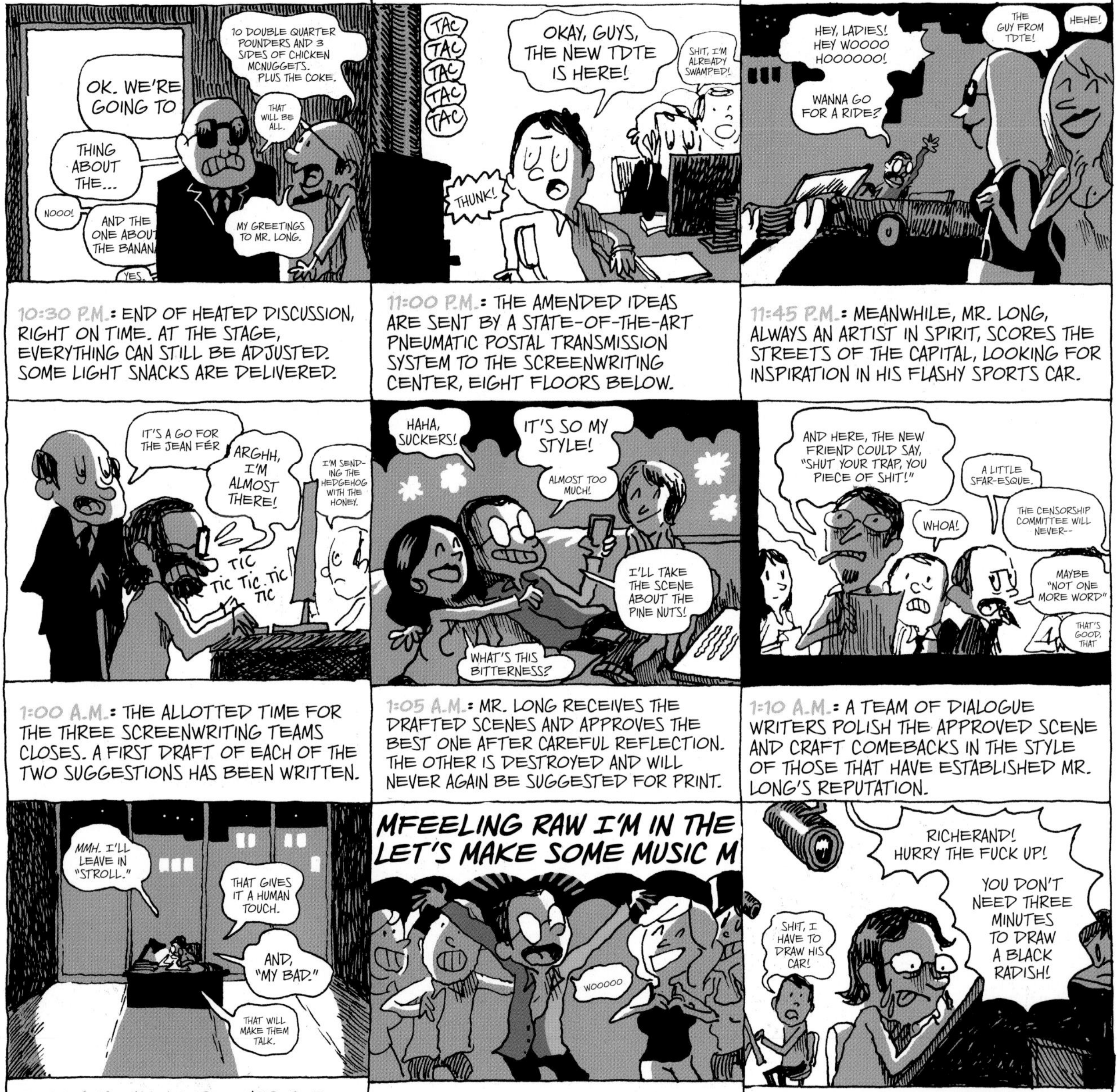
OK. WE'RE GOING TO
THING ABOUT THE...
10 DOUBLE QUARTER POUNDERS AND 3 SIDES OF CHICKEN MCNUGGETS. PLUS THE COKE.
THAT WILL BE ALL.
NOOO!
AND THE ONE ABOUT THE BANANA
MY GREETINGS TO MR. LONG.
YES.
10:30 P.M.: END OF HEATED DISCUSSION, RIGHT ON TIME. AT THE STAGE, EVERYTHING CAN STILL BE ADJUSTED. SOME LIGHT SNACKS ARE DELIVERED.
TAC TAC TAC TAC TAC
OKAY, GUYS, THE NEW TDTE IS HERE!
SHIT, I'M ALREADY SWAMPED!
THUNK!
11:00 P.M.: THE AMENDED IDEAS ARE SENT BY A STATE-OF-THE-ART PNEUMATIC POSTAL TRANSMISSION SYSTEM TO THE SCREENWRITING CENTER, EIGHT FLOORS BELOW.
HEY, LADIES! HEY WOOOO HOOOOOO!
THE GUY FROM TDTE!
HEHE!
WANNA GO FOR A RIDE?
11:45 P.M.: MEANWHILE, MR. LONG, ALWAYS AN ARTIST IN SPIRIT, SCORES THE STREETS OF THE CAPITAL, LOOKING FOR INSPIRATION IN HIS FLASHY SPORTS CAR.
IT'S A GO FOR THE JEAN FÉR
ARGHH, I'M ALMOST THERE!
I'M SENDING THE HEDGEHOG WITH THE HONEY.
TIC TIC TIC TIC TIC
1:00 A.M.: THE ALLOTTED TIME FOR THE THREE SCREENWRITING TEAMS CLOSES. A FIRST DRAFT OF EACH OF THE TWO SUGGESTIONS HAS BEEN WRITTEN.
HAHA, SUCKERS!
IT'S SO MY STYLE!
ALMOST TOO MUCH!
I'LL TAKE THE SCENE ABOUT THE PINE NUTS!
WHAT'S THIS BITTERNESS?
1:05 A.M.: MR. LONG RECEIVES THE DRAFTED SCENES AND APPROVES THE BEST ONE AFTER CAREFUL REFLECTION. THE OTHER IS DESTROYED AND WILL NEVER AGAIN BE SUGGESTED FOR PRINT.
AND HERE, THE NEW FRIEND COULD SAY, "SHUT YOUR TRAP, YOU PIECE OF SHIT!"
A LITTLE SFAR-ESQUE.
WHOA!
THE CENSORSHIP COMMITTEE WILL NEVER--
MAYBE "NOT ONE MORE WORD"
THAT'S GOOD, THAT
1:10 A.M.: A TEAM OF DIALOGUE WRITERS POLISH THE APPROVED SCENE AND CRAFT COMEBACKS IN THE STYLE OF THOSE THAT HAVE ESTABLISHED MR. LONG'S REPUTATION.
MMH. I'LL LEAVE IN "STROLL."
THAT GIVES IT A HUMAN TOUCH.
AND, "MY BAD."
THAT WILL MAKE THEM TALK.
3:00 A.M.: ALL LOOSE ENDS TIED UP, THE SCRIPT IS SENT TO THE PROOFREADER, ONE FLOOR ABOVE, WHO ENSURES THE HUMANNESS OF THE PROPOSED SYNTAX.
MFEELING RAW I'M IN THE
LET'S MAKE SOME MUSIC M
WOOOOO
3:30 A.M.: STILL GOING STRONG, MR. LONG ENJOYS OBSERVING THE EXCESSES OF HIS CONTEMPORARIES, WHICH HE WILL TRANSCRIBE LATER INTO A FUTURE LITTLE STORY WHOSE TRUTHS ARE ONLY HIS TO KNOW.
RICHERAND! HURRY THE FUCK UP!
YOU DON'T NEED THREE MINUTES TO DRAW A BLACK RADISH!
SHIT, I HAVE TO DRAW HIS CAR!
4:00 A.M.: IN THE BASEMENT OF TDTE, THE DEFT LITTLE HANDS OF THE GRAPHICS TEAM BRING TO LIFE THE SCRIPT OF THE NIGHT. MAGIC OF CREATION, BREATHTAKING BIRTH OF ART.

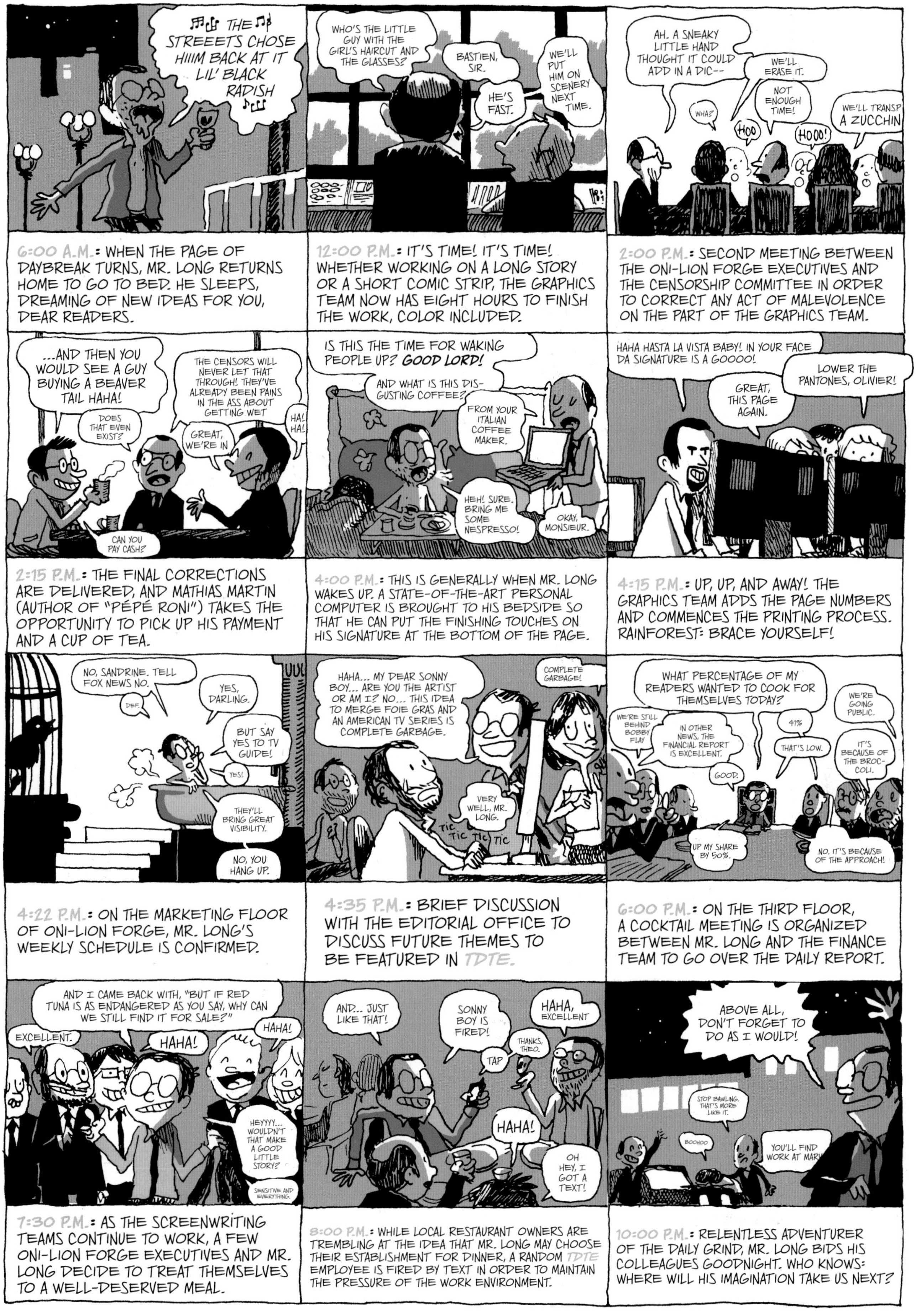
♫ THE ♫ STREEETS CHOSE HIIIM BACK AT IT LIL' BLACK RADISH ♫
6:00 A.M.: WHEN THE PAGE OF DAYBREAK TURNS, MR. LONG RETURNS HOME TO GO TO BED. HE SLEEPS, DREAMING OF NEW IDEAS FOR YOU, DEAR READERS.
WHO'S THE LITTLE GUY WITH THE GIRL'S HAIRCUT AND THE GLASSES?
BASTIEN, SIR.
HE'S FAST.
WE'LL PUT HIM ON SCENERY NEXT TIME.
12:00 P.M.: IT'S TIME! IT'S TIME! WHETHER WORKING ON A LONG STORY OR A SHORT COMIC STRIP, THE GRAPHICS TEAM NOW HAS EIGHT HOURS TO FINISH THE WORK, COLOR INCLUDED.
AH. A SNEAKY LITTLE HAND THOUGHT IT COULD ADD IN A DIC--
WHA?
WE'LL ERASE IT.
HOO
NOT ENOUGH TIME!
HOOO!
WE'LL TRANSP A ZUCCHIN
2:00 P.M.: SECOND MEETING BETWEEN THE ONI-LION FORGE EXECUTIVES AND THE CENSORSHIP COMMITTEE IN ORDER TO CORRECT ANY ACT OF MALEVOLENCE ON THE PART OF THE GRAPHICS TEAM.
...AND THEN YOU WOULD SEE A GUY BUYING A BEAVER TAIL HAHA!
DOES THAT EVEN EXIST?
THE CENSORS WILL NEVER LET THAT THROUGH! THEY'VE ALREADY BEEN PAINS IN THE ASS ABOUT GETTING WET
GREAT, WE'RE IN
HA! HA!
CAN YOU PAY CASH?
2:15 P.M.: THE FINAL CORRECTIONS ARE DELIVERED, AND MATHIAS MARTIN (AUTHOR OF "PÉPÉ RONI") TAKES THE OPPORTUNITY TO PICK UP HIS PAYMENT AND A CUP OF TEA.
IS THIS THE TIME FOR WAKING PEOPLE UP? GOOD LORD!
AND WHAT IS THIS DISGUSTING COFFEE?
FROM YOUR ITALIAN COFFEE MAKER.
HEH! SURE. BRING ME SOME NESPRESSO!
OKAY, MONSIEUR.
4:00 P.M.: THIS IS GENERALLY WHEN MR. LONG WAKES UP. A STATE-OF-THE-ART PERSONAL COMPUTER IS BROUGHT TO HIS BEDSIDE SO THAT HE CAN PUT THE FINISHING TOUCHES ON HIS SIGNATURE AT THE BOTTOM OF THE PAGE.
HAHA HASTA LA VISTA BABY! IN YOUR FACE DA SIGNATURE IS A GOOOO!
GREAT, THIS PAGE AGAIN.
LOWER THE PANTONES, OLIVIER!
4:15 P.M.: UP, UP, AND AWAY! THE GRAPHICS TEAM ADDS THE PAGE NUMBERS AND COMMENCES THE PRINTING PROCESS. RAINFOREST: BRACE YOURSELF!
NO, SANDRINE. TELL FOX NEWS NO.
DEF.
YES, DARLING.
BUT SAY YES TO TV GUIDE!
YES!
THEY'LL BRING GREAT VISIBILITY.
NO, YOU HANG UP.
4:22 P.M.: ON THE MARKETING FLOOR OF ONI-LION FORGE, MR. LONG'S WEEKLY SCHEDULE IS CONFIRMED.
HAHA... MY DEAR SONNY BOY... ARE YOU THE ARTIST OR AM I? NO... THIS IDEA TO MERGE FOIE GRAS AND AN AMERICAN TV SERIES IS COMPLETE GARBAGE.
COMPLETE GARBAGE!
VERY WELL, MR. LONG.
TIC TIC TIC TIC
4:35 P.M.: BRIEF DISCUSSION WITH THE EDITORIAL OFFICE TO DISCUSS FUTURE THEMES TO BE FEATURED IN TDTE.
WHAT PERCENTAGE OF MY READERS WANTED TO COOK FOR THEMSELVES TODAY?
WE'RE STILL BEHIND BOBBY FLAY
IN OTHER NEWS, THE FINANCIAL REPORT IS EXCELLENT.
GOOD.
41%
THAT'S LOW.
WE'RE GOING PUBLIC.
IT'S BECAUSE OF THE BROCCOLI.
UP MY SHARE BY 50%.
NO. IT'S BECAUSE OF THE APPROACH!
6:00 P.M.: ON THE THIRD FLOOR, A COCKTAIL MEETING IS ORGANIZED BETWEEN MR. LONG AND THE FINANCE TEAM TO GO OVER THE DAILY REPORT.
AND I CAME BACK WITH, "BUT IF RED TUNA IS AS ENDANGERED AS YOU SAY, WHY CAN WE STILL FIND IT FOR SALE?"
EXCELLENT.
HAHA!
HAHA!
HEYYYY... WOULDN'T THAT MAKE A GOOD LITTLE STORY?
SENSITIVE AND EVERYTHING.
7:30 P.M.: AS THE SCREENWRITING TEAMS CONTINUE TO WORK, A FEW ONI-LION FORGE EXECUTIVES AND MR. LONG DECIDE TO TREAT THEMSELVES TO A WELL-DESERVED MEAL.
AND... JUST LIKE THAT!
SONNY BOY IS FIRED!
HAHA, EXCELLENT
THANKS, THEO.
TAP
HAHA!
OH HEY, I GOT A TEXT!
8:00 P.M.: WHILE LOCAL RESTAURANT OWNERS ARE TREMBLING AT THE IDEA THAT MR. LONG MAY CHOOSE THEIR ESTABLISHMENT FOR DINNER, A RANDOM TDTE EMPLOYEE IS FIRED BY TEXT IN ORDER TO MAINTAIN THE PRESSURE OF THE WORK ENVIRONMENT.
ABOVE ALL, DON'T FORGET TO DO AS I WOULD!
STOP BAWLING. THAT'S MORE LIKE IT.
BOOHOO
YOU'LL FIND WORK AT MAR
10:00 P.M.: RELENTLESS ADVENTURER OF THE DAILY GRIND, MR. LONG BIDS HIS COLLEAGUES GOODNIGHT. WHO KNOWS: WHERE WILL HIS IMAGINATION TAKE US NEXT?

To Drink and To Eat

more meals and mischief from a French Kitchen

— GUILLAUME LONG —

Volume 2

Colors by Céline Badarous Denizon
and Guillaume Long

AN ONI PRESS PUBLICATION

This book is dedicated to all those who kept me from
having a heart attack after I screwed up a recipe.

G. L.

English Translation by Sylvia M. Grove
Lettering by AndWorld Design's DC Hopkins
Colors by Céline Badarous Denizon and Guillaume Long
Cover Art by Guillaume Long
Front Cover Design by Robin Allen
Cover Jacket Design by Sonja Synak
Interior Design by Sonja Synak

The "Pépé Roni" comic strips are the work of artist Mathias Martin and originally appeared in the magazine *French Cuisine*.

A thank you to Capucine (p. 108-109) as well as Dominique Goblet and Nancy Peña (p. 28) for their beautiful drawings.
Thanks also to Olivier Merlin for the subtitle.

Published by Oni-Lion Forge Publishing Group, LLC

James Lucas Jones, president & publisher • Sarah Gaydos, editor in chief • Charlie Chu, e.v.p. of creative & business development
Brad Rooks, director of operations • Amber O'Neill, special projects manager • Harris Fish, events manager • Margot Wood, director of
marketing & sales • Devin Funches, sales & marketing manager • Katie Sainz, marketing manager • Tara Lehmann, publicist • Troy Look,
director of design & production • Kate Z. Stone, senior graphic designer • Sonja Synak, graphic designer • Hilary Thompson, graphic
designer • Sarah Rockwell, junior graphic designer • Angie Knowles, digital prepress lead • Vincent Kukua, digital prepress technician
Jasmine Amiri, senior editor • Shawna Gore, senior editor • Amanda Meadows, senior editor • Robert Meyers, senior editor, licensing •
Grace Bornhoft, editor • Zack Soto, editor • Chris Cerasi, editorial coordinator • Steve Ellis, vice president of games • Ben Eisner, game
developer Michelle Nguyen, executive assistant • Jung Lee, logistics coordinator

Joe Nozemack, publisher emeritus

1319 SE Martin Luther King, Jr. Blvd.
Suite 240
Portland, OR 97214

onipress.com 🅕 🅨 🅞 lionforge.com

lemonde.fr/blog/long
facebook.com/0c0ABAM
twitter.com/0c0ABAM
instagram.com/0c0ABAM

First Edition: January 2021

ISBN: 978-1-62010-855-0
eISBN: 978-1-62010-856-7

1 2 3 4 5 6 7 8 9 10

Library of Congress Control Number 2019945813

Printed in China.

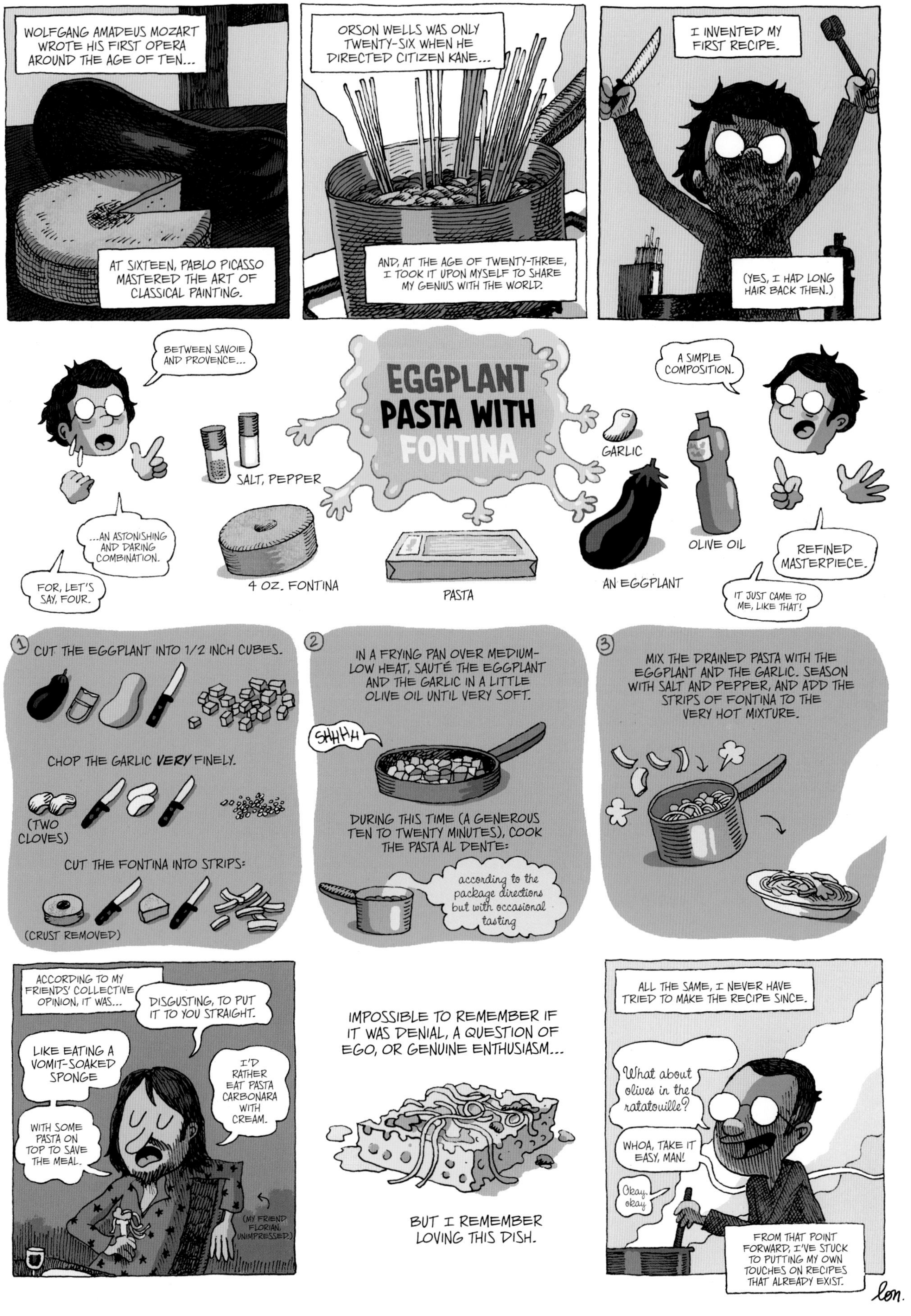
WOLFGANG AMADEUS MOZART WROTE HIS FIRST OPERA AROUND THE AGE OF TEN...
AT SIXTEEN, PABLO PICASSO MASTERED THE ART OF CLASSICAL PAINTING.
ORSON WELLS WAS ONLY TWENTY-SIX WHEN HE DIRECTED CITIZEN KANE...
AND, AT THE AGE OF TWENTY-THREE, I TOOK IT UPON MYSELF TO SHARE MY GENIUS WITH THE WORLD.
I INVENTED MY FIRST RECIPE.
(YES, I HAD LONG HAIR BACK THEN.)
BETWEEN SAVOIE AND PROVENCE...
...AN ASTONISHING AND DARING COMBINATION.
FOR, LET'S SAY, FOUR.
EGGPLANT PASTA WITH FONTINA
SALT, PEPPER
4 OZ. FONTINA
PASTA
GARLIC
AN EGGPLANT
OLIVE OIL
A SIMPLE COMPOSITION.
REFINED MASTERPIECE.
IT JUST CAME TO ME, LIKE THAT!
1 CUT THE EGGPLANT INTO 1/2 INCH CUBES.
CHOP THE GARLIC VERY FINELY.
(TWO CLOVES)
CUT THE FONTINA INTO STRIPS:
(CRUST REMOVED)
2 IN A FRYING PAN OVER MEDIUM-LOW HEAT, SAUTÉ THE EGGPLANT AND THE GARLIC IN A LITTLE OLIVE OIL UNTIL VERY SOFT.
SHHHH
DURING THIS TIME (A GENEROUS TEN TO TWENTY MINUTES), COOK THE PASTA AL DENTE:
according to the package directions but with occasional tasting
3 MIX THE DRAINED PASTA WITH THE EGGPLANT AND THE GARLIC. SEASON WITH SALT AND PEPPER, AND ADD THE STRIPS OF FONTINA TO THE VERY HOT MIXTURE.
ACCORDING TO MY FRIENDS' COLLECTIVE OPINION, IT WAS...
DISGUSTING, TO PUT IT TO YOU STRAIGHT.
LIKE EATING A VOMIT-SOAKED SPONGE
I'D RATHER EAT PASTA CARBONARA WITH CREAM.
WITH SOME PASTA ON TOP TO SAVE THE MEAL.
(MY FRIEND FLORIAN, UNIMPRESSED)
IMPOSSIBLE TO REMEMBER IF IT WAS DENIAL, A QUESTION OF EGO, OR GENUINE ENTHUSIASM...
BUT I REMEMBER LOVING THIS DISH.
ALL THE SAME, I NEVER HAVE TRIED TO MAKE THE RECIPE SINCE.
What about olives in the ratatouille?
WHOA, TAKE IT EASY, MAN!
Okay, okay
FROM THAT POINT FORWARD, I'VE STUCK TO PUTTING MY OWN TOUCHES ON RECIPES THAT ALREADY EXIST.
lon.

Contents

Manual

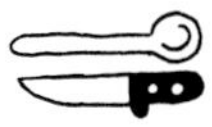

Level 1: Recipes requiring no cooking experience. Quick, with no actual cooking involved.

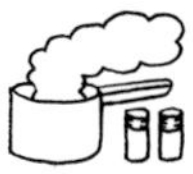

Level 2: Recipes that are slightly more involved, take some time, and require some cooking.

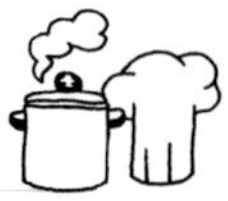

Level 3: Very difficult recipes (only sometimes; I'm mostly joking).

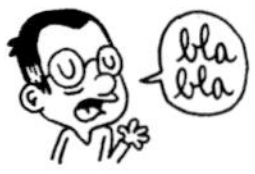
bla bla

Egotrip: Stories that feature my mug(shot).

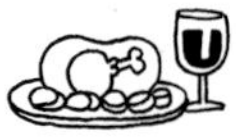

Restaurant: Stories of meals in places that I like.

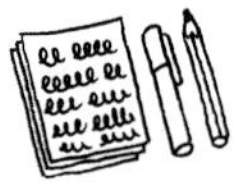

Inventory: Useful lists for foodies.

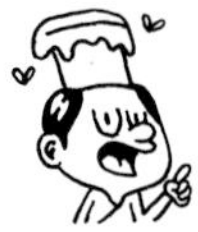

Joël Reblochon: Cooking tips and history presented by the late Joël Reblochon.

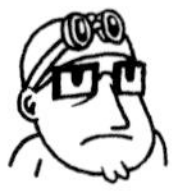

New Friend: Cooking commentary provided by my friend Florian.

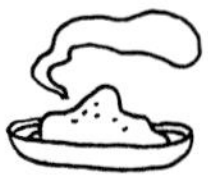

Leftovers: Everything else that doesn't fit into the other categories of this book.

Spring

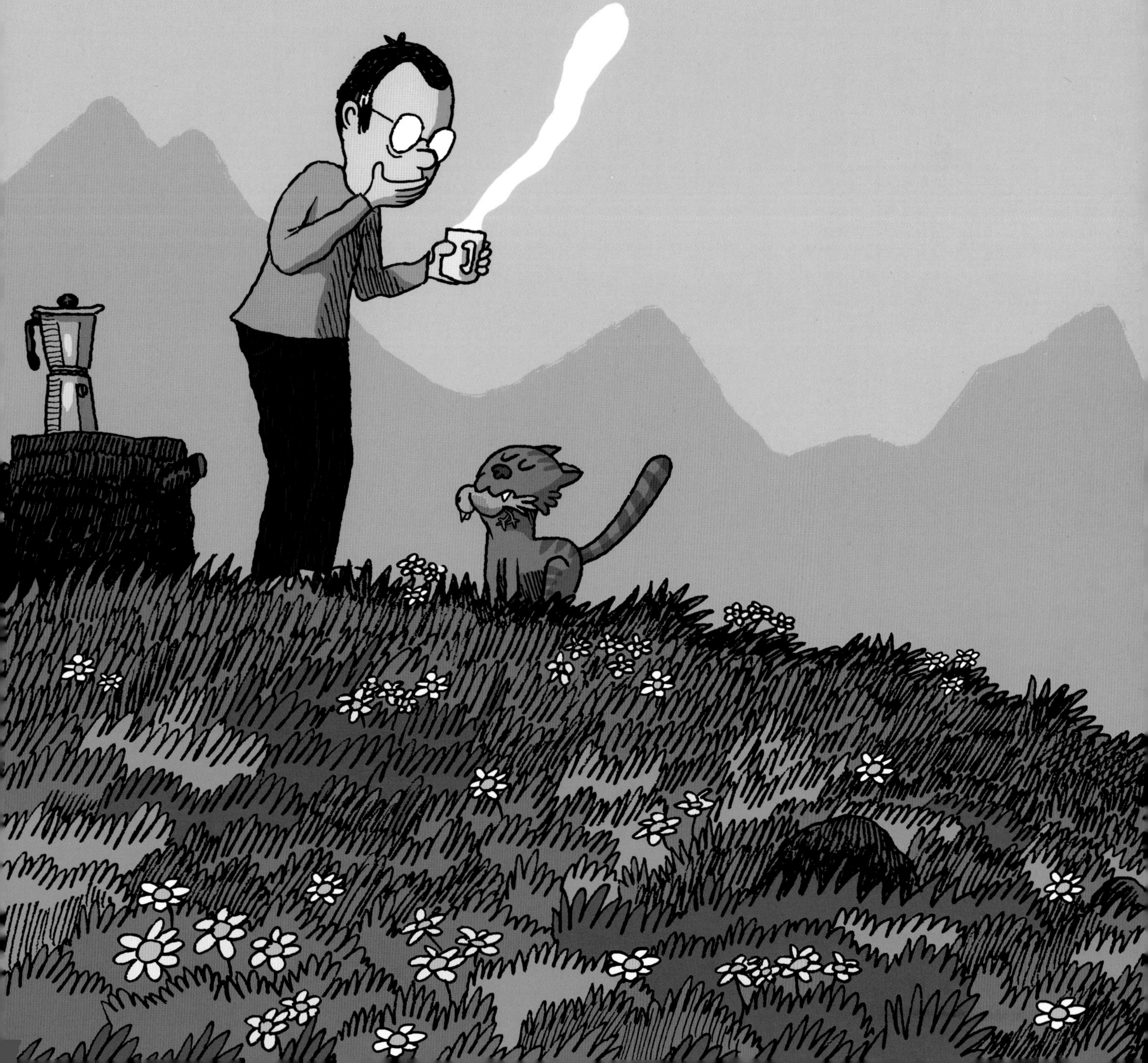

Every morning presents me with the horrendous ordeal of getting out of my cozy bed and waking up.

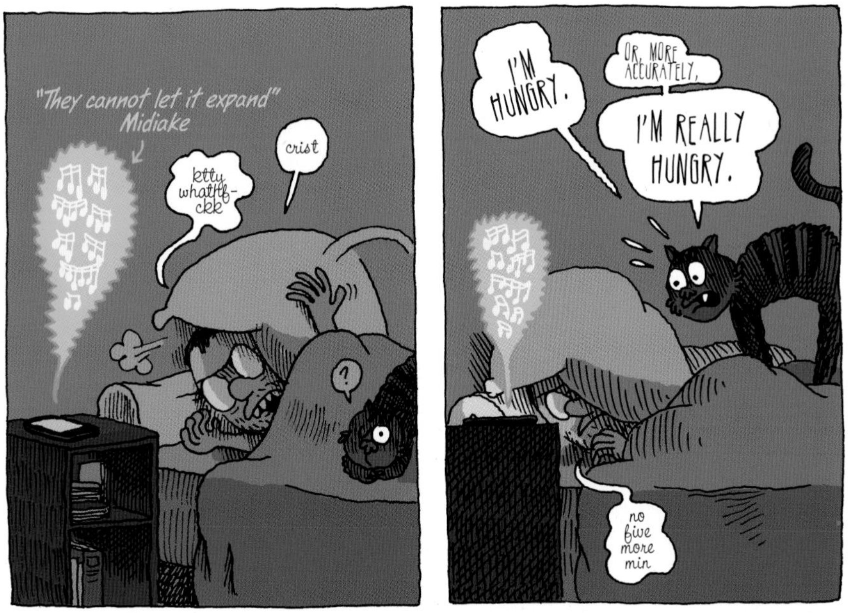
"They cannot let it expand"
Midiake
crist
I'M HUNGRY.
OR, MORE ACCURATELY,
I'M REALLY HUNGRY.
no five more min

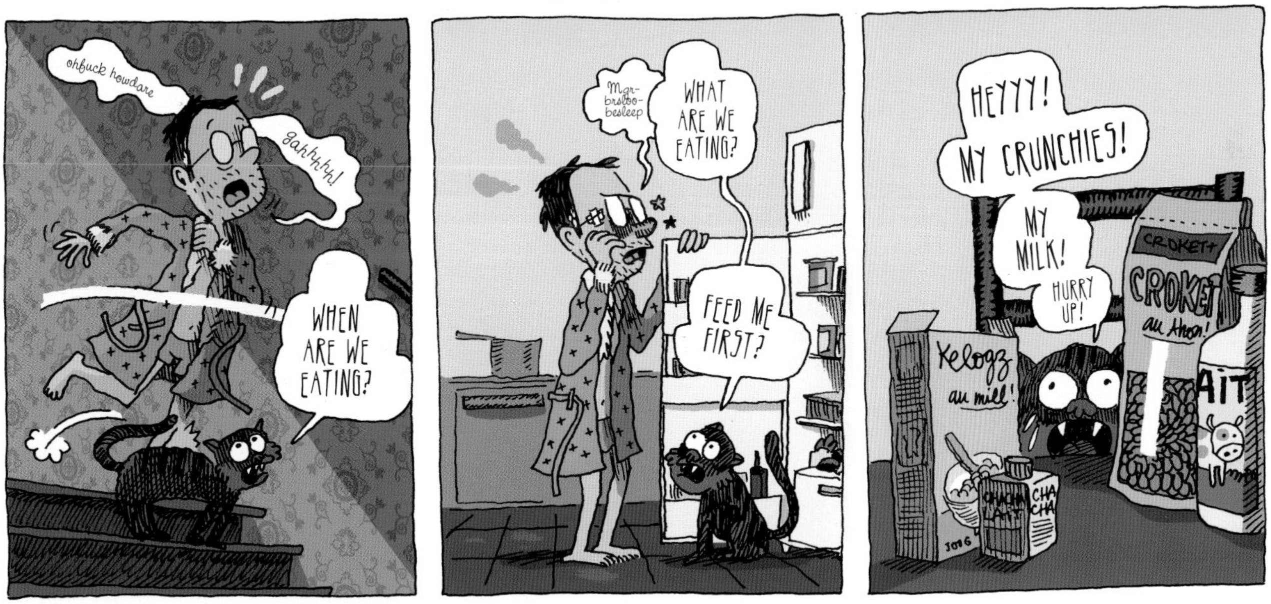
ohfuck howdare
gahhhh!
WHEN ARE WE EATING?
Mgr-brsboo-besleep
WHAT ARE WE EATING?
FEED ME FIRST?
HEYYY! MY CRUNCHIES!
MY MILK!
HURRY UP!
Kelogz au miel!
CROKETT
CROKET au thon!
LAIT

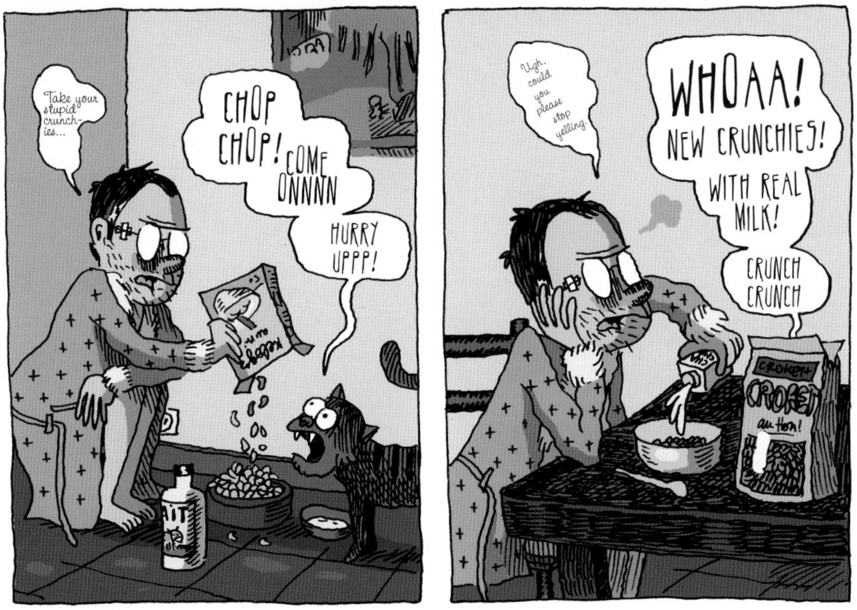
Take your stupid crunch-ies...
CHOP CHOP!
COME ONNNN
HURRY UPPP!
Ugh. could you please stop yelling
WHOAA! NEW CRUNCHIES!
WITH REAL MILK!
CRUNCH CRUNCH
CROKET
CROKET au thon!

But the real challenge of each day? Not mistaking my cat's tail for my paint brushes.

lon.

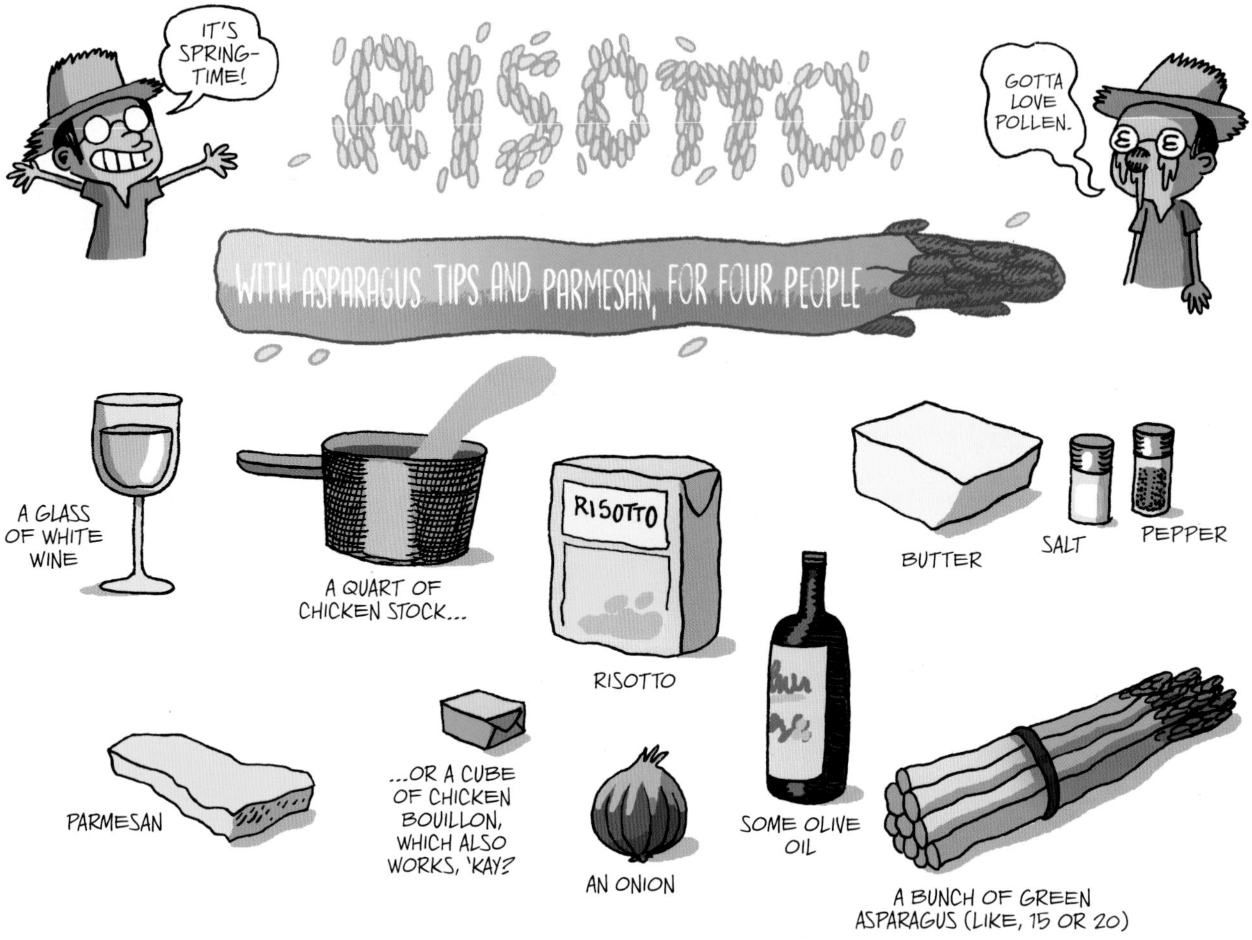
IT'S SPRING-TIME!
RISOTTO
GOTTA LOVE POLLEN.
WITH ASPARAGUS TIPS AND PARMESAN, FOR FOUR PEOPLE
A GLASS OF WHITE WINE
A QUART OF CHICKEN STOCK...
RISOTTO
RISOTTO
BUTTER
SALT
PEPPER
PARMESAN
...OR A CUBE OF CHICKEN BOUILLON, WHICH ALSO WORKS, 'KAY?
AN ONION
SOME OLIVE OIL
A BUNCH OF GREEN ASPARAGUS (LIKE, 15 OR 20)

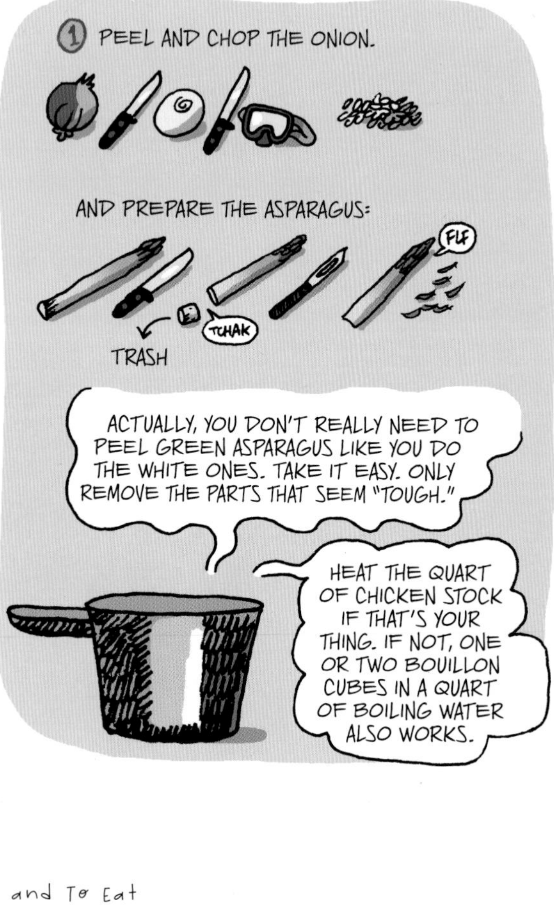
1 PEEL AND CHOP THE ONION.
AND PREPARE THE ASPARAGUS:
FLF
TCHAK
TRASH
ACTUALLY, YOU DON'T REALLY NEED TO PEEL GREEN ASPARAGUS LIKE YOU DO THE WHITE ONES. TAKE IT EASY. ONLY REMOVE THE PARTS THAT SEEM "TOUGH."
HEAT THE QUART OF CHICKEN STOCK IF THAT'S YOUR THING. IF NOT, ONE OR TWO BOUILLON CUBES IN A QUART OF BOILING WATER ALSO WORKS.

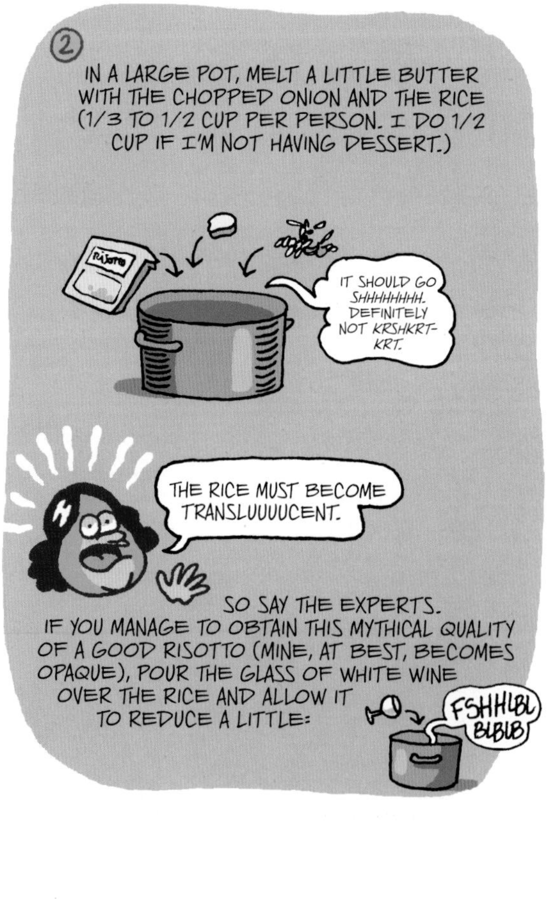
2 IN A LARGE POT, MELT A LITTLE BUTTER WITH THE CHOPPED ONION AND THE RICE (1/3 TO 1/2 CUP PER PERSON. I DO 1/2 CUP IF I'M NOT HAVING DESSERT.)
RISOTTO
IT SHOULD GO SHHHHHHHH. DEFINITELY NOT KRSHKRT-KRT.
THE RICE MUST BECOME TRANSLUUUUCENT.
SO SAY THE EXPERTS.
IF YOU MANAGE TO OBTAIN THIS MYTHICAL QUALITY OF A GOOD RISOTTO (MINE, AT BEST, BECOMES OPAQUE), POUR THE GLASS OF WHITE WINE OVER THE RICE AND ALLOW IT TO REDUCE A LITTLE:
FSHHLBL BLBLB

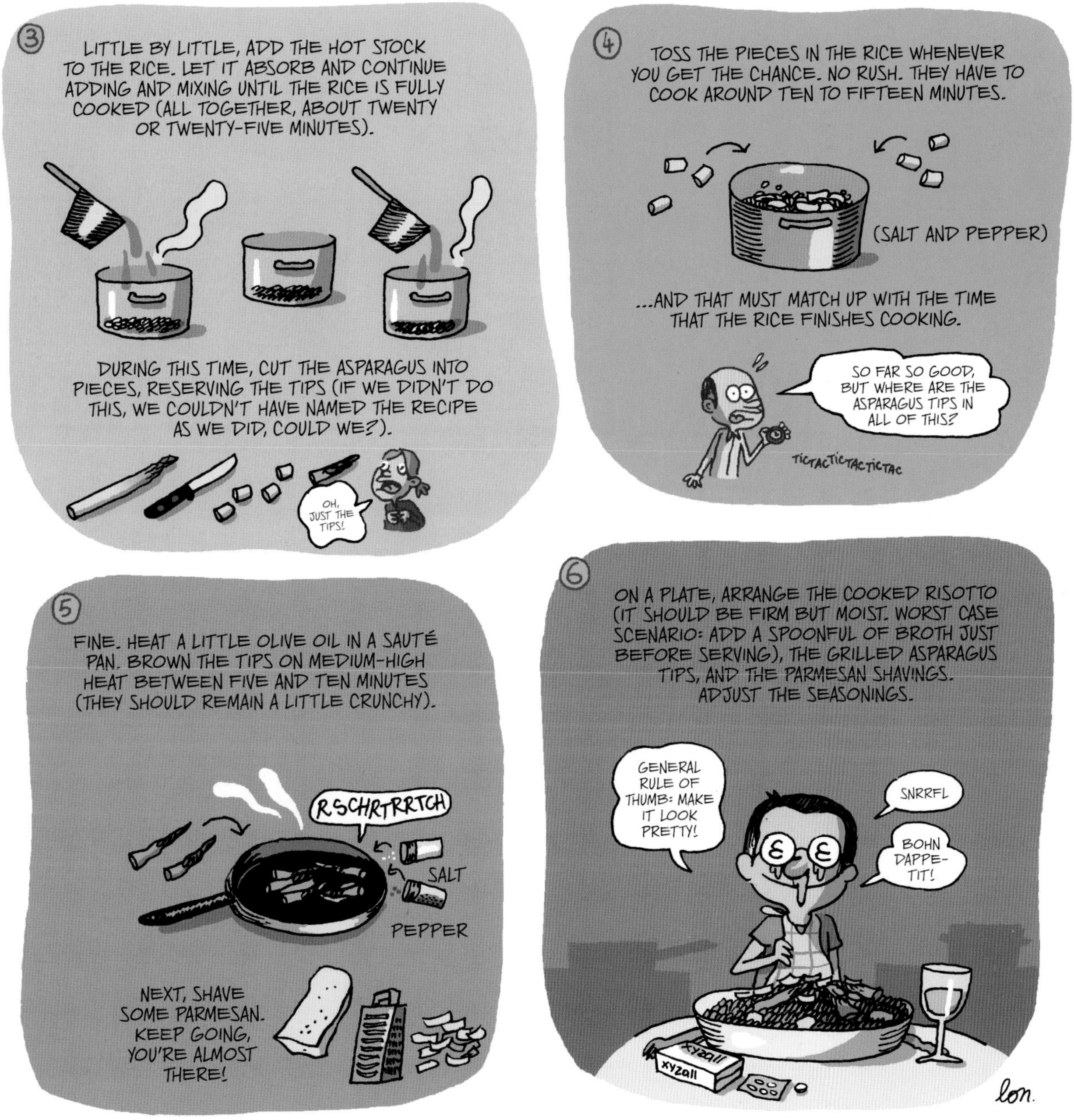
3
LITTLE BY LITTLE, ADD THE HOT STOCK TO THE RICE. LET IT ABSORB AND CONTINUE ADDING AND MIXING UNTIL THE RICE IS FULLY COOKED (ALL TOGETHER, ABOUT TWENTY OR TWENTY-FIVE MINUTES).
DURING THIS TIME, CUT THE ASPARAGUS INTO PIECES, RESERVING THE TIPS (IF WE DIDN'T DO THIS, WE COULDN'T HAVE NAMED THE RECIPE AS WE DID, COULD WE?).
OH, JUST THE TIPS!
4
TOSS THE PIECES IN THE RICE WHENEVER YOU GET THE CHANCE. NO RUSH. THEY HAVE TO COOK AROUND TEN TO FIFTEEN MINUTES.
(SALT AND PEPPER)
...AND THAT MUST MATCH UP WITH THE TIME THAT THE RICE FINISHES COOKING.
SO FAR SO GOOD, BUT WHERE ARE THE ASPARAGUS TIPS IN ALL OF THIS?
TICTACTICTACTICTAC
5
FINE. HEAT A LITTLE OLIVE OIL IN A SAUTÉ PAN. BROWN THE TIPS ON MEDIUM-HIGH HEAT BETWEEN FIVE AND TEN MINUTES (THEY SHOULD REMAIN A LITTLE CRUNCHY).
RSCHRTRRTCH
SALT
PEPPER
NEXT, SHAVE SOME PARMESAN. KEEP GOING, YOU'RE ALMOST THERE!
6
ON A PLATE, ARRANGE THE COOKED RISOTTO (IT SHOULD BE FIRM BUT MOIST. WORST CASE SCENARIO: ADD A SPOONFUL OF BROTH JUST BEFORE SERVING), THE GRILLED ASPARAGUS TIPS, AND THE PARMESAN SHAVINGS. ADJUST THE SEASONINGS.
GENERAL RULE OF THUMB: MAKE IT LOOK PRETTY!
SNRRFL
BOHN DAPPE-TIT!
xyzall
lon.

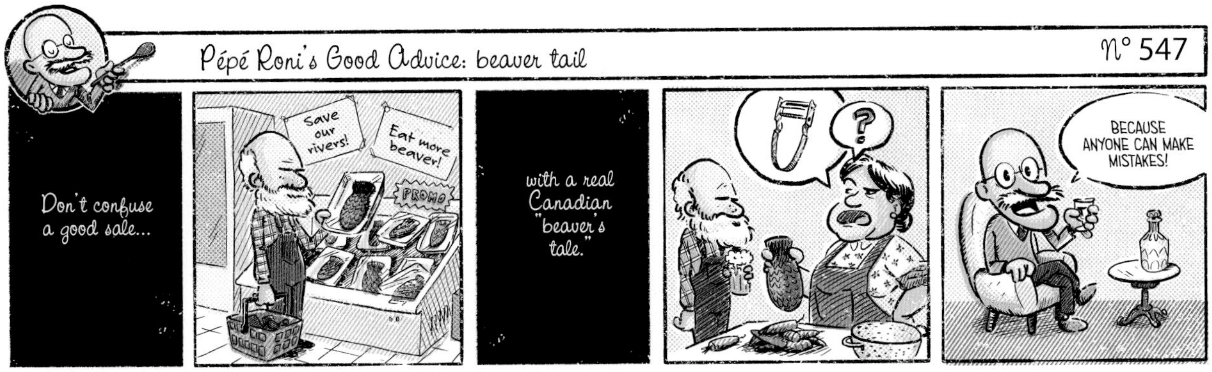
Pépé Roni's Good Advice: beaver tail
N° 547
Don't confuse a good sale...
Save our rivers!
Eat more beaver!
PROMO
with a real Canadian "beaver's tale."
?
BECAUSE ANYONE CAN MAKE MISTAKES!

Beaver Tail: A classic oblong fried pastry served in Canada, often garnished with cinnamon and sugar.

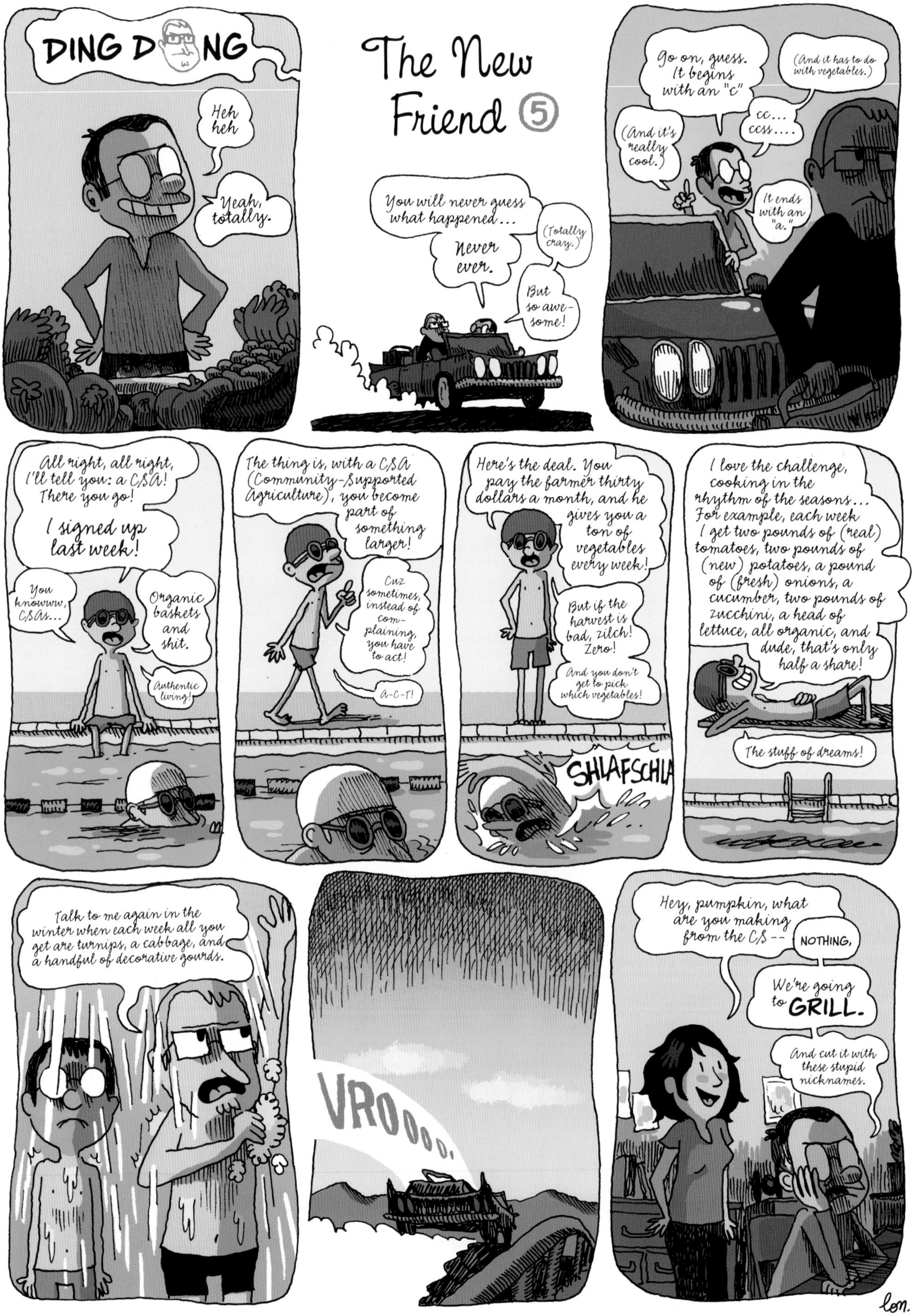
DING DONG
The New Friend 5
Heh heh
Yeah, totally.
You will never guess what happened...
Never ever.
(Totally crazy.)
But so awesome!
Go on, guess. It begins with an "c"
(And it has to do with vegetables.)
(And it's really cool.)
cc... ccss....
It ends with an "a."
All right, all right, I'll tell you: a CSA! There you go!
I signed up last week!
You knowww, CSAs...
Organic baskets and shit.
Authentic living!
The thing is, with a CSA (Community-Supported Agriculture), you become part of something larger!
Cuz sometimes, instead of complaining, you have to act!
A-C-T!
Here's the deal. You pay the farmer thirty dollars a month, and he gives you a ton of vegetables every week!
But if the harvest is bad, zilch! Zero!
And you don't get to pick which vegetables!
SHLAFSCHLA
I love the challenge, cooking in the rhythm of the seasons... For example, each week I get two pounds of (real) tomatoes, two pounds of (new) potatoes, a pound of (fresh) onions, a cucumber, two pounds of zucchini, a head of lettuce, all organic, and dude, that's only half a share!
The stuff of dreams!
Talk to me again in the winter when each week all you get are turnips, a cabbage, and a handful of decorative gourds.
VROOooo.
Hey, pumpkin, what are you making from the CS --
NOTHING,
We're going to GRILL.
And cut it with these stupid nicknames.
len.

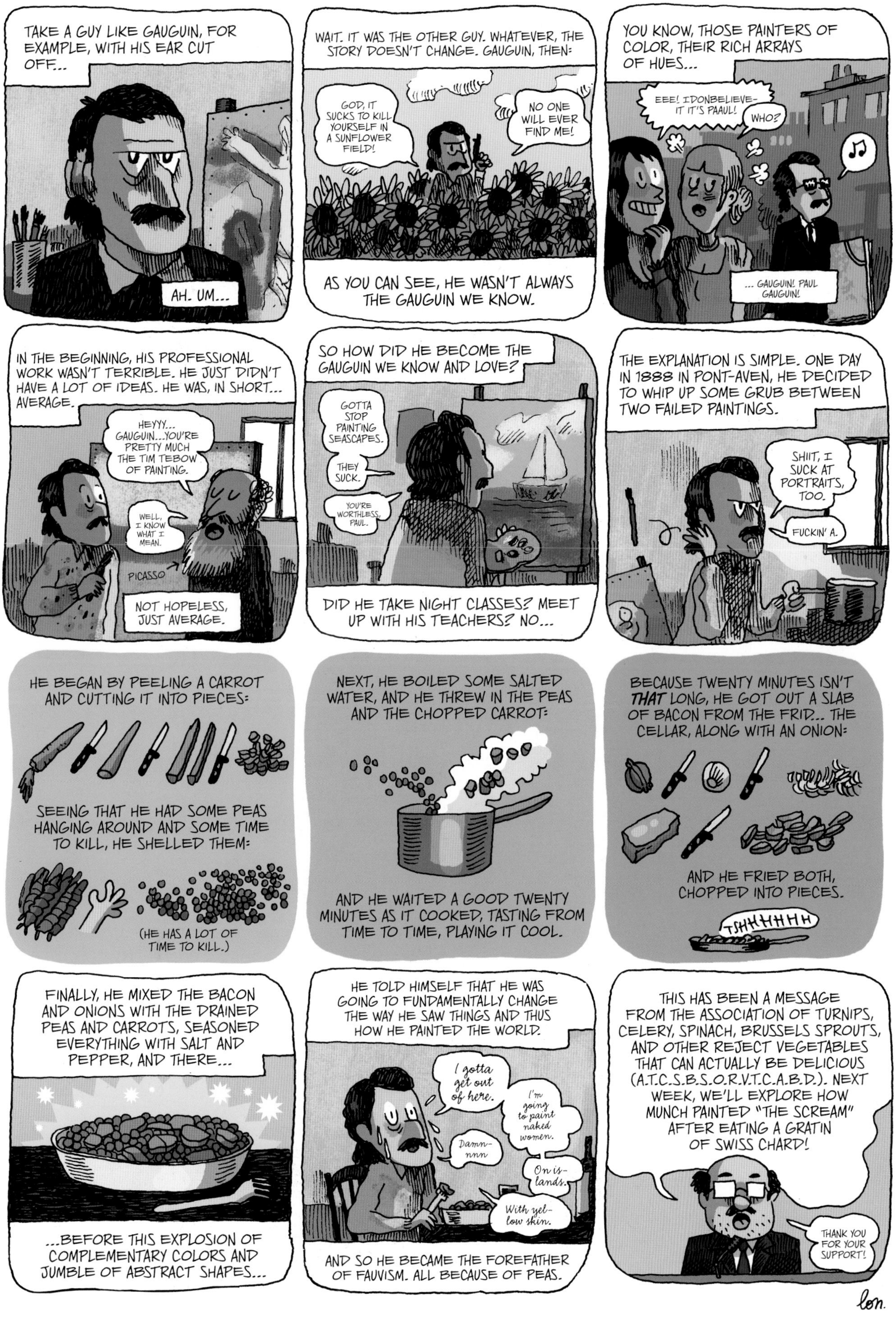
TAKE A GUY LIKE GAUGUIN, FOR EXAMPLE, WITH HIS EAR CUT OFF...
AH. UM...
WAIT. IT WAS THE OTHER GUY. WHATEVER, THE STORY DOESN'T CHANGE. GAUGUIN, THEN:
GOD, IT SUCKS TO KILL YOURSELF IN A SUNFLOWER FIELD!
NO ONE WILL EVER FIND ME!
AS YOU CAN SEE, HE WASN'T ALWAYS THE GAUGUIN WE KNOW.
YOU KNOW, THOSE PAINTERS OF COLOR, THEIR RICH ARRAYS OF HUES...
EEE! IDONBELIEVE-IT IT'S PAAUL!
WHO?
... GAUGUIN! PAUL GAUGUIN!
IN THE BEGINNING, HIS PROFESSIONAL WORK WASN'T TERRIBLE. HE JUST DIDN'T HAVE A LOT OF IDEAS. HE WAS, IN SHORT... AVERAGE.
HEYYY... GAUGUIN...YOU'RE PRETTY MUCH THE TIM TEBOW OF PAINTING.
WELL, I KNOW WHAT I MEAN.
PICASSO
NOT HOPELESS, JUST AVERAGE.
SO HOW DID HE BECOME THE GAUGUIN WE KNOW AND LOVE?
GOTTA STOP PAINTING SEASCAPES.
THEY SUCK.
YOU'RE WORTHLESS, PAUL.
DID HE TAKE NIGHT CLASSES? MEET UP WITH HIS TEACHERS? NO...
THE EXPLANATION IS SIMPLE. ONE DAY IN 1888 IN PONT-AVEN, HE DECIDED TO WHIP UP SOME GRUB BETWEEN TWO FAILED PAINTINGS.
SHIIT, I SUCK AT PORTRAITS, TOO.
FUCKIN' A.
HE BEGAN BY PEELING A CARROT AND CUTTING IT INTO PIECES:
SEEING THAT HE HAD SOME PEAS HANGING AROUND AND SOME TIME TO KILL, HE SHELLED THEM:
(HE HAS A LOT OF TIME TO KILL.)
NEXT, HE BOILED SOME SALTED WATER, AND HE THREW IN THE PEAS AND THE CHOPPED CARROT:
AND HE WAITED A GOOD TWENTY MINUTES AS IT COOKED, TASTING FROM TIME TO TIME, PLAYING IT COOL.
BECAUSE TWENTY MINUTES ISN'T THAT LONG, HE GOT OUT A SLAB OF BACON FROM THE FRID... THE CELLAR, ALONG WITH AN ONION:
AND HE FRIED BOTH, CHOPPED INTO PIECES.
TSHHHHHH
FINALLY, HE MIXED THE BACON AND ONIONS WITH THE DRAINED PEAS AND CARROTS, SEASONED EVERYTHING WITH SALT AND PEPPER, AND THERE...
...BEFORE THIS EXPLOSION OF COMPLEMENTARY COLORS AND JUMBLE OF ABSTRACT SHAPES...
HE TOLD HIMSELF THAT HE WAS GOING TO FUNDAMENTALLY CHANGE THE WAY HE SAW THINGS AND THUS HOW HE PAINTED THE WORLD.
I gotta get out of here.
I'm going to paint naked women.
Damn-nnn
On is-lands.
With yel-low skin.
AND SO HE BECAME THE FOREFATHER OF FAUVISM. ALL BECAUSE OF PEAS.
THIS HAS BEEN A MESSAGE FROM THE ASSOCIATION OF TURNIPS, CELERY, SPINACH, BRUSSELS SPROUTS, AND OTHER REJECT VEGETABLES THAT CAN ACTUALLY BE DELICIOUS (A.T.C.S.B.S.O.R.V.T.C.A.B.D.). NEXT WEEK, WE'LL EXPLORE HOW MUNCH PAINTED "THE SCREAM" AFTER EATING A GRATIN OF SWISS CHARD!
THANK YOU FOR YOUR SUPPORT!
lon.

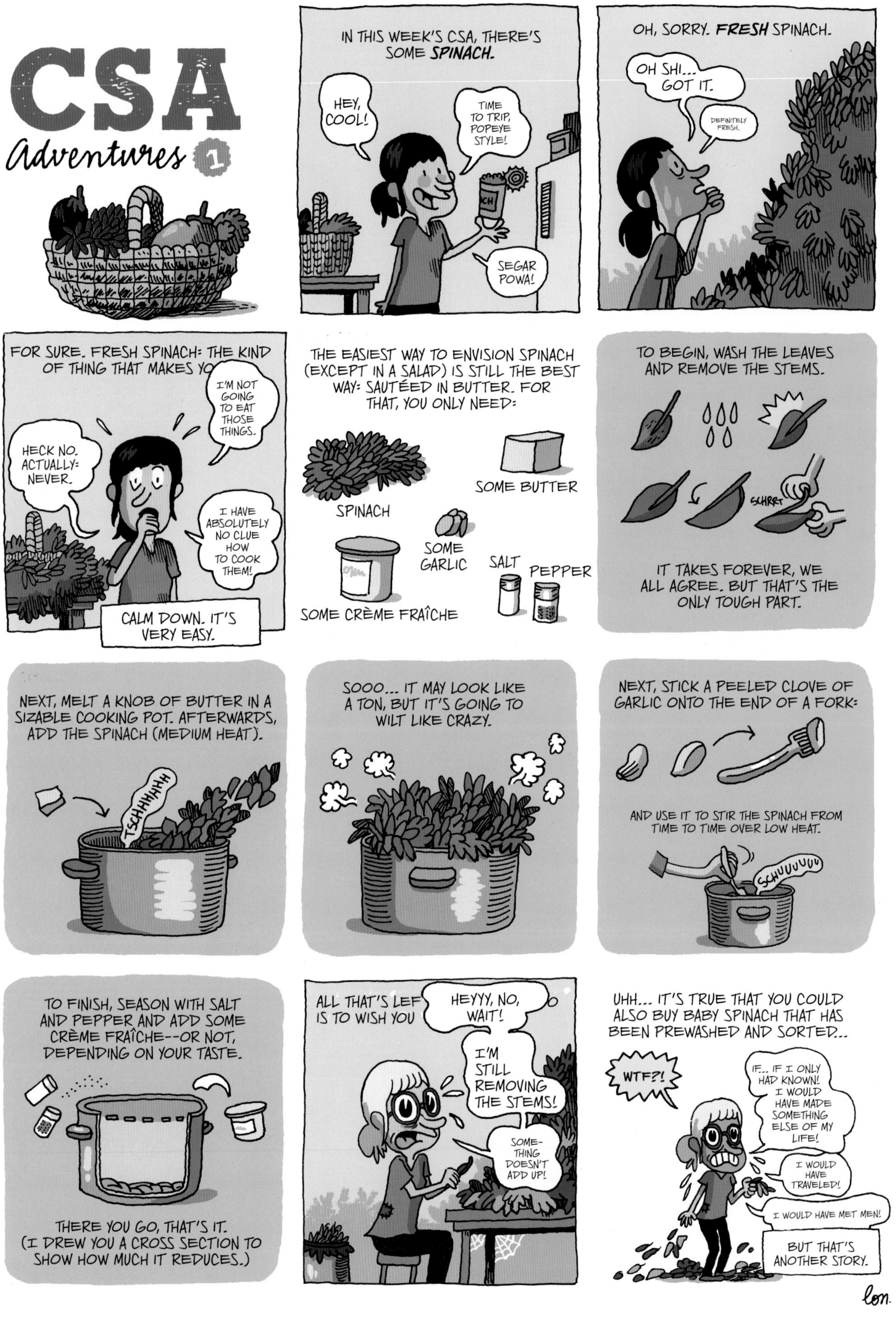
CSA
Adventures 1
IN THIS WEEK'S CSA, THERE'S SOME SPINACH.
HEY, COOL!
TIME TO TRIP, POPEYE STYLE!
SEGAR POWA!
OH, SORRY. FRESH SPINACH.
OH SHI... GOT IT.
DEFINITELY FRESH.
FOR SURE. FRESH SPINACH: THE KIND OF THING THAT MAKES YO
I'M NOT GOING TO EAT THOSE THINGS.
HECK NO. ACTUALLY: NEVER.
I HAVE ABSOLUTELY NO CLUE HOW TO COOK THEM!
CALM DOWN. IT'S VERY EASY.
THE EASIEST WAY TO ENVISION SPINACH (EXCEPT IN A SALAD) IS STILL THE BEST WAY: SAUTÉED IN BUTTER. FOR THAT, YOU ONLY NEED:
SPINACH
SOME BUTTER
SOME GARLIC
SALT
PEPPER
SOME CRÈME FRAÎCHE
TO BEGIN, WASH THE LEAVES AND REMOVE THE STEMS.
SCHRRT
IT TAKES FOREVER, WE ALL AGREE. BUT THAT'S THE ONLY TOUGH PART.
NEXT, MELT A KNOB OF BUTTER IN A SIZABLE COOKING POT. AFTERWARDS, ADD THE SPINACH (MEDIUM HEAT).
TSCHHHHHH
SOOO... IT MAY LOOK LIKE A TON, BUT IT'S GOING TO WILT LIKE CRAZY.
NEXT, STICK A PEELED CLOVE OF GARLIC ONTO THE END OF A FORK:
AND USE IT TO STIR THE SPINACH FROM TIME TO TIME OVER LOW HEAT.
SCHUUUUUU
TO FINISH, SEASON WITH SALT AND PEPPER AND ADD SOME CRÈME FRAÎCHE--OR NOT, DEPENDING ON YOUR TASTE.
THERE YOU GO, THAT'S IT. (I DREW YOU A CROSS SECTION TO SHOW HOW MUCH IT REDUCES.)
ALL THAT'S LEF IS TO WISH YOU
HEYYY, NO, WAIT!
I'M STILL REMOVING THE STEMS!
SOME-THING DOESN'T ADD UP!
UHH... IT'S TRUE THAT YOU COULD ALSO BUY BABY SPINACH THAT HAS BEEN PREWASHED AND SORTED...
WTF?!
IF... IF I ONLY HAD KNOWN! I WOULD HAVE MADE SOMETHING ELSE OF MY LIFE!
I WOULD HAVE TRAVELED!
I WOULD HAVE MET MEN!
BUT THAT'S ANOTHER STORY.
lon.

BEER-BRAISED
RABBIT

SALT AND PEPPER

A LITTLE FLOUR

FOR FOUR ANIMAL-LOVING FRIENDS

DEFINITELY SLOSHED!

SOME HONEY

BAY LEAVES AND SAGE

TWO ONIONS

7 OZ. PORK BELLY OR DICED PANCETTA

SOME OLIVE OIL

A PACKET OF SLIVERED ALMONDS

ONE BUNNY...

...IN THE FORM OF FOUR DEBONED FILLETS

32 OZ. BLOND ALE

1 CUT THE PORK BELLY INTO STRIPS...

OR JUST OPEN THE PACKAGE OF DICED PANCETTA (DEFINITELY LESS WORK). PEEL AND MINCE THE ONIONS,

AND ROLL THE RABBIT FILLETS IN FLOUR.

? POUF POUF POUF POUF FOOLED AGAIN!

2 IN A SAUCEPAN (OR A STOCKPOT), COOK THE DICED PANCETTA AND SET THEM ASIDE.

TSHHH

NEXT, ADD ENOUGH OLIVE OIL TO SEAR THE RABBIT FILLETS ON ALL SIDES. REDUCE THE HEAT AND ADD THE CHOPPED ONION. SWEAT GENTLY.

FLOUTCH   SHHHHH   PFFF (I'VE HAD ENOUGH!)

3 STIR CAREFULLY; NEXT, ADD ENOUGH BEER (WHAT BRAND? SHEESH, NO CLUE, SORRY!) TO COMPLETELY COVER THE FILLETS.

ADD ONE OR TWO BAY LEAVES AND SOME SAGE (WELL... IT'S OPTIONAL, BUT WHATEVER YOU DO, USE FRESH HERBS, NOT DRIED). SIMMER, COVERED, FOR A GOOD TWENTY MINUTES.

SALT AND PEPPER!

4 WHILE IT COOKS, WHAT TO DO? WELL, WE COULD TOAST THE ALMONDS IN A PAN (NO OIL) OVER HIGH HEAT, BUT BE CAREFUL: THEY CAN BURN, FAST.

Wiiiiii

FINALLY, WHEN THE RABBIT IS COOKED AND THE BEER HAS SIGNIFICANTLY REDUCED, ADD THE DICED PANCETTA AND ALMONDS INTO THE SAUCE. FINISH WITH A GENEROUS SPOONFUL OF HONEY.

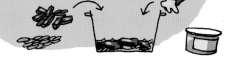

AFTER A FEW MORE MINUTES OVER LOW HEAT AND A LITTLE STIRRING, IT'S READY TO SERVE!

BONUS

BECAUSE THERE'S MORE TO LIFE THAN MEAT, YOU COULD SERVE THIS DISH WITH BRAISED ENDIVES, WHICH MAKE AN AWESOME SIDE:

TSHH   (OIL)

FLIP FLIP

COOK TEN MINUTES IN THE BEER WITH THE RABBIT, STILL COVERED.

SALT   PEPPER

URRHAK*G   CRAP! THE BAY LEAF!   TEHEHE

lon.

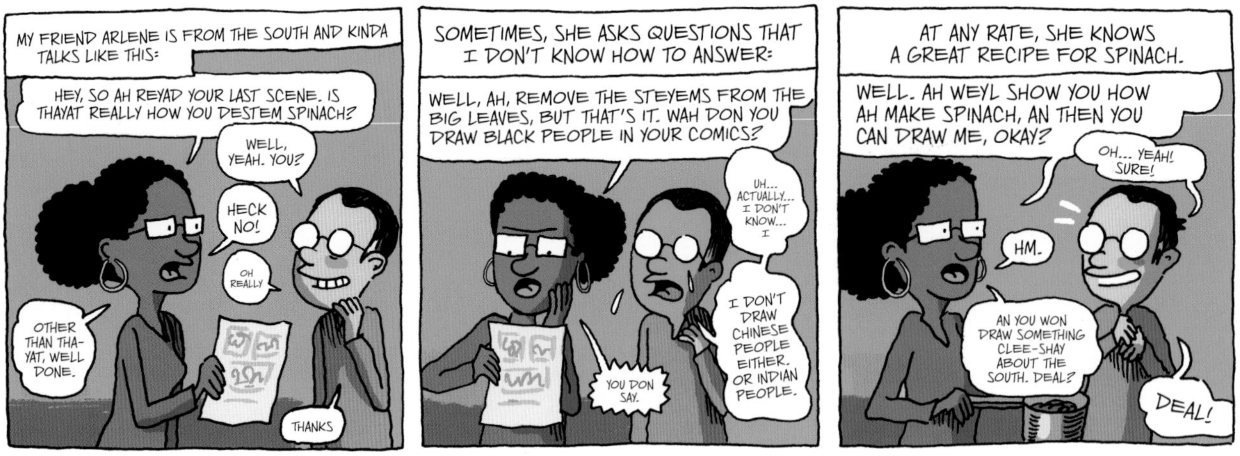
MY FRIEND ARLENE IS FROM THE SOUTH AND KINDA TALKS LIKE THIS:
HEY, SO AH REYAD YOUR LAST SCENE. IS THAYAT REALLY HOW YOU DESTEM SPINACH?
WELL, YEAH. YOU?
HECK NO!
OH REALLY
OTHER THAN THA-YAT, WELL DONE.
THANKS
SOMETIMES, SHE ASKS QUESTIONS THAT I DON'T KNOW HOW TO ANSWER:
WELL, AH, REMOVE THE STEYEMS FROM THE BIG LEAVES, BUT THAT'S IT. WAH DON YOU DRAW BLACK PEOPLE IN YOUR COMICS?
UH... ACTUALLY... I DON'T KNOW... I
I DON'T DRAW CHINESE PEOPLE EITHER. OR INDIAN PEOPLE.
YOU DON SAY.
AT ANY RATE, SHE KNOWS A GREAT RECIPE FOR SPINACH.
WELL. AH WEYL SHOW YOU HOW AH MAKE SPINACH, AN THEN YOU CAN DRAW ME, OKAY?
OH... YEAH! SURE!
HM.
AN YOU WON DRAW SOMETHING CLEE-SHAY ABOUT THE SOUTH. DEAL?
DEAL!

Arlene's SPINACH AND Rahce

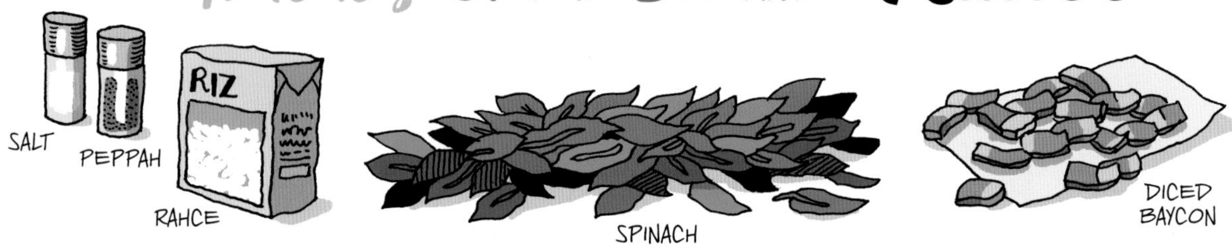
SALT
PEPPAH
RIZ
RAHCE
SPINACH
DICED BAYCON

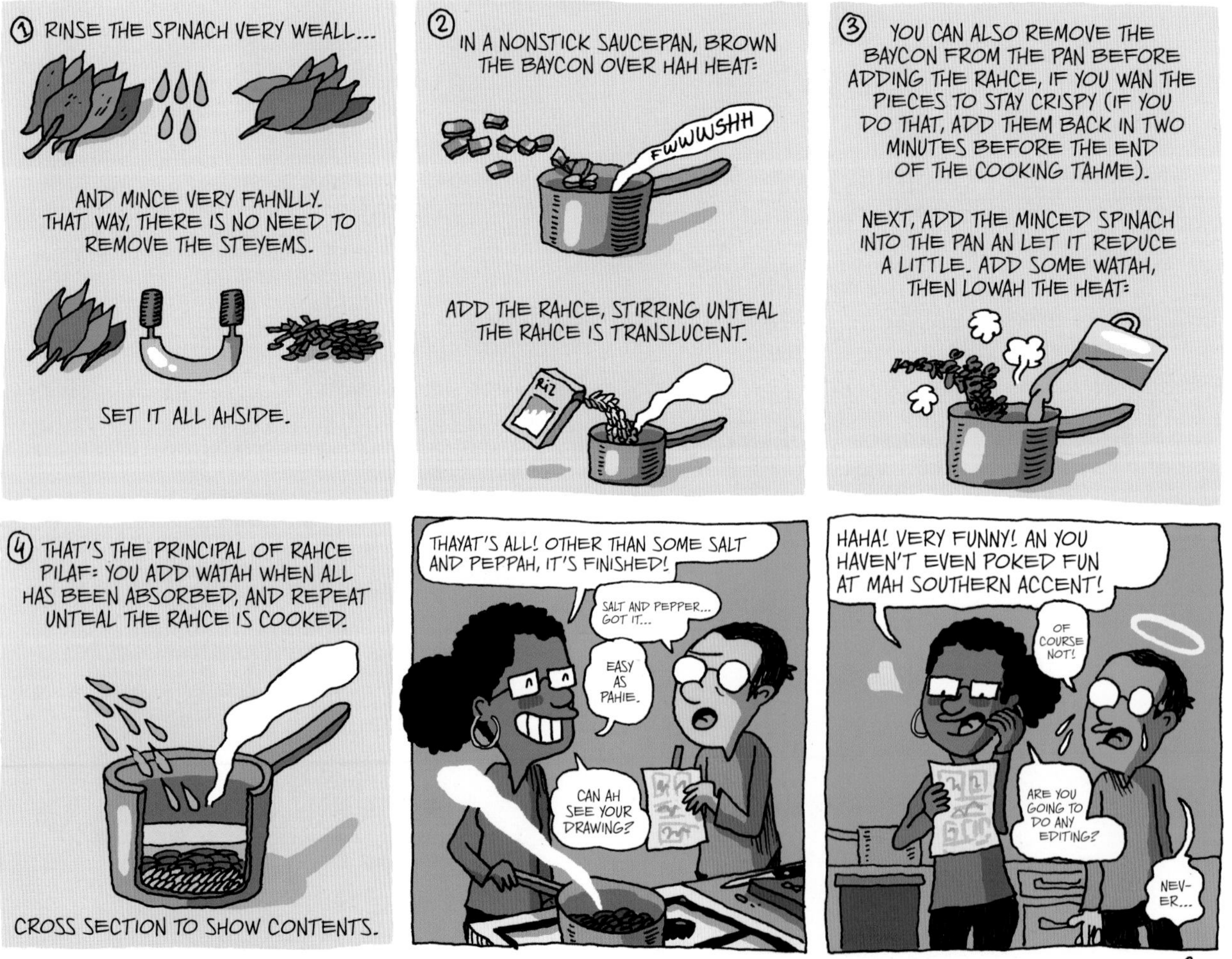
① RINSE THE SPINACH VERY WEALL...
AND MINCE VERY FAHNLLY. THAT WAY, THERE IS NO NEED TO REMOVE THE STEYEMS.
SET IT ALL AHSIDE.
② IN A NONSTICK SAUCEPAN, BROWN THE BAYCON OVER HAH HEAT:
FWWWSHH
ADD THE RAHCE, STIRRING UNTEAL THE RAHCE IS TRANSLUCENT.
RIZ
③ YOU CAN ALSO REMOVE THE BAYCON FROM THE PAN BEFORE ADDING THE RAHCE, IF YOU WAN THE PIECES TO STAY CRISPY (IF YOU DO THAT, ADD THEM BACK IN TWO MINUTES BEFORE THE END OF THE COOKING TAHME).
NEXT, ADD THE MINCED SPINACH INTO THE PAN AN LET IT REDUCE A LITTLE. ADD SOME WATAH, THEN LOWAH THE HEAT:
④ THAT'S THE PRINCIPAL OF RAHCE PILAF: YOU ADD WATAH WHEN ALL HAS BEEN ABSORBED, AND REPEAT UNTEAL THE RAHCE IS COOKED.
CROSS SECTION TO SHOW CONTENTS.
THAYAT'S ALL! OTHER THAN SOME SALT AND PEPPAH, IT'S FINISHED!
SALT AND PEPPER... GOT IT...
EASY AS PAHIE.
CAN AH SEE YOUR DRAWING?
HAHA! VERY FUNNY! AN YOU HAVEN'T EVEN POKED FUN AT MAH SOUTHERN ACCENT!
OF COURSE NOT!
ARE YOU GOING TO DO ANY EDITING?
NEV-ER...
lon.

AT THE GROCERY STORE, A LABEL CATCHES YOUR EYE. PRODUCE SECTION.

YOU KNOW THE WORD, BUT THE IMAGE DOESN'T MATCH UP WITH WHAT YOU'RE REMEMBERING.

BECAUSE IT LOOKS A LITTLE WEIRD, A MYSTERY TO THE AVERAGE GUY, YOU BUY:

a bunch of (raw)
SALSIFY

YOU KNOW, THOSE BITTER, LIMP, WHITE PIECES FROM A CAN THAT DEFINED YOUR CHILDHOOD:

GO ON!

THINK ABOUT THE STARVING CHILDREN IN AFRICA!

HEY! YOU! DON'T YOU DARE THROW THEM IN THE TRASH. DON'T YOU REMEMBER THE *BROCOLOUNGE©?* WASN'T THAT GOOD?

YEAH, WELL... HEY, NOW.

WE'RE NOT GOING TO MAKE SOME SALSIFY©, ARE WE?

WHY NOT? SALSIFY, OFTEN MISTAKEN FOR HIS COUSIN, BLACK SALSIFY (OR SCORZONERA)* HAS BECOME INCREASINGLY RARE IN THE LAST DECADES. IT'S A FOOD THAT'S PARTICULARLY UNREWARDING TO PREPARE... AND EVEN SO...

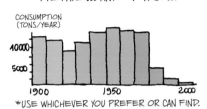

CONSUMPTION (TONS/YEAR)

*USE WHICHEVER YOU PREFER OR CAN FIND.

TAKE YOUR BUNCH OF SALSIFY AND BEGIN BY REMOVING THE LEAVES IF THERE HAPPEN TO BE ANY:

ONCE WASHED AND SORTED, THEY WILL UPGRADE ANY OF YOUR SALADS.

NEXT, WASH THE SALSIFY AND SOAK THEM IN WATER FOR TWO OR THREE MINUTES. THAT WILL MAKE THEM EASIER TO PEEL.

NEXT COMES THE THANKLESS PART: PEELING THEM. YOU MAY SAY THAT'S EASY, BUT SALSIFY'S NO CARROT OR POTATO. WITH SALSIFY...

PEELING MAKES YOUR HANDS INDESCRIBABLY GROSS, AND YOU WASTE 40% OF THE VEGETABLE IN THE PROCESS. ONE IDEA WOULD BE TO USE GLOVES OR TO FIND YOURSELF SOME ORGANIC SALSIFY. LESS OF A NEED TO PEEL.

CHOP THE SALSIFY INTO PIECES.

(1 INCH)

AND NEXT, EITHER COOK THEM IMMEDIATELY IN BOILING WATER FOR THIRTY MINUTES,

OR SOAK THEM IN WATER WITH SOME LEMON JUICE TO MAKE SURE THEY DON'T TURN BROWN. (YOU HAVEN'T DONE ALL THAT WORK TO LET THEM LOOK UGLY ON THE DINNER TABLE, RIGHT?)

FINALLY, WHEN THEY'RE COOKED (TENDER WHEN PIERCED WITH A FORK), TWO EASY PREPARATIONS:

PARSLEY

① SALSIFIES

TEN MINUTES

OIL

②

HEAVY CREAM

TEN MINUTES

PARMESAN

A SUBTLE TASTE, SWEET AND FINE, RESEMBLING THAT OF ARTICHOKES... UNDOUBTEDLY, YOU'RE GOING TO SAVOR SALSIFY THIS TIME!

WHOAAA

← (NOT AT ALL LIKE THE CANNED ONES)

SALSIFY IS BECOMING EXTINCT FROM OUR WAY OF EATING. COOKING THEM BECOMES A POLITICAL ACT! THERE'S A TON OF PEOPLE FIGHTING TO SAVE THE STUPID PANDAS, AND YOU CAN'T EVEN EAT THEM!

BUT NOBODY'S STANDING UP FOR SALSIFY! NOBODY!

ADOPT ME!

THIS HAS BEEN A MESSAGE FROM THE ASSOCIATION OF TURNIPS, CELERY, SPINACH, BRUSSELS SPROUTS, AND OTHER REJECT VEGETABLES THAT CAN ACTUALLY BE DELICIOUS.

(A.T.C.S.B.S.O.R.V.T.C.A.B.D.).

OUR SUP-PORT IS GROWING, THANKS TO YOU!

THE STRUGGLE CONTINUES!

lon.

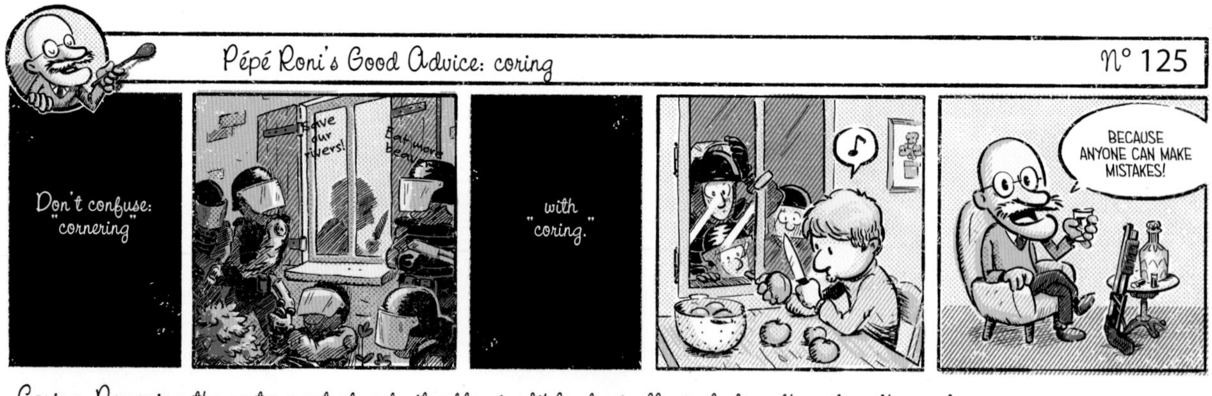
Pépé Roni's Good Advice: coring
N° 125
Don't confuse: "cornering"
Save our rivers!
Eat more
with "coring."
BECAUSE ANYONE CAN MAKE MISTAKES!

Coring: Removing the center part of a fruit, often inedible, typically including the pit or the seeds.

JOURNAL
FROM
STOCKHOLM

TRIP TO STOCKHOLM

I'M ACCOMPANYING NANCY TO THE "SMALL PRESS EXPOSITION"* WHERE SHE HAS BEEN INVITED DUE TO THE TRANSLATION OF ONE OF HER BOOKS INTO SWEDISH.

*FESTIVAL OF INDIE COMICS, CARTOONING, & GRAPHIC NOVELS

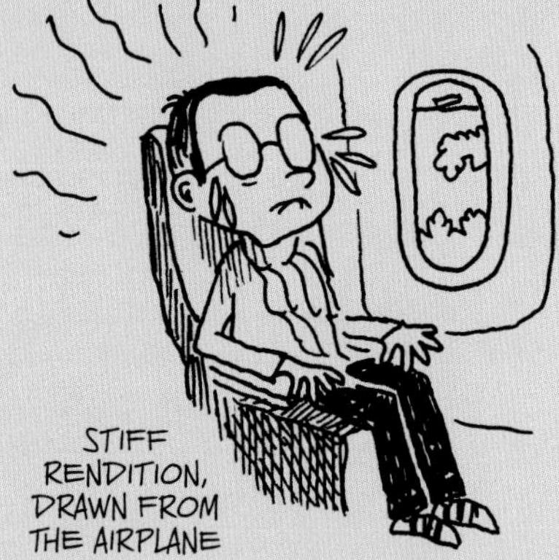

STIFF RENDITION, DRAWN FROM THE AIRPLANE

A gruyere, bresaola, and lettuce sandwich made by my mom

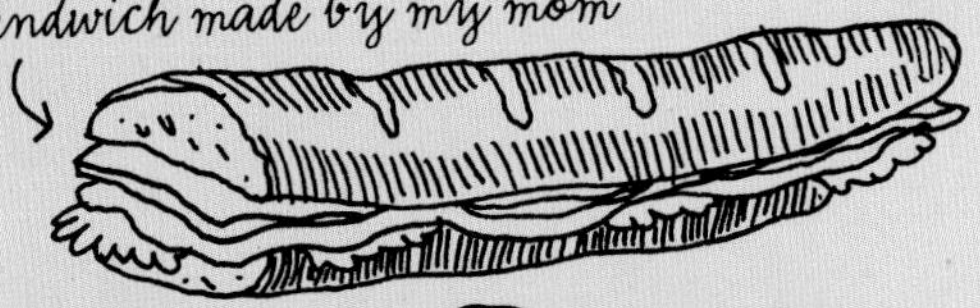

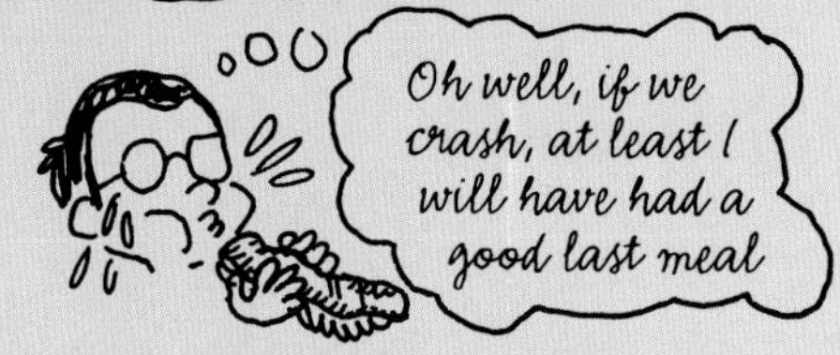

Oh well, if we crash, at least I will have had a good last meal

(To give you an idea of the taste, it's like horse meat dipped in a good fondue.)

SWEDISH WORDS I KNOW:

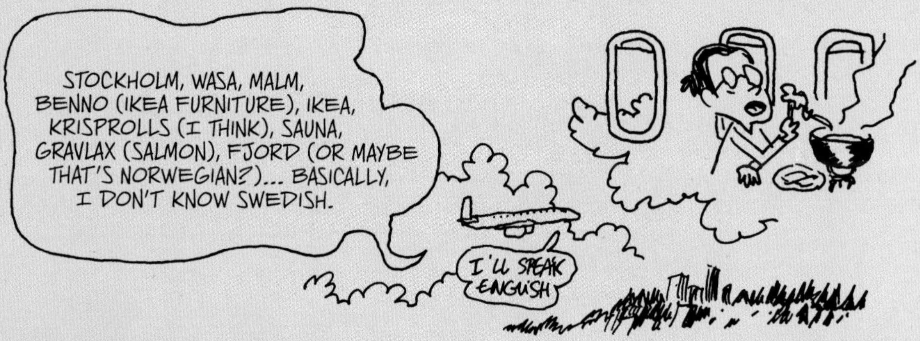

STOCKHOLM, WASA, MALM, BENNO (IKEA FURNITURE), IKEA, KRISPROLLS (I THINK), SAUNA, GRAVLAX (SALMON), FJORD (OR MAYBE THAT'S NORWEGIAN?)... BASICALLY, I DON'T KNOW SWEDISH.
I'LL SPEAK ENGLISH

DAY 1

OKAY, TWO THINGS TO DRAW THAT ARE TYPICALLY SWEDISH

1

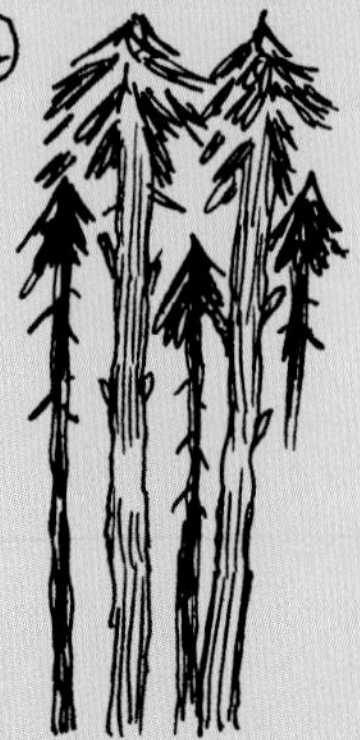

THIS KIND OF TREE

2

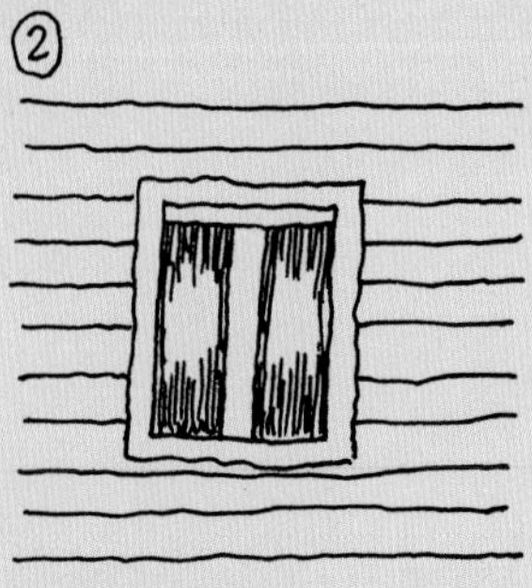

THIS KIND OF WINDOW

WHEN I ARRIVE IN STOCKHOLM, I REALIZE THAT I HAVEN'T REALLY TAKEN INTO ACCOUNT THAT IT'S STILL WINTER...33°F

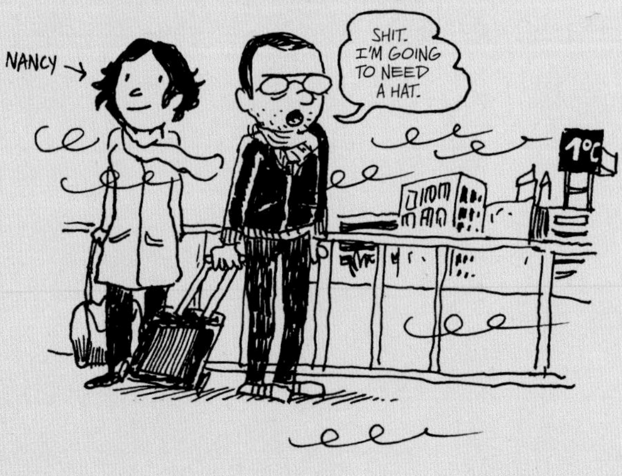

NANCY
SHIT. I'M GOING TO NEED A HAT.
1°C

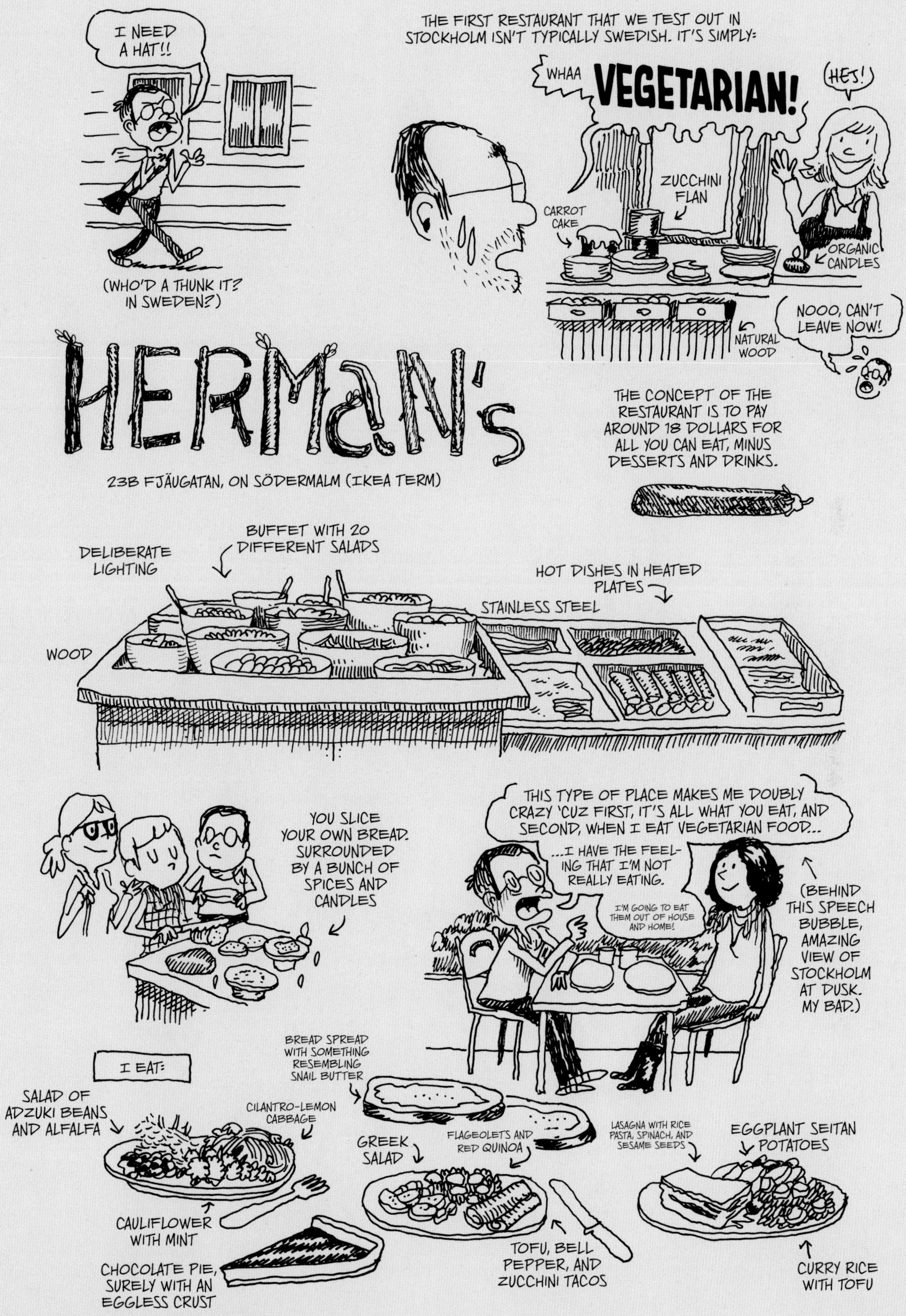
THE FIRST RESTAURANT THAT WE TEST OUT IN STOCKHOLM ISN'T TYPICALLY SWEDISH. IT'S SIMPLY:
I NEED A HAT!!
(WHO'D A THUNK IT? IN SWEDEN?)
WHAA VEGETARIAN!
HEJ!
ZUCCHINI FLAN
CARROT CAKE
ORGANIC CANDLES
NATURAL WOOD
NOOO, CAN'T LEAVE NOW!
HERMAN'S
23B FJÄUGATAN, ON SÖDERMALM (IKEA TERM)
THE CONCEPT OF THE RESTAURANT IS TO PAY AROUND 18 DOLLARS FOR ALL YOU CAN EAT, MINUS DESSERTS AND DRINKS.
DELIBERATE LIGHTING
BUFFET WITH 20 DIFFERENT SALADS
HOT DISHES IN HEATED PLATES
STAINLESS STEEL
WOOD
YOU SLICE YOUR OWN BREAD. SURROUNDED BY A BUNCH OF SPICES AND CANDLES
THIS TYPE OF PLACE MAKES ME DOUBLY CRAZY 'CUZ FIRST, IT'S ALL WHAT YOU EAT, AND SECOND, WHEN I EAT VEGETARIAN FOOD...
...I HAVE THE FEELING THAT I'M NOT REALLY EATING.
I'M GOING TO EAT THEM OUT OF HOUSE AND HOME!
(BEHIND THIS SPEECH BUBBLE, AMAZING VIEW OF STOCKHOLM AT DUSK. MY BAD.)
I EAT:
BREAD SPREAD WITH SOMETHING RESEMBLING SNAIL BUTTER
SALAD OF ADZUKI BEANS AND ALFALFA
CILANTRO-LEMON CABBAGE
GREEK SALAD
FLAGEOLETS AND RED QUINOA
LASAGNA WITH RICE PASTA, SPINACH, AND SESAME SEEDS
EGGPLANT SEITAN POTATOES
CAULIFLOWER WITH MINT
CHOCOLATE PIE, SURELY WITH AN EGGLESS CRUST
TOFU, BELL PEPPER, AND ZUCCHINI TACOS
CURRY RICE WITH TOFU

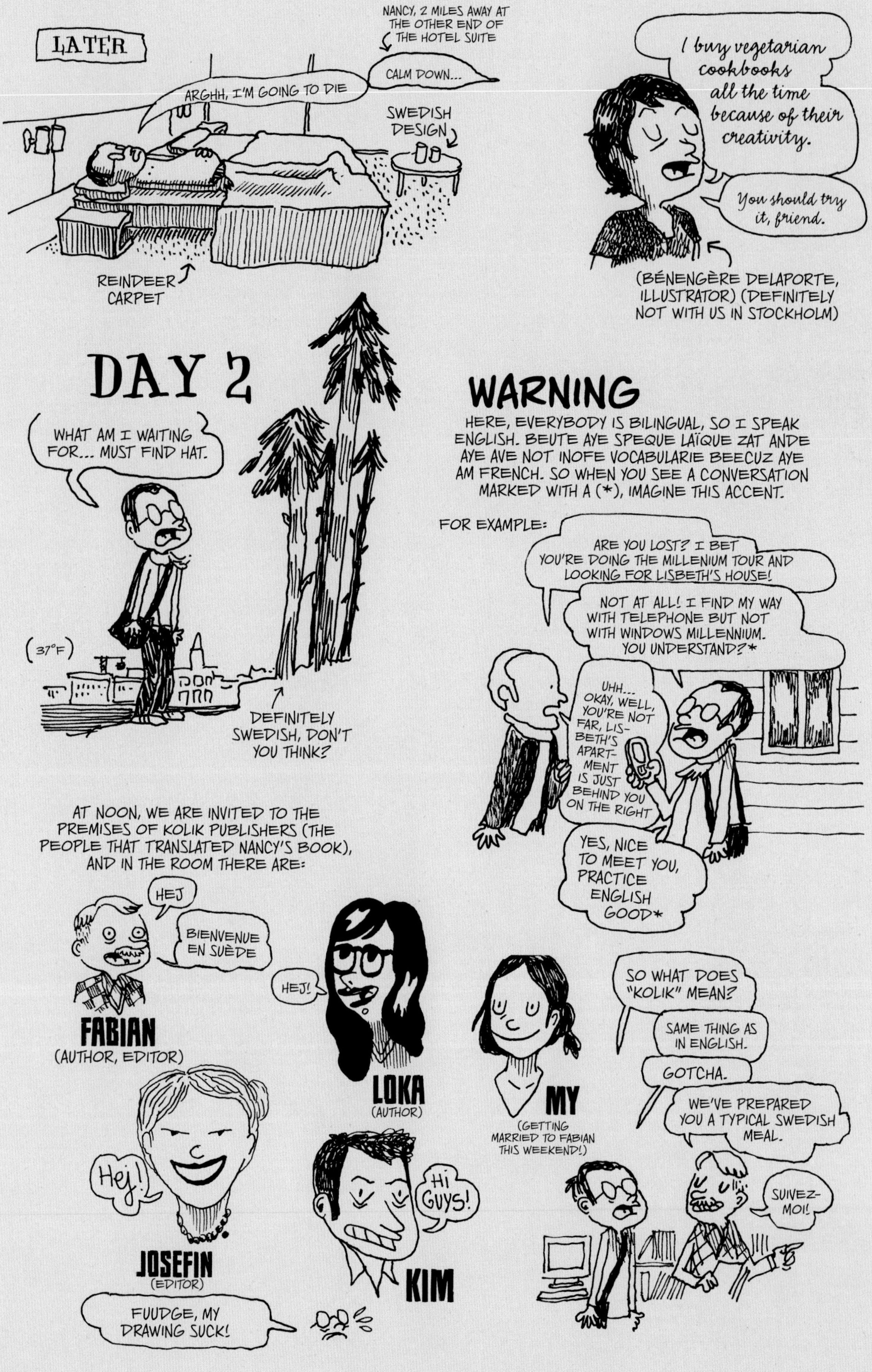

LATER
NANCY, 2 MILES AWAY AT THE OTHER END OF THE HOTEL SUITE
CALM DOWN...
ARGHH, I'M GOING TO DIE
SWEDISH DESIGN
REINDEER CARPET
I buy vegetarian cookbooks all the time because of their creativity.
You should try it, friend.
(BÉNENGÈRE DELAPORTE, ILLUSTRATOR) (DEFINITELY NOT WITH US IN STOCKHOLM)
DAY 2
WHAT AM I WAITING FOR... MUST FIND HAT.
(37°F)
DEFINITELY SWEDISH, DON'T YOU THINK?
WARNING
HERE, EVERYBODY IS BILINGUAL, SO I SPEAK ENGLISH. BEUTE AYE SPEQUE LAÏQUE ZAT ANDE AYE AVE NOT INOFE VOCABULARIE BEECUZ AYE AM FRENCH. SO WHEN YOU SEE A CONVERSATION MARKED WITH A (*), IMAGINE THIS ACCENT.
FOR EXAMPLE:
ARE YOU LOST? I BET YOU'RE DOING THE MILLENIUM TOUR AND LOOKING FOR LISBETH'S HOUSE!
NOT AT ALL! I FIND MY WAY WITH TELEPHONE BUT NOT WITH WINDOWS MILLENNIUM. YOU UNDERSTAND?*
UHH... OKAY, WELL, YOU'RE NOT FAR, LISBETH'S APARTMENT IS JUST BEHIND YOU ON THE RIGHT
YES, NICE TO MEET YOU, PRACTICE ENGLISH GOOD*
AT NOON, WE ARE INVITED TO THE PREMISES OF KOLIK PUBLISHERS (THE PEOPLE THAT TRANSLATED NANCY'S BOOK), AND IN THE ROOM THERE ARE:
HEJ
BIENVENUE EN SUÈDE
FABIAN
(AUTHOR, EDITOR)
HEJ!
LOKA
(AUTHOR)
MY
(GETTING MARRIED TO FABIAN THIS WEEKEND!)
Hej!
JOSEFIN
(EDITOR)
Hi GUYS!
KIM
FUUDGE, MY DRAWING SUCK!
SO WHAT DOES "KOLIK" MEAN?
SAME THING AS IN ENGLISH.
GOTCHA.
WE'VE PREPARED YOU A TYPICAL SWEDISH MEAL.
SUIVEZ-MOI!

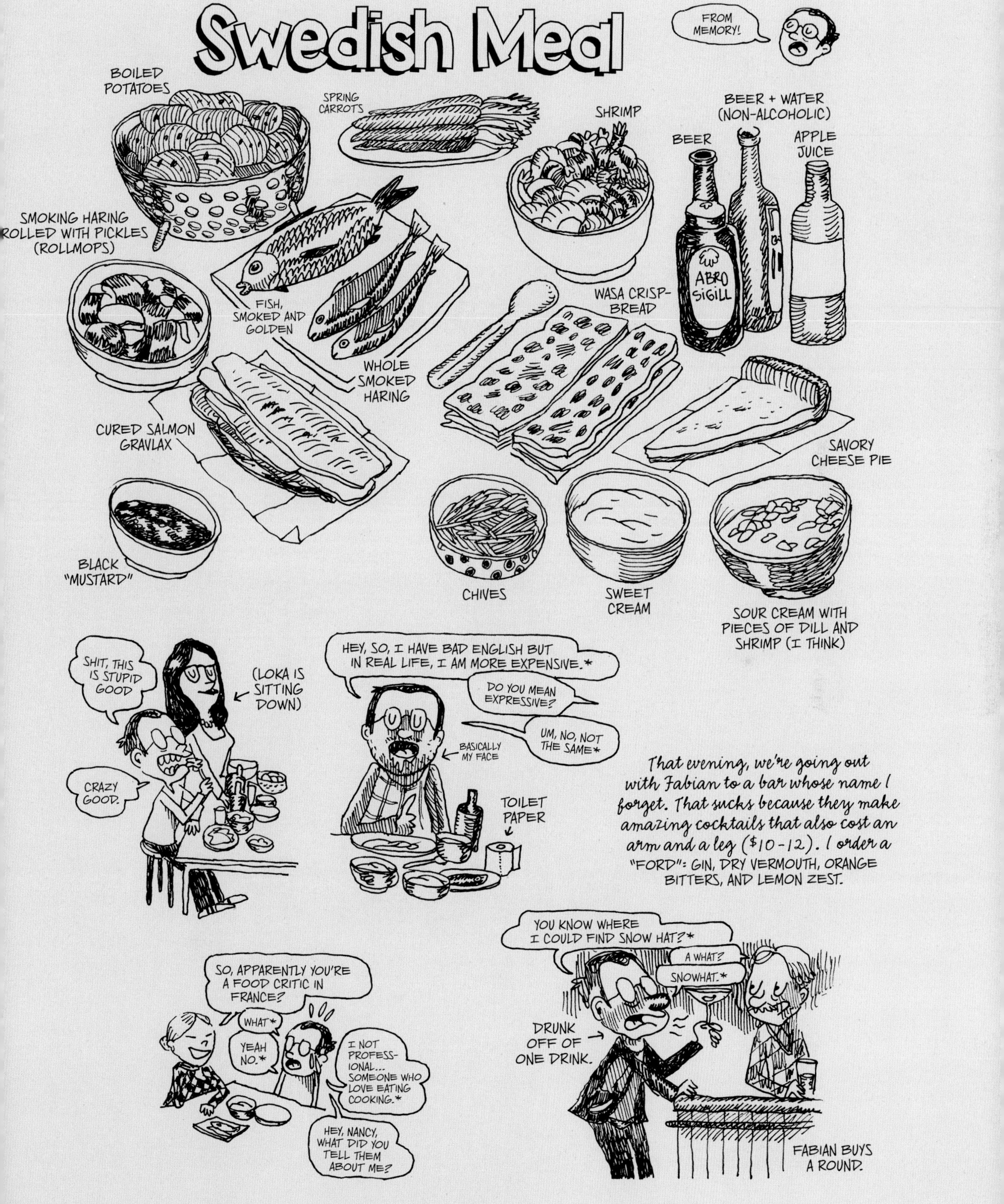
Swedish Meal
FROM MEMORY!
BOILED POTATOES
SPRING CARROTS
SHRIMP
BEER + WATER (NON-ALCOHOLIC)
BEER
APPLE JUICE
ABRO SIGILL
SMOKING HARING ROLLED WITH PICKLES (ROLLMOPS)
FISH, SMOKED AND GOLDEN
WASA CRISP-BREAD
WHOLE SMOKED HARING
CURED SALMON GRAVLAX
SAVORY CHEESE PIE
BLACK "MUSTARD"
CHIVES
SWEET CREAM
SOUR CREAM WITH PIECES OF DILL AND SHRIMP (I THINK)
SHIT, THIS IS STUPID GOOD
(LOKA IS SITTING DOWN)
CRAZY GOOD.
HEY, SO, I HAVE BAD ENGLISH BUT IN REAL LIFE, I AM MORE EXPENSIVE.*
DO YOU MEAN EXPRESSIVE?
UM, NO, NOT THE SAME*
BASICALLY MY FACE
TOILET PAPER
That evening, we're going out with Fabian to a bar whose name I forget. That sucks because they make amazing cocktails that also cost an arm and a leg ($10-12). I order a "FORD": GIN, DRY VERMOUTH, ORANGE BITTERS, AND LEMON ZEST.
SO, APPARENTLY YOU'RE A FOOD CRITIC IN FRANCE?
WHAT*
YEAH NO.*
I NOT PROFESS-IONAL... SOMEONE WHO LOVE EATING COOKING.*
HEY, NANCY, WHAT DID YOU TELL THEM ABOUT ME?
YOU KNOW WHERE I COULD FIND SNOW HAT?*
A WHAT?
SNOWHAT.*
DRUNK OFF OF ONE DRINK.
FABIAN BUYS A ROUND.

DAY 3

Stockholm

FOR BREAKFAST:
BUCKWHEAT CRÊPES,
SMOKED SALMON,
HARING WITH JUNIPER
BERRIES, AND CAVIAR,
WHICH HERE MEANS
SHRIMP ROE.

Breakfast shared with Dominique Goblet et Nancy Peña

At breakfast, I only want to eat black bread.

But I'm not the only one.

TUSAN OCKSÅ!

*TRANSLATION: DAMN IT!

Goodness me!

LIKE USUAL IN THIS KIND OF HOTEL
(SEE BUDAPEST, VOLUME 1), I EAT
A BREAKFAST OF CHAMPIONS:

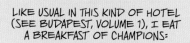

ORANGE JUICE

COFFEE

KIWI

MUESLI

WASA

CROISSANT

TOAST WITH
MARMALADE

BOILED
EGGS AND
BACON

WHEN I SPEND TIME WITH OTHER WRITERS AT A FESTIVAL OR
ELSEWHERE, I LOVE TALKING ABOUT TONS OF THINGS, DEFINITELY
NOT ABOUT WORK. I GET EXACTLY WHAT I ASKED FOR:

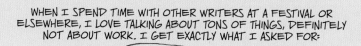

LAPLAND'S
CRAZY, MAN! YOU
CATCH FISH COD
THE SIZE
OF DOGS
BLABLABLA
FORESTS

HEHHH
TROOO
GOOD

REINDEER
PELTS
FOR $25!

YEP

A VIKING
WITH A
YOUTH
HOSTEL!

AND LUCKY FOR THAT
BREAKFAST, BECAUSE,
WHEN TRAVELING, NANCY ALWAYS
WANTS TO VISIT A MILLION
THINGS, AND WE'LL INEVITABLY
FIND OURSELVES WITH AN
IMPOSSIBLE DILEMMA:

WAIT JUST ONE MOMENT, YOU KNOW
THAT IT'S IMPOSSIBLE FOR ME
TO NOT EAT LUNCH AT NOON!

WE'RE
GOING TO
DIE OF
HUNGER!

WE'RE GOING
TO LOSE OUR
ABILITY TO
TASTE!

CALM DOWN,
IT'S 12:30.

IF YOU MADE
OUR ITINERARY,
WE WOULD
NEVER GET
ANYWHERE.
WE'D SPEND
OUR VACATION
IN SPECIALTY
SHOPS OR
RESTAURANTS.

OR AQUARIUMS.

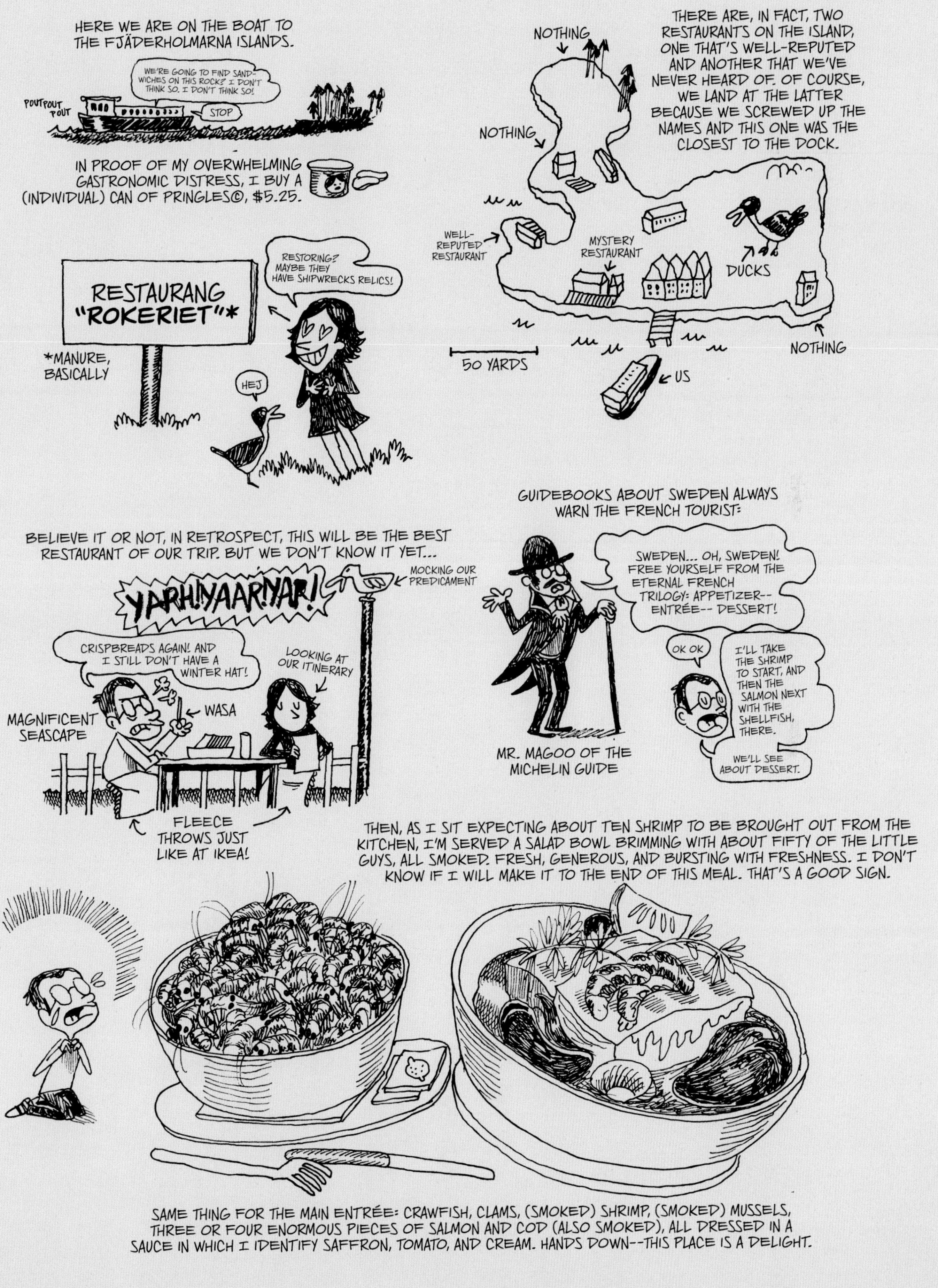
HERE WE ARE ON THE BOAT TO THE FJÄDERHOLMARNA ISLANDS.
WE'RE GOING TO FIND SANDWICHES ON THIS ROCK? I DON'T THINK SO. I DON'T THINK SO!
POUTPOUT POUT
STOP
IN PROOF OF MY OVERWHELMING GASTRONOMIC DISTRESS, I BUY A (INDIVIDUAL) CAN OF PRINGLES©, $5.25.
THERE ARE, IN FACT, TWO RESTAURANTS ON THE ISLAND, ONE THAT'S WELL-REPUTED AND ANOTHER THAT WE'VE NEVER HEARD OF. OF COURSE, WE LAND AT THE LATTER BECAUSE WE SCREWED UP THE NAMES AND THIS ONE WAS THE CLOSEST TO THE DOCK.
NOTHING
NOTHING
WELL-REPUTED RESTAURANT
MYSTERY RESTAURANT
DUCKS
NOTHING
50 YARDS
US
RESTAURANG "ROKERIET"*
*MANURE, BASICALLY
RESTORING? MAYBE THEY HAVE SHIPWRECKS RELICS!
HEJ
BELIEVE IT OR NOT, IN RETROSPECT, THIS WILL BE THE BEST RESTAURANT OF OUR TRIP. BUT WE DON'T KNOW IT YET...
YARH!YAAR!YAR!
MOCKING OUR PREDICAMENT
CRISPBREADS AGAIN! AND I STILL DON'T HAVE A WINTER HAT!
LOOKING AT OUR ITINERARY
WASA
MAGNIFICENT SEASCAPE
FLEECE THROWS JUST LIKE AT IKEA!
GUIDEBOOKS ABOUT SWEDEN ALWAYS WARN THE FRENCH TOURIST:
SWEDEN... OH, SWEDEN! FREE YOURSELF FROM THE ETERNAL FRENCH TRILOGY: APPETIZER-- ENTRÉE-- DESSERT!
MR. MAGOO OF THE MICHELIN GUIDE
OK OK
I'LL TAKE THE SHRIMP TO START, AND THEN THE SALMON NEXT WITH THE SHELLFISH, THERE.
WE'LL SEE ABOUT DESSERT.
THEN, AS I SIT EXPECTING ABOUT TEN SHRIMP TO BE BROUGHT OUT FROM THE KITCHEN, I'M SERVED A SALAD BOWL BRIMMING WITH ABOUT FIFTY OF THE LITTLE GUYS, ALL SMOKED. FRESH, GENEROUS, AND BURSTING WITH FRESHNESS. I DON'T KNOW IF I WILL MAKE IT TO THE END OF THIS MEAL. THAT'S A GOOD SIGN.
SAME THING FOR THE MAIN ENTRÉE: CRAWFISH, CLAMS, (SMOKED) SHRIMP, (SMOKED) MUSSELS, THREE OR FOUR ENORMOUS PIECES OF SALMON AND COD (ALSO SMOKED), ALL DRESSED IN A SAUCE IN WHICH I IDENTIFY SAFFRON, TOMATO, AND CREAM. HANDS DOWN--THIS PLACE IS A DELIGHT.

NO JOKE: I REALLY LOVED THIS MOMENT. THE SETTING WAS MAGNIFICENT, THE FOOD WAS EXCELLENT, AND ABOVE ALL (THIS MADE THE TRIP WORTH IT), I DISCOVERED A NEW TASTE: FRESH AND SMOKED FISH. I LIKE KNOWING THAT MY TASTE BUDS CAN STILL BE TAKEN ON AN ADVENTURE, EVEN AT THIRTY-THREE YEARS OLD.

DRAWING REPRESENTING THE POSTCARDS SENT TO VARIOUS FRIENDS. SLIGHT RESEMBLANCE TO THE COVER OF MANDRYKA'S "CLOPINETTES."

$45! I CAN'T BELIEVE THAT IT WAS THAT FREAKIN GOOD AND FILLING!

AND I DIDN'T EVEN ORDER DESSERT.

HEYY!

SPORTS 2000

EXCUSE ME LOOK FOR A HAT SNOW.*

WHAT?

HAT, FOR SNOW, KNOW WHAT I MEAN?*

AH! A WINTER HAT!

BECAUSE NEED MAGNIFI-CENT EAR-FLAPS.*

1956-2012

This is Kristiina. She worked at the Kulturhuset and managed the festival (because of her generosity, I could come on this trip). Thank you, Kristiina, for everything.

THAT EVENING, WE EAT VERY LATE FOR STOCKHOLM (11 P.M.)* IN A DISGUSTING SUSHI RESTAURANT THAT NEVERTHELESS HAD THE KINDNESS TO SERVE US BEFORE CLOSING.

WHAT'S THIS? TOMATOES, ARTICHOKE HEARTS, BABY CORN, AND IMITATION CRAB IN A DISH OF NOODLES AND PORK TERIYAKI? CLEARLY, I'M HUNGRY.

SMWEEK SMWEEK

IT'S NOT THAT DIFFICULT TO MAKE A BOWL OF NOODLES AND PORK!

CAN YOU STOP TALKING ABOUT FOOD FOR TWO SECONDS?

YOU HAVEN'T TOLD ME WHAT YOU THINK OF MY HAT!

*IN SWEDEN, EVERYTHING CLOSES EARLY--NOT LIKE FRANCE. HERE PEOPLE GENERALLY EAT DINNER AROUND 6 P.M.!

Day 4

WHAAAA I DON'T BELIEVE IIIIT!

NANCY, COME SEEEE!

OKAY WHAT

THERE ON THE CORNER!!

THE H&M?

NO, BEHIND IT!

OKAY WHAT

THERE

PFFF

ON THE STREET CORNER, BEHIND THE H&M, VISIBLE WHEN LEANING YOUR HEAD OUT OF THE WINDOW OF THE HOTEL ROOM SUITE.

WHAT, THE JUNK FOOD?

THE BURGER KING!

YEAH, THAT'S JUNK FOOD.

COME ONNN...

YOU'RE BEING ANTI-AMERICAN!

NO, I JUST DON'T LIKE GROSS STUFF. SLIGHT DIFFERENCE.

BA-BUM, BA-BUM.

BUT A BURGER KING! FINALLY! THE STUFF OF FRENCH LEGENDS! I'M NOT TALKING ABOUT ANY OLD MCDONALD'S. BURGER KING IS SUPER HIP WITH THESE AMAZING FRIES AND BURGERS THA MELT IN YOUR MOUTH!

♪ LALALA I CAN'T HEAR YOU ♪♪

THE LAST ONE NEAREST TO ME JUST CLOSED! I NEVER DARED TO HOPE THAT I'D FIND IT HERE, OF ALL PLACES!

AT NOON, WE EAT LUNCH IN THE BASEMENT OF THE HÖTORGSHALLEN NEAR THE KONSERHUSET (CONCERT HALL).

HÖTORGSHALLEN, AN INDOOR MARKET WITH GRUB AS FAR AS THE EYE CAN SEE...

"Hell and wild dens salute you."

Or something like that.

AT... **KAJSAS FISK**

... YOU EAT REALLY WELL FOR CHEAP:

(DÉCO-CHEAP, LIKE AT A SUPERMARKET CAFÉ)

IT'S CRAZY TO THINK THAT I'M EATING THIS EXCELLENT FISH SOUP IN THIS MARKET WHEN, IN MARSEILLES, IT'S IMPOSSIBLE TO FIND A BOUILLABAISSE THAT'S HALF AS GOOD FOR TWICE THE PRICE!

GULP!

85 KR ($10)
REAL FISH SOUP WITH REAL PIECES OF FISH

REAL BREAD WITH REAL AIOLI

REAL SWEDISH TABLE

SO BECAUSE WE'VE ONLY EATEN SOUP...

WE COULD GO GET A LITTLE *BURGER KING*...

STILL CAN'T HEE-EEEAR YOU

HÖTORGSHALLEN

ESRO

SUSHI BAR

FISKEHAGET 006

IN THE AFTERNOON, I GO TO THE BAR ON THE TOP FLOOR OF THE KULTURHUSET TO DRAW DAY 2 OF MY JOURNAL.

NANCY SIGNING BOOKS ON THE FOURTH FLOOR

KULTURH

KULTUR HUSE

AS I WAIT FOR MY SERVER, I OBSERVE A GUY ON THE SQUARE FAR BELOW, DOING TAI-CHI WHILE BALANCING BEER CANS ON HIS HEAD...

IT CAN'T BE THAT HARD, BUT THE GUY IS REALLY ZONED IN.

I WAIT FOREVER FOR THE SERVER, TRYING FROM TIME TO TIME TO GET HIS ATTENTION. BUT I'M USED TO NOT BEING NOTICED AT BARS. I'M LEFT EVEN MORE ALONE WHEN I DRAW.

EXCUSE ME, I WANT DRINK.*

AFTER SOME TIME, I FIGURE OUT THAT I'M IN A SELF-SERVICE BAR. GO FIGURE!

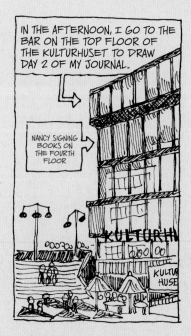

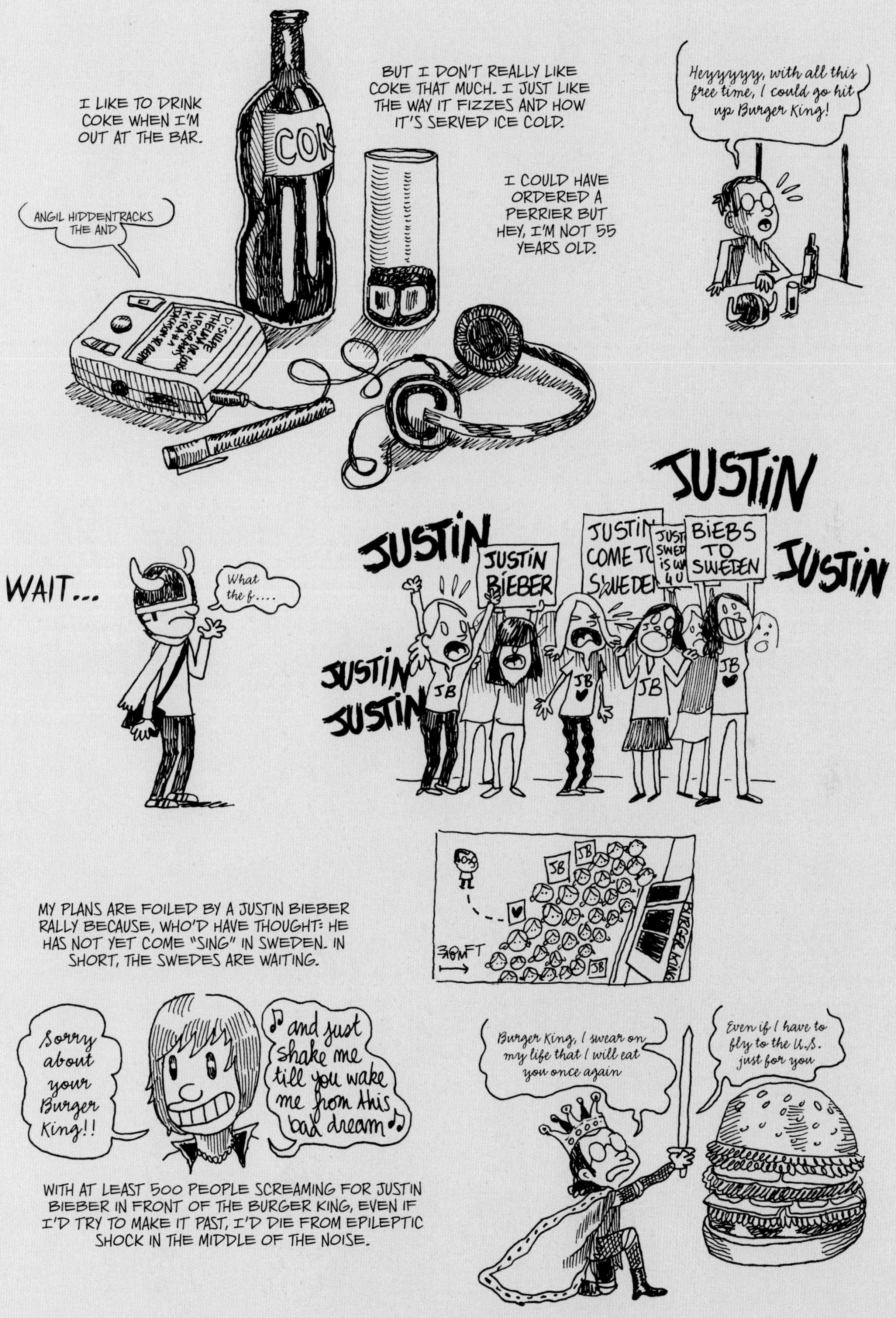

I LIKE TO DRINK COKE WHEN I'M OUT AT THE BAR.
BUT I DON'T REALLY LIKE COKE THAT MUCH. I JUST LIKE THE WAY IT FIZZES AND HOW IT'S SERVED ICE COLD.
COK
ANGIL HIDDENTRACKS THE AND
I COULD HAVE ORDERED A PERRIER BUT HEY, I'M NOT 55 YEARS OLD.
Heyyyyyy, with all this free time, I could go hit up Burger King!
WAIT...
What the f....
JUSTIN
JUSTIN BIEBER
JUSTIN COME TO SWEDEN
BIEBS TO SWEDEN
JUSTIN
JUSTIN
JUSTIN
JUSTIN
JB
JB
JB
MY PLANS ARE FOILED BY A JUSTIN BIEBER RALLY BECAUSE, WHO'D HAVE THOUGHT: HE HAS NOT YET COME "SING" IN SWEDEN. IN SHORT, THE SWEDES ARE WAITING.
JB
30 FT
BURGER KING
Sorry about your Burger King!!
and just shake me till you wake me from this bad dream
WITH AT LEAST 500 PEOPLE SCREAMING FOR JUSTIN BIEBER IN FRONT OF THE BURGER KING, EVEN IF I'D TRY TO MAKE IT PAST, I'D DIE FROM EPILEPTIC SHOCK IN THE MIDDLE OF THE NOISE.
Burger King, I swear on my life that I will eat you once again
Even if I have to fly to the U.S. just for you

That evening, we look for somewhere nice to eat but everything's already booked up:

WE SETTLE ON
DE SVARTA FÅREN

The black sheep

What you mean, no reservations? You don't know who I am?*

Mean nothing to you, journalist for Le Monde?*

Yes, French newspaper. With news.*

You not? Oh okay*

I get out of the shower like Dominque-Strauss Kahn. You'll see!

Cheap candles everywhere... I smell tourist trap.

Yeah and a menu in three languages.

At least we tried.

SO WE ORDER:

① GRILLAD HALLOUMIOST MED TOMAT, BASILIKA OCH OLIVOLJA PÅ ROSTAT BONDBRÖD

② ÄLGCARPACCIO MED BASILIKA, PIN-JENÖTTER, RIVEN PARMESAN TOPPAT MED OLIVOLJA & BALSAMICO

③ KLASSISK BIFF A LA' RYDBERG, TÄRNAD OXFILÉ OCH POTATIS SERVERAS MED ROSTAD LÖK, SENAPSCRÈME SAMT ÄGGULA

① DECENT APPETIZER. THE TOMATOES HAVE NO TASTE, BUT IT WILL DO WHEN PAIRED WITH THE BASIL... THE HALLOUMI CHEESE IS A BIG THING IN SWEDEN, BUT IT'S ACTUALLY FROM CYPRUS. IN SUM, NOT BAD. BUT KINDA MELTED.

② MOOSE CARPACCIO! PINE NUTS. I CROSS MY FINGERS THAT THEY'RE NOT FROM CHINA. IT'S BETTER THAN THE BEEF, PROBABLY BECAUSE OF ITS ORIGINALITY.

③ BEEF RYDBERG, A CLASSIC DISH WITH PIECES OF BRAISED MEAT, COOKED EGG, CHEESE SAUCE, POTATOES IN THEIR SKINS, AND SOME GRAVY. GOOD, BUT JUST A BIT TOO MUCH.

Come on, little guy

Wanna make a carpaccio with Michel?

SPEAKING OBJECTIVELY, DE SVARTA FÅREN WASN'T BAD. JUST A LITTLE TOO GUIDEBOOK-ESQUE TO REALLY BE MY CUP OF TEA.

Do you think that Burger King makes moose hamburgers up here?

♪lalalaaa♪

TAC TAC TAC TAC TAC TAC

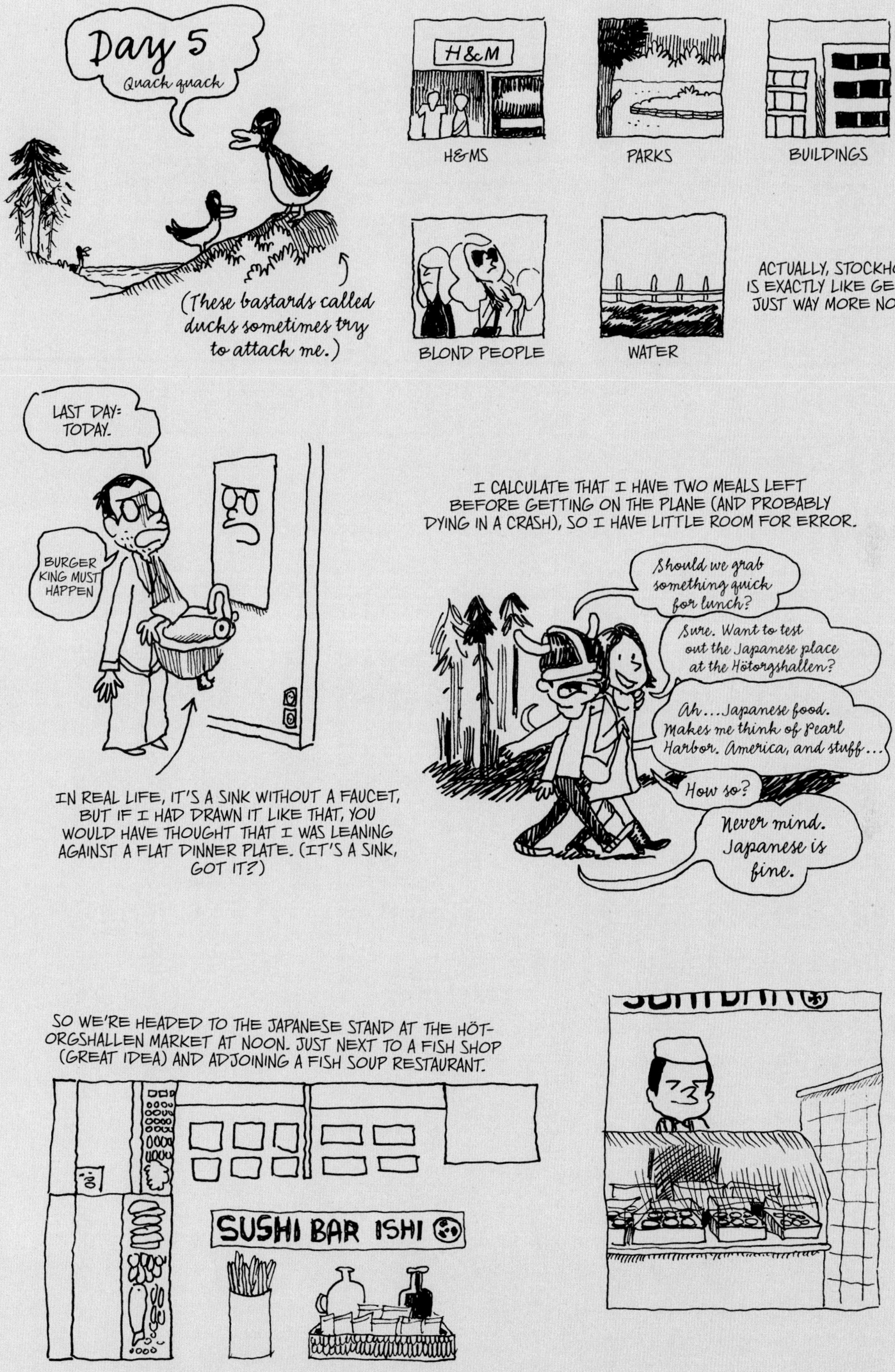

Day 5
Quack quack
(These bastards called ducks sometimes try to attack me.)
H&M
H&MS
PARKS
BUILDINGS
BLOND PEOPLE
WATER
ACTUALLY, STOCKHOLM IS EXACTLY LIKE GENEVA, JUST WAY MORE NORTH.
LAST DAY: TODAY.
BURGER KING MUST HAPPEN
IN REAL LIFE, IT'S A SINK WITHOUT A FAUCET, BUT IF I HAD DRAWN IT LIKE THAT, YOU WOULD HAVE THOUGHT THAT I WAS LEANING AGAINST A FLAT DINNER PLATE. (IT'S A SINK, GOT IT?)
I CALCULATE THAT I HAVE TWO MEALS LEFT BEFORE GETTING ON THE PLANE (AND PROBABLY DYING IN A CRASH), SO I HAVE LITTLE ROOM FOR ERROR.
Should we grab something quick for lunch?
Sure. Want to test out the Japanese place at the Hötorgshallen?
Ah... Japanese food. Makes me think of Pearl Harbor. America, and stuff...
How so?
Never mind. Japanese is fine.
SO WE'RE HEADED TO THE JAPANESE STAND AT THE HÖT-ORGSHALLEN MARKET AT NOON. JUST NEXT TO A FISH SHOP (GREAT IDEA) AND ADJOINING A FISH SOUP RESTAURANT.
SUSHI BAR ISHI

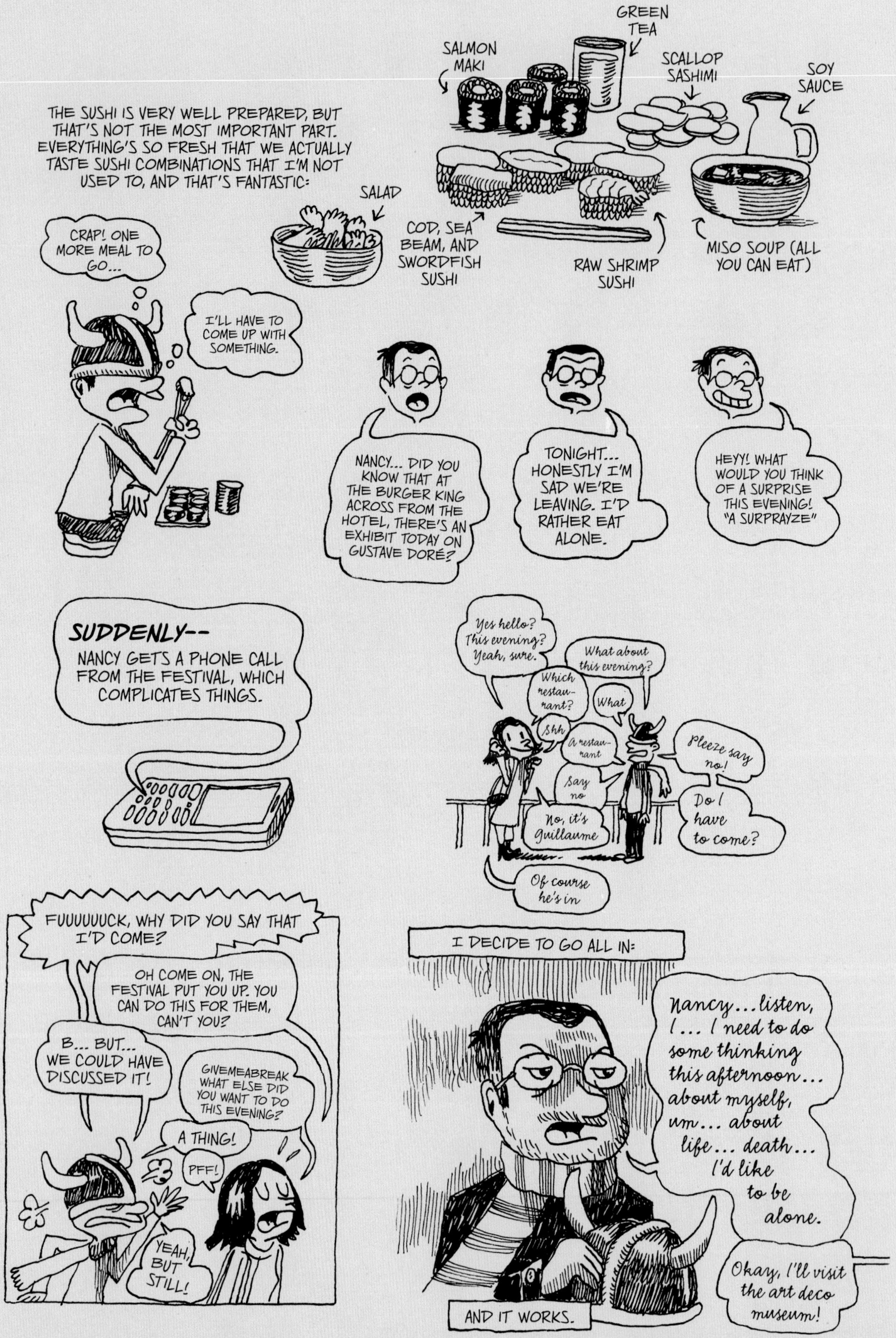
THE SUSHI IS VERY WELL PREPARED, BUT THAT'S NOT THE MOST IMPORTANT PART. EVERYTHING'S SO FRESH THAT WE ACTUALLY TASTE SUSHI COMBINATIONS THAT I'M NOT USED TO, AND THAT'S FANTASTIC:
GREEN TEA
SALMON MAKI
SCALLOP SASHIMI
SOY SAUCE
SALAD
COD, SEA BEAM, AND SWORDFISH SUSHI
RAW SHRIMP SUSHI
MISO SOUP (ALL YOU CAN EAT)
CRAP! ONE MORE MEAL TO GO...
I'LL HAVE TO COME UP WITH SOMETHING.
NANCY... DID YOU KNOW THAT AT THE BURGER KING ACROSS FROM THE HOTEL, THERE'S AN EXHIBIT TODAY ON GUSTAVE DORÉ?
TONIGHT... HONESTLY I'M SAD WE'RE LEAVING. I'D RATHER EAT ALONE.
HEYY! WHAT WOULD YOU THINK OF A SURPRISE THIS EVENING! "A SURPRAYZE"
SUDDENLY--
NANCY GETS A PHONE CALL FROM THE FESTIVAL, WHICH COMPLICATES THINGS.
Yes hello? This evening? Yeah, sure.
What about this evening?
Which restaurant?
What
Shh
A restaurant
Pleeze say no!
Say no
No, it's Guillaume
Do I have to come?
Of course he's in
FUUUUUUCK, WHY DID YOU SAY THAT I'D COME?
OH COME ON, THE FESTIVAL PUT YOU UP. YOU CAN DO THIS FOR THEM, CAN'T YOU?
B... BUT... WE COULD HAVE DISCUSSED IT!
GIVEMEABREAK WHAT ELSE DID YOU WANT TO DO THIS EVENING?
A THING!
PFF!
YEAH, BUT STILL!
I DECIDE TO GO ALL IN:
Nancy... listen, I... I need to do some thinking this afternoon... about myself, um... about life... death... I'd like to be alone.
Okay, I'll visit the art deco museum!
AND IT WORKS.

YEEESSS!!!!

The Burger King Dance

B
U
R
G
E
R
K
i
N
G

FINALLY, I HEAD TOWARDS THE ***BURGER KING*** NEAR THE HOTEL. I'M NOT REALLY HUNGRY BUT SEEING THAT I KNOW NOTHING ABOUT THIS EVENING'S RESTAURANT, IT'S BETTER TO EAT TWICE.

BUT WHEN I ARRIVE BEFORE THE FAST-FOOD MYTH, EVERYTHING'S DARK AND THERE'S THIS SMALL SIGN ON THE DOOR:

STÄNGT
LEDSEN!

THIS CAN'T
HAPPENING

Whyyyyyyy but whyyyyyyy
?

IT'S CLOSED. GAME OVER. I'M FINISHED. I WILL NOT BE EATING BURGER KING TODAY. MAYBE EVER. I'M COLD, I'M ALONE IN THIS CITY THAT'S EXACTLY LIKE GENEVA, JUST WAY MORE NORTH. WITHOUT BURGER KING.

NO.
I CAN
NOT.

FOR THE REST OF AFTERNOON, I WANDER SADLY THROUGH THE STREETS OF STOCKHOLM. I BUY SOME GRUB TO TAKE HOME.

Cans of rollmops

Fresh smoked salmon

A reindeer roast

sardines

Crispbread. Go ahead, say it.

Wasa

Halloumi cheese

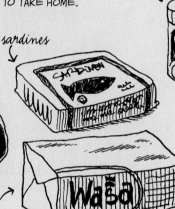

I also buy a reindeer pelt.

The chatterbox from breakfast the other day really had a point.

Cuz when I can't eat what I want, I go a little crazy and shit.

THE EVENING
I meet up with Nancy at the restaurant along with the others from the festival.

SNF SNF

?

YOU SMELL LIKE MCDONALD'S. DID YOU GET SOME WHEN YOU WERE OUT?

PFFFFF!

OR ELSE I'D SAY YOU MADE OUT WITH A TRASHCAN...

UGHHH!

LIKE I THOUGHT, THE RESTAURANT REALLY ISN'T THAT GOOD.

BLÅ DÖRREN   KROG

ACROSS FROM ME AT THE TABLE, THERE'S THIS GUY, THIERRY GROENSTEEN. HE'S A HISTORIAN OF FRENCH-LANGUAGE COMICS AND A PUBLISHER AT ACTES SUD... IN SHORT, HE'S UP IN THE FIELD. AT ONE POINT, HE TAKES MY JOURNAL AND SAYS:

Ohhh, you recommend stuff to drink and to eat in here!

Well hey, I've never heard of your work, even though I'm up in this field!

Hey speaking of that...

Are you gonna draw me in your journal?

Hm? Hm?

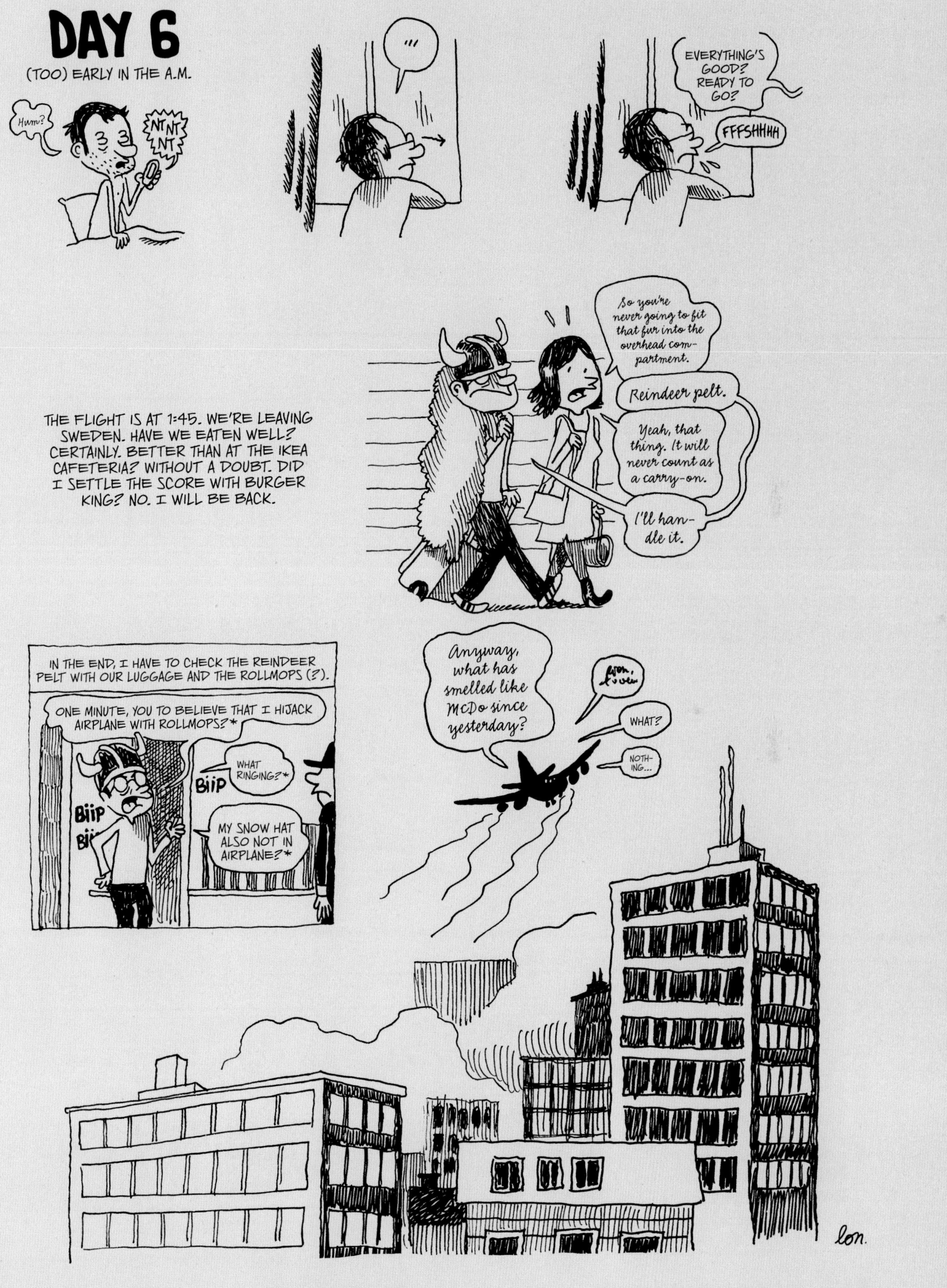
DAY 6
(TOO) EARLY IN THE A.M.
Hum?
NT NT NT
"
EVERYTHING'S GOOD? READY TO GO?
FFFSHHHH
THE FLIGHT IS AT 1:45. WE'RE LEAVING SWEDEN. HAVE WE EATEN WELL? CERTAINLY. BETTER THAN AT THE IKEA CAFETERIA? WITHOUT A DOUBT. DID I SETTLE THE SCORE WITH BURGER KING? NO. I WILL BE BACK.
So you're never going to fit that fur into the overhead compartment.
Reindeer pelt.
Yeah, that thing. It will never count as a carry-on.
I'll handle it.
IN THE END, I HAVE TO CHECK THE REINDEER PELT WITH OUR LUGGAGE AND THE ROLLMOPS (?).
ONE MINUTE, YOU TO BELIEVE THAT I HIJACK AIRPLANE WITH ROLLMOPS?*
BIIP
BIIP
WHAT RINGING?*
MY SNOW HAT ALSO NOT IN AIRPLANE?*
Anyway, what has smelled like McDo since yesterday?
WHAT?
NOTHING...
lon.

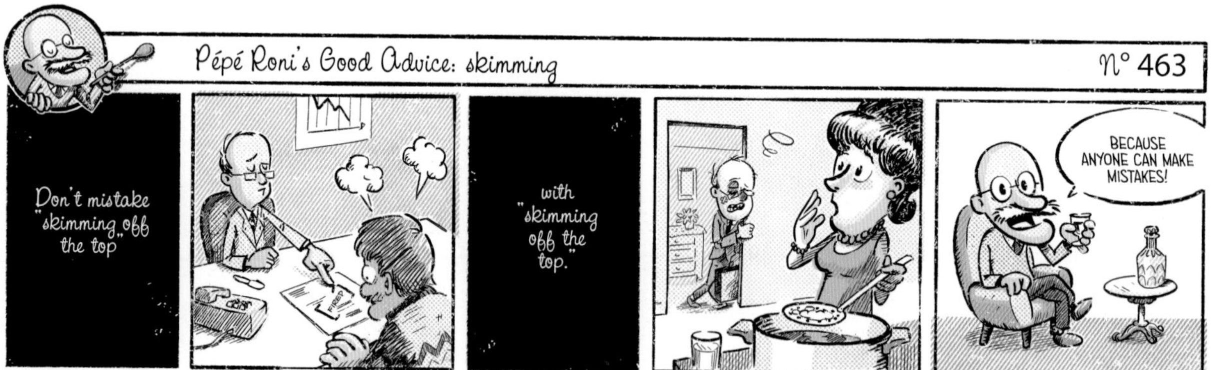
Pépé Roni's Good Advice: skimming
N° 463
Don't mistake "skimming off the top"
with "skimming off the top."
BECAUSE ANYONE CAN MAKE MISTAKES!
Skimming: Removing the layer of fat that collects on the surface of a sauce, stock, or broth (easiest to do when chilled).

Summer

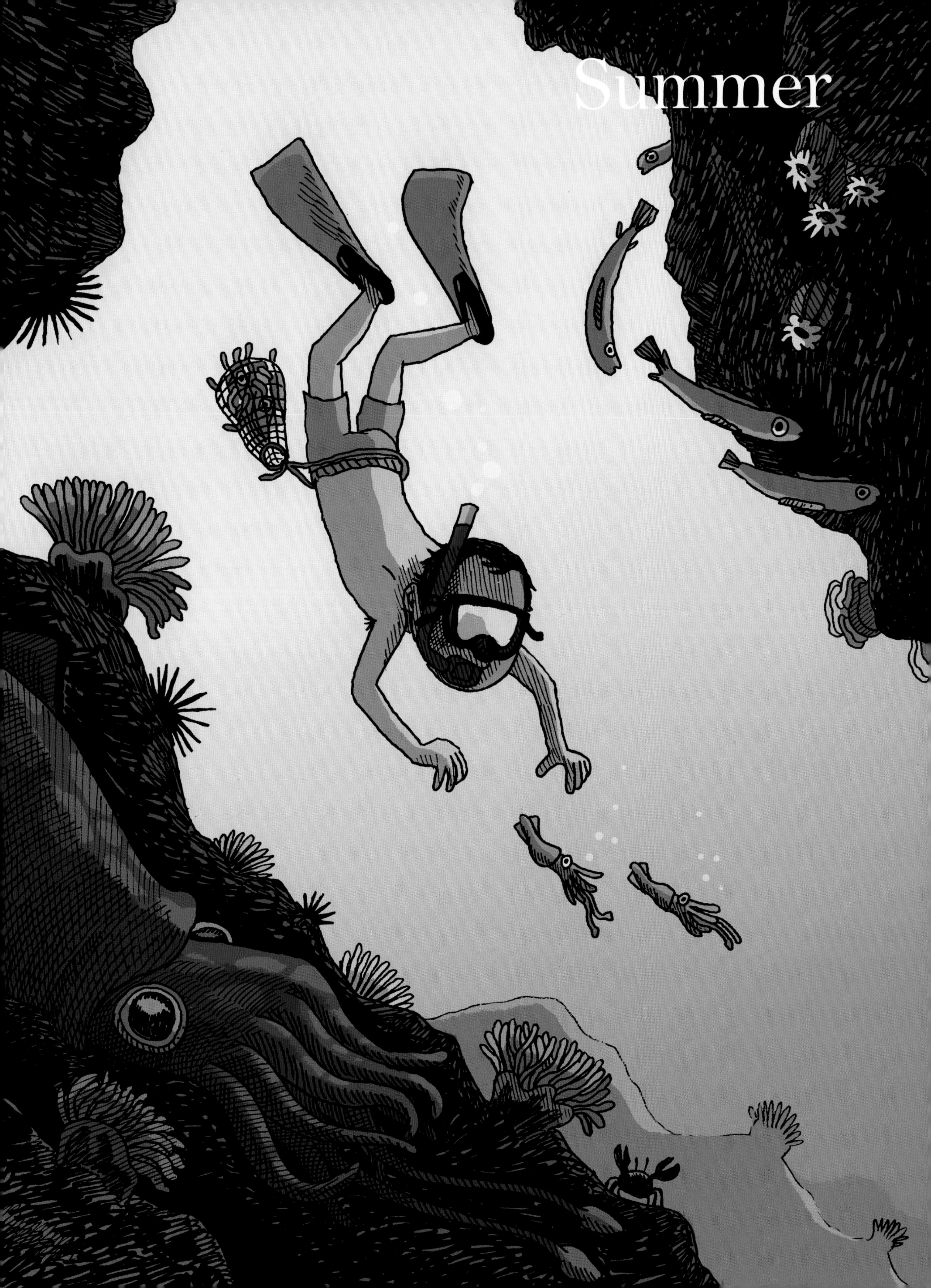

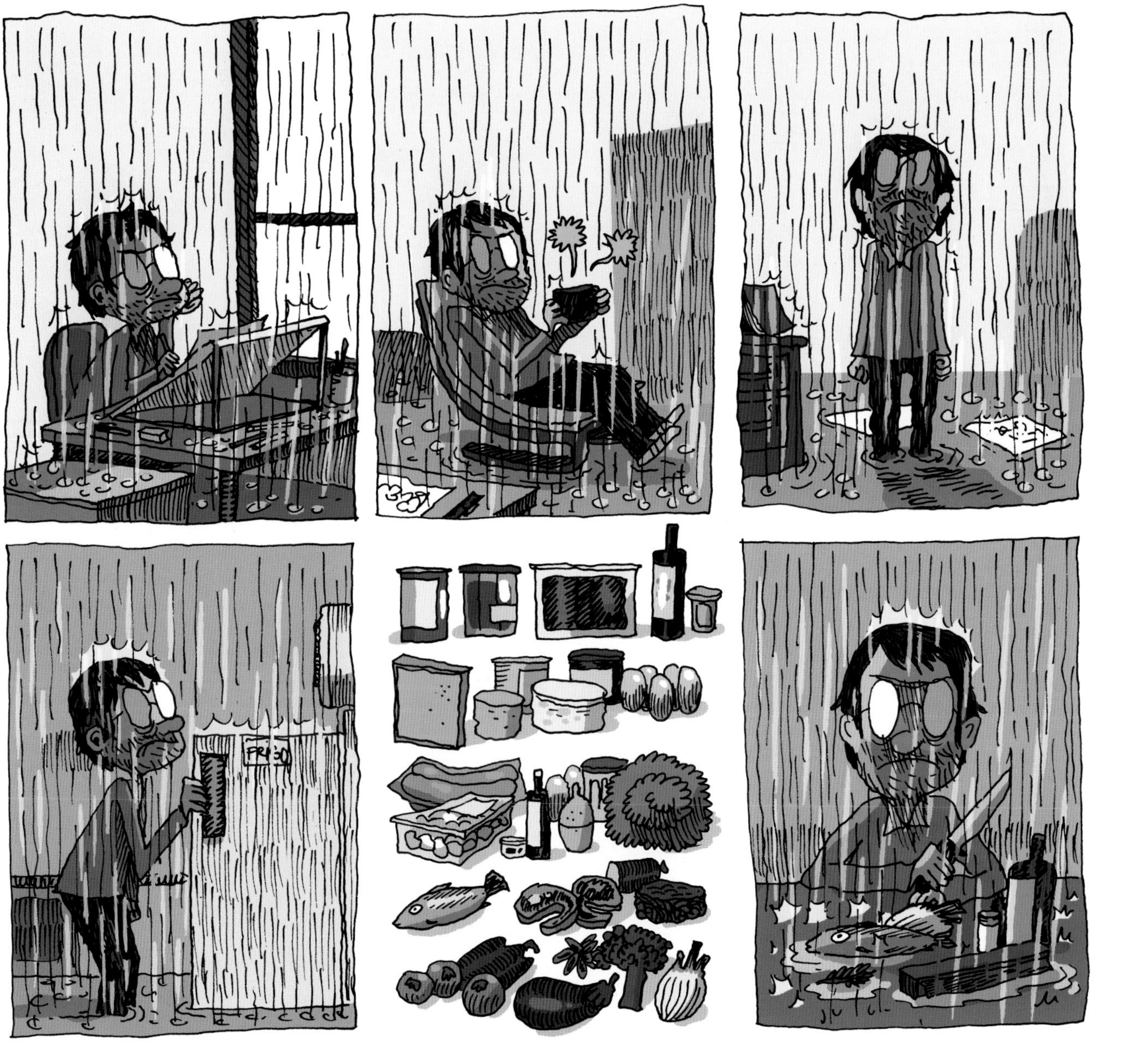

SOME DAYS, YOU JUST NEED THINGS TO BE EASY. A TROUT IS EASY ENOUGH, RIGHT? BUY IT GUTTED AND SCALED. IF YOU CAN, GO FOR A RIVER TROUT BECAUSE A RAINBOW TROUT, DESPITE ITS NAME, LACKS FLAVOR. STUFF HIM WITH A SPRIG OF ROSEMARY (OR THYME OR SAGE) LIKE THIS:

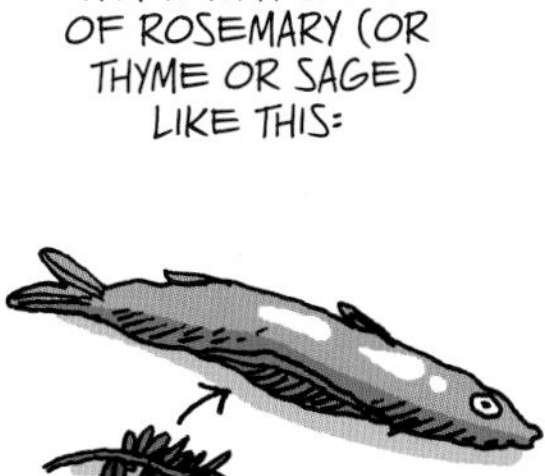

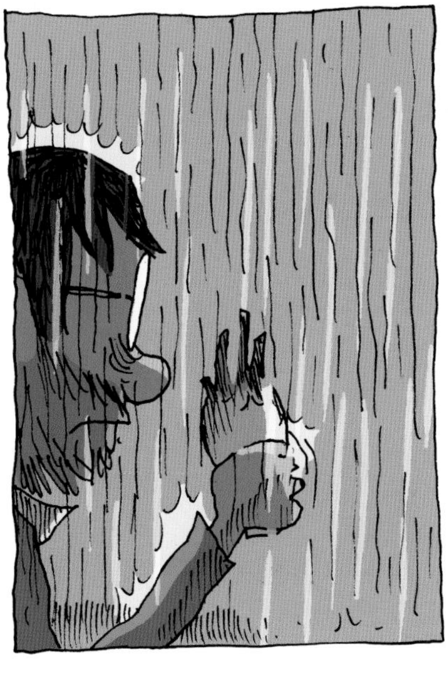

TURN YOUR OVEN TO BROIL. AS IT HEATS, TAKE CARE OF THE FENNEL:

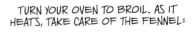

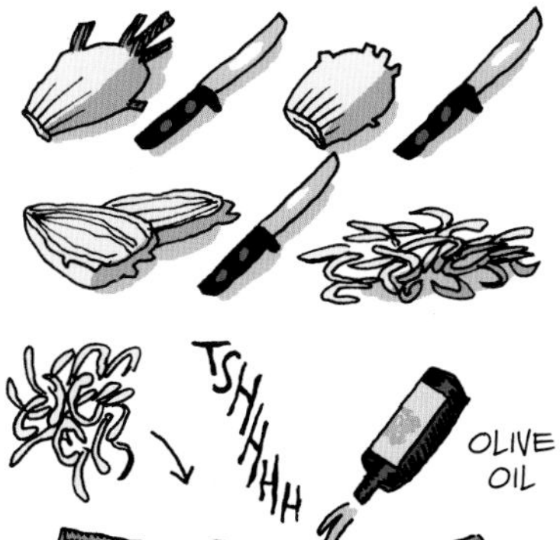
TSHHHH
OLIVE OIL

(OVER HIGH HEAT FOR THREE MINUTES, STIRRING OCCASIONALLY)

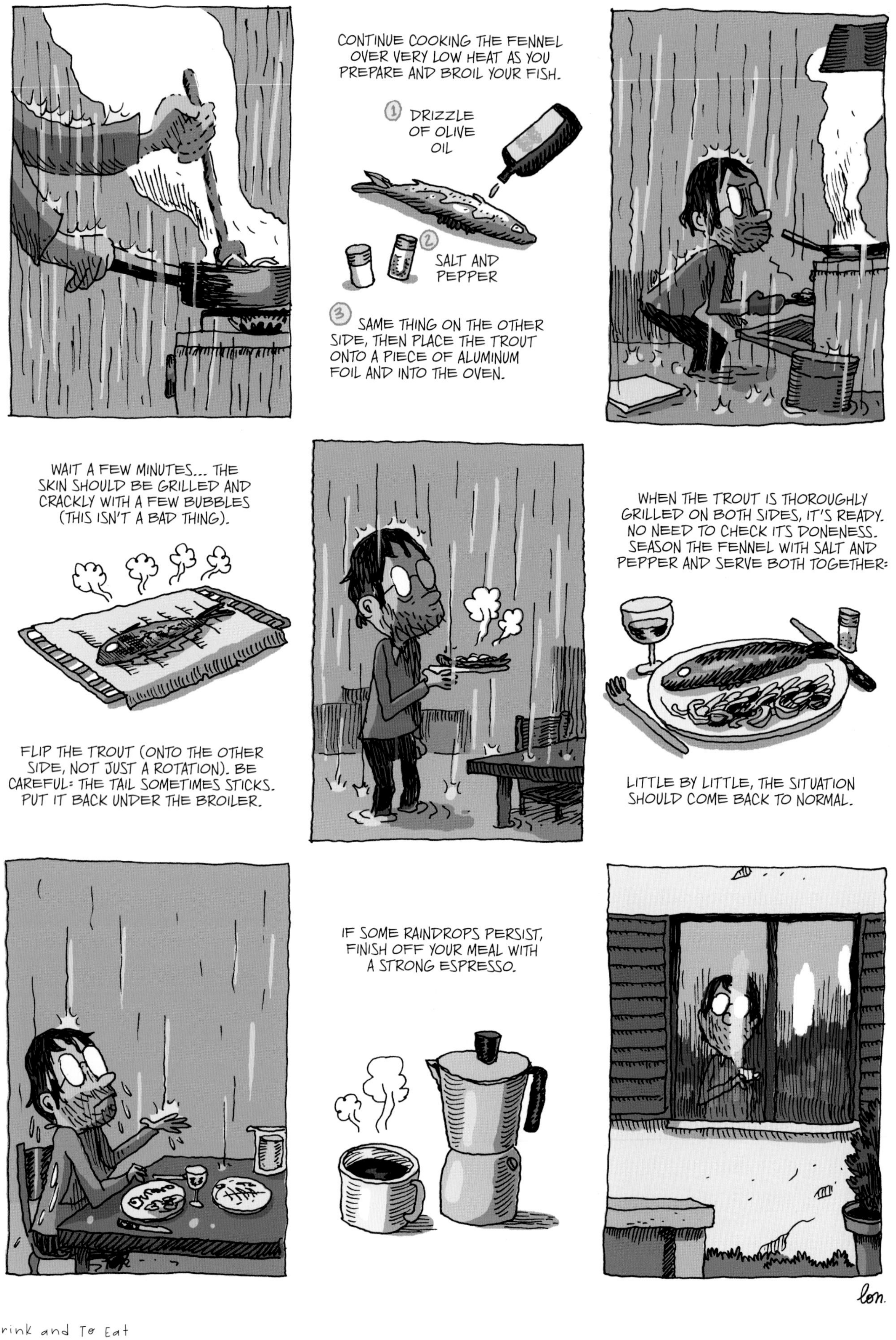
CONTINUE COOKING THE FENNEL OVER VERY LOW HEAT AS YOU PREPARE AND BROIL YOUR FISH.
1 DRIZZLE OF OLIVE OIL
2 SALT AND PEPPER
3 SAME THING ON THE OTHER SIDE, THEN PLACE THE TROUT ONTO A PIECE OF ALUMINUM FOIL AND INTO THE OVEN.
WAIT A FEW MINUTES... THE SKIN SHOULD BE GRILLED AND CRACKLY WITH A FEW BUBBLES (THIS ISN'T A BAD THING).
FLIP THE TROUT (ONTO THE OTHER SIDE, NOT JUST A ROTATION). BE CAREFUL: THE TAIL SOMETIMES STICKS. PUT IT BACK UNDER THE BROILER.
WHEN THE TROUT IS THOROUGHLY GRILLED ON BOTH SIDES, IT'S READY. NO NEED TO CHECK ITS DONENESS. SEASON THE FENNEL WITH SALT AND PEPPER AND SERVE BOTH TOGETHER:
LITTLE BY LITTLE, THE SITUATION SHOULD COME BACK TO NORMAL.
IF SOME RAINDROPS PERSIST, FINISH OFF YOUR MEAL WITH A STRONG ESPRESSO.
lon.

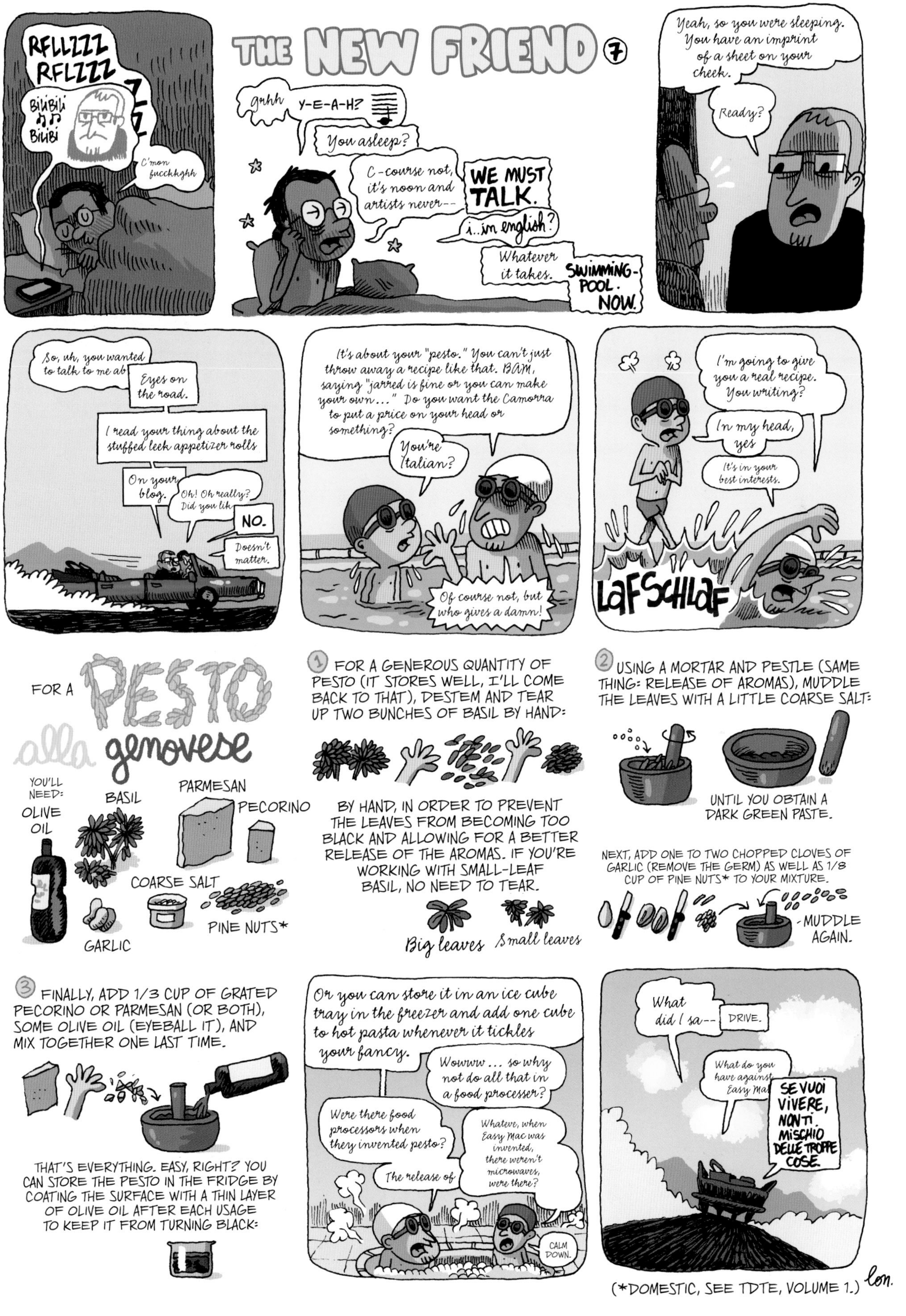
RFLLZZZ
RFLZZZ
BiLiBiLi ♫♪ BiLiBi
C'mon fucchhghh
THE NEW FRIEND 7
grhh
Y-E-A-H?
You asleep?
C-course not, it's noon and artists never--
WE MUST TALK.
i..in english?
Whatever it takes.
SWIMMING-POOL. NOW.
Yeah, so you were sleeping. You have an imprint of a sheet on your cheek.
Ready?
So, uh, you wanted to talk to me ab
Eyes on the road.
I read your thing about the stuffed leek appetizer rolls
On your blog.
Oh! Oh really? Did you lik
NO.
Doesn't matter.
It's about your "pesto." You can't just throw away a recipe like that. BAM, saying "jarred is fine or you can make your own..." Do you want the Camorra to put a price on your head or something?
You're Italian?
Of course not, but who gives a damn!
I'm going to give you a real recipe. You writing?
In my head, yes
It's in your best interests.
LAFSCHLAF
FOR A PESTO alla genovese
YOU'LL NEED:
OLIVE OIL
BASIL
PARMESAN
PECORINO
COARSE SALT
GARLIC
PINE NUTS*
1 FOR A GENEROUS QUANTITY OF PESTO (IT STORES WELL, I'LL COME BACK TO THAT), DESTEM AND TEAR UP TWO BUNCHES OF BASIL BY HAND:
BY HAND, IN ORDER TO PREVENT THE LEAVES FROM BECOMING TOO BLACK AND ALLOWING FOR A BETTER RELEASE OF THE AROMAS. IF YOU'RE WORKING WITH SMALL-LEAF BASIL, NO NEED TO TEAR.
Big leaves
Small leaves
2 USING A MORTAR AND PESTLE (SAME THING: RELEASE OF AROMAS), MUDDLE THE LEAVES WITH A LITTLE COARSE SALT:
UNTIL YOU OBTAIN A DARK GREEN PASTE.
NEXT, ADD ONE TO TWO CHOPPED CLOVES OF GARLIC (REMOVE THE GERM) AS WELL AS 1/8 CUP OF PINE NUTS* TO YOUR MIXTURE.
-MUDDLE AGAIN.
3 FINALLY, ADD 1/3 CUP OF GRATED PECORINO OR PARMESAN (OR BOTH), SOME OLIVE OIL (EYEBALL IT), AND MIX TOGETHER ONE LAST TIME.
THAT'S EVERYTHING. EASY, RIGHT? YOU CAN STORE THE PESTO IN THE FRIDGE BY COATING THE SURFACE WITH A THIN LAYER OF OLIVE OIL AFTER EACH USAGE TO KEEP IT FROM TURNING BLACK:
Or you can store it in an ice cube tray in the freezer and add one cube to hot pasta whenever it tickles your fancy.
Wowww... so why not do all that in a food processer?
Were there food processors when they invented pesto?
Whateve, when Easy Mac was invented, there weren't microwaves, were there?
The release of
CALM DOWN.
What did I sa--
DRIVE.
What do you have against Easy Ma
SE VUOI VIVERE, NON TI MISCHIO DELLE TROPPE COSE.
(*DOMESTIC, SEE TDTE, VOLUME 1.)
Lon.

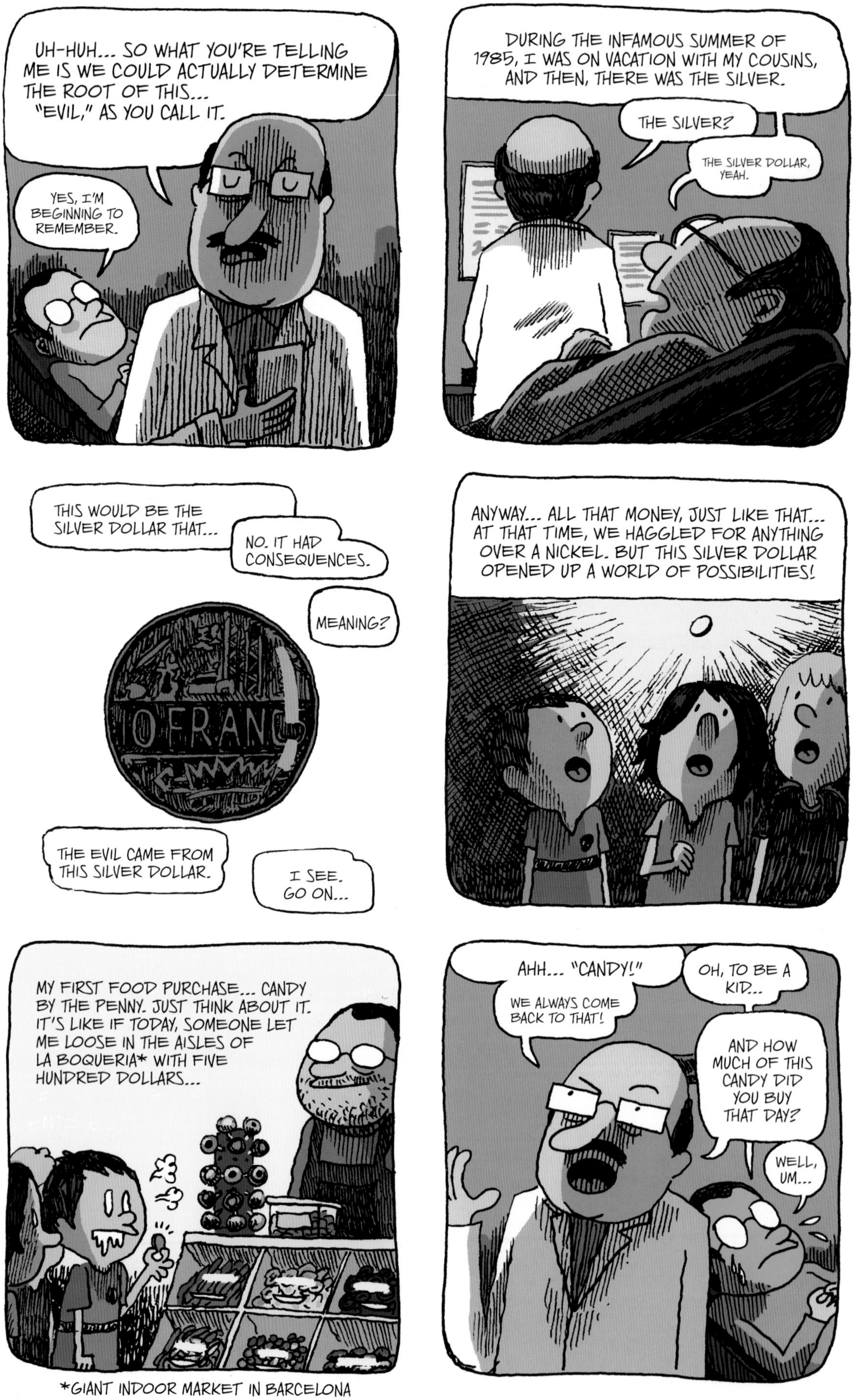
UH-HUH... SO WHAT YOU'RE TELLING ME IS WE COULD ACTUALLY DETERMINE THE ROOT OF THIS... "EVIL," AS YOU CALL IT.
YES, I'M BEGINNING TO REMEMBER.
DURING THE INFAMOUS SUMMER OF 1985, I WAS ON VACATION WITH MY COUSINS, AND THEN, THERE WAS THE SILVER.
THE SILVER?
THE SILVER DOLLAR, YEAH.
THIS WOULD BE THE SILVER DOLLAR THAT...
NO. IT HAD CONSEQUENCES.
MEANING?
10 FRANC
THE EVIL CAME FROM THIS SILVER DOLLAR.
I SEE. GO ON...
ANYWAY... ALL THAT MONEY, JUST LIKE THAT... AT THAT TIME, WE HAGGLED FOR ANYTHING OVER A NICKEL. BUT THIS SILVER DOLLAR OPENED UP A WORLD OF POSSIBILITIES!
MY FIRST FOOD PURCHASE... CANDY BY THE PENNY. JUST THINK ABOUT IT. IT'S LIKE IF TODAY, SOMEONE LET ME LOOSE IN THE AISLES OF LA BOQUERIA* WITH FIVE HUNDRED DOLLARS...
AHH... "CANDY!"
WE ALWAYS COME BACK TO THAT!
OH, TO BE A KID...
AND HOW MUCH OF THIS CANDY DID YOU BUY THAT DAY?
WELL, UM...

*GIANT INDOOR MARKET IN BARCELONA

AS I REMEMBER IT, WE COMPLETELY LOST OUR MINDS. LET'S SEE, ABOUT FIFTEEN SOUR FRUITY FRIES...

THE ACIDITY GOT EVERYONE ON THE SAME PAGE.

AND A COUPLE OF GUMMY BEARS... WE LIKED TO PLAY SURGERY WITH THEIR HEADS.

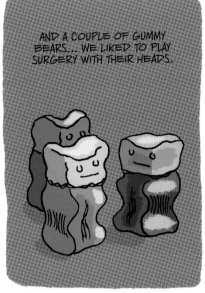

ON THAT NOTE, WE ALSO GOT SOME GUMMY CROCODILES. BUT I WASN'T A BIG FAN OF THE WHITE PART UNDERNEATH.

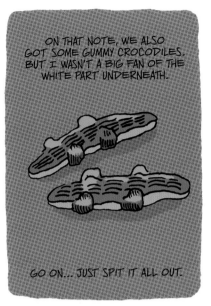

GO ON... JUST SPIT IT ALL OUT.

THANK YOU, DOCTOR... OH! THERE WERE ALSO SMURFS, BUT AT TEN CENTS A POP, THAT SOMEWHAT SHATTERED OUR BUDGET.

MAYBE THREE OR FOUR...

AT THE SAME PRICE, THERE WERE ALSO GUMMY LACES. WE LIKED THE RED ONES BEST.

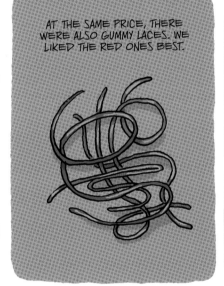

GOOD. ONE MOMENT--I BELIEVE I KNOW WHERE THIS IS COMING FROM. OKAY--GO ON.

OH... DID I TALK ABOUT THE GIANT TOOTSIE ROLLS?

NOW THAT WAS NEAT. FIFTEEN CENTS, BUT SO MUCH BETTER THAN THE REGULAR-SIZED ONES.

AHH! MALABAR GUM! TWENTY-FIVE CENTS, DOUBLE FLAVOR, AND A COMIC STRIP INSIDE! OR A TATTOO!

WE WAFFLED BETWEEN TUBBLE GUM OR HUBBA BUBBA FOR FIFTY CENTS, JUST TO BE COOL.

CHEWING GUM? UH-HUH. WE'RE MAKING HEADWAY.

REALLY? YOU THINK THAT COULD BE...

NO, BUT IT'S THE CLINCHER. IT COULD SINGLE-HANDEDLY BE THE SOURCE OF THIS "EVIL," AS YOU CALL IT... BUT I SUPPOSE THAT'S NOT EVERYTHING, RIGHT?

WELL ACTUALLY... NO, YOU'RE RIGHT. SHOULD I GO ON?

UP TO YOU. YOUR APPOINTMENT IS ALMOST UP.

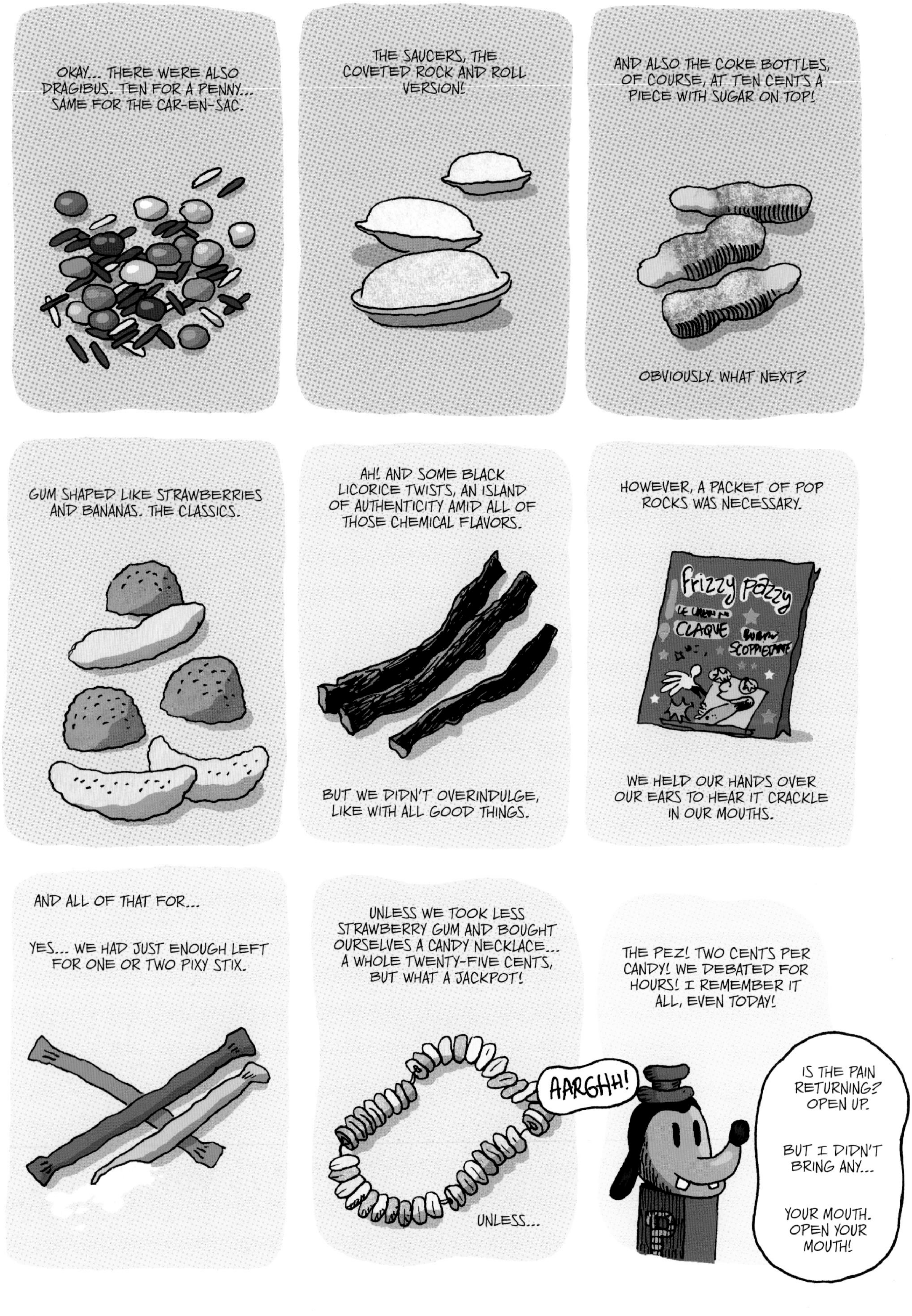
OKAY... THERE WERE ALSO DRAGIBUS. TEN FOR A PENNY... SAME FOR THE CAR-EN-SAC.
THE SAUCERS, THE COVETED ROCK AND ROLL VERSION!
AND ALSO THE COKE BOTTLES, OF COURSE, AT TEN CENTS A PIECE WITH SUGAR ON TOP!
OBVIOUSLY. WHAT NEXT?
GUM SHAPED LIKE STRAWBERRIES AND BANANAS. THE CLASSICS.
AH! AND SOME BLACK LICORICE TWISTS, AN ISLAND OF AUTHENTICITY AMID ALL OF THOSE CHEMICAL FLAVORS.
BUT WE DIDN'T OVERINDULGE, LIKE WITH ALL GOOD THINGS.
HOWEVER, A PACKET OF POP ROCKS WAS NECESSARY.
Frizzy Pazzy
CLAQUE
SCOPPIETTANTE
WE HELD OUR HANDS OVER OUR EARS TO HEAR IT CRACKLE IN OUR MOUTHS.
AND ALL OF THAT FOR...
YES... WE HAD JUST ENOUGH LEFT FOR ONE OR TWO PIXY STIX.
UNLESS WE TOOK LESS STRAWBERRY GUM AND BOUGHT OURSELVES A CANDY NECKLACE... A WHOLE TWENTY-FIVE CENTS, BUT WHAT A JACKPOT!
UNLESS...
THE PEZ! TWO CENTS PER CANDY! WE DEBATED FOR HOURS! I REMEMBER IT ALL, EVEN TODAY!
AARGHH!
IS THE PAIN RETURNING? OPEN UP.
BUT I DIDN'T BRING ANY...
YOUR MOUTH. OPEN YOUR MOUTH!

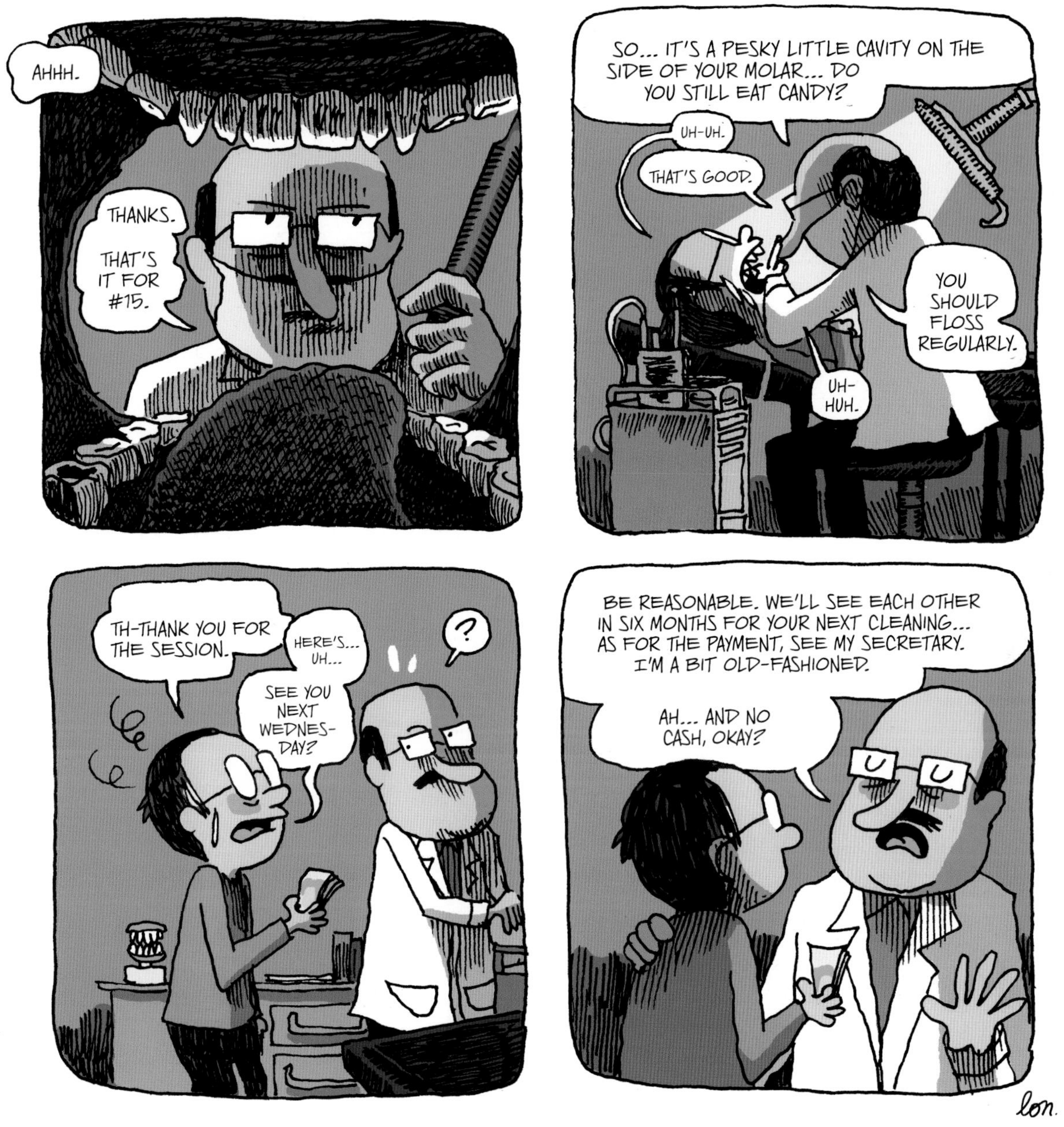
AHHH.
THANKS.
THAT'S IT FOR #15.
SO... IT'S A PESKY LITTLE CAVITY ON THE SIDE OF YOUR MOLAR... DO YOU STILL EAT CANDY?
UH-UH.
THAT'S GOOD.
YOU SHOULD FLOSS REGULARLY.
UH-HUH.
TH-THANK YOU FOR THE SESSION.
HERE'S... UH...
SEE YOU NEXT WEDNES-DAY?
?
BE REASONABLE. WE'LL SEE EACH OTHER IN SIX MONTHS FOR YOUR NEXT CLEANING... AS FOR THE PAYMENT, SEE MY SECRETARY. I'M A BIT OLD-FASHIONED.
AH... AND NO CASH, OKAY?
lon.

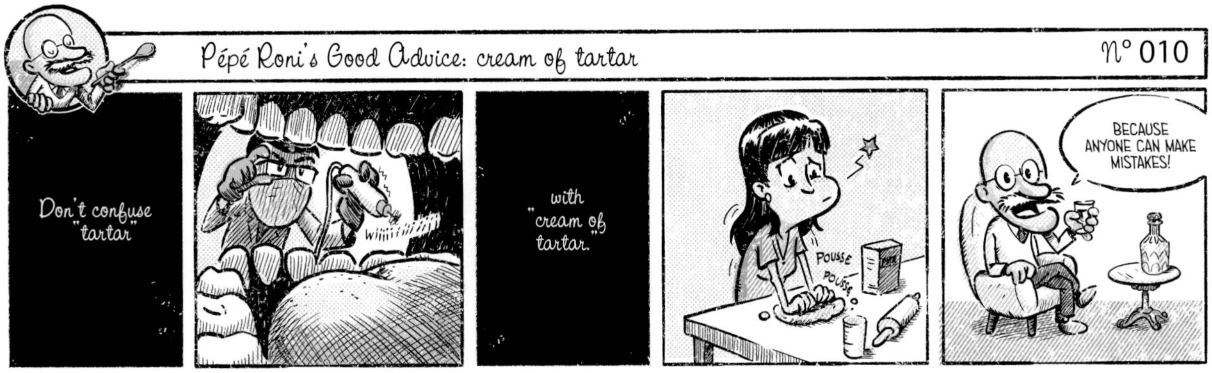
Pépé Roni's Good Advice: cream of tartar
N° 010
Don't confuse "tartar"
with "cream of tartar."
POUSSE
POUSSE
BECAUSE ANYONE CAN MAKE MISTAKES!

Cream of Tartar: An acid, purified into powder, that acts as a stabilizing agent or volume enhancer for egg whites and baked goods.

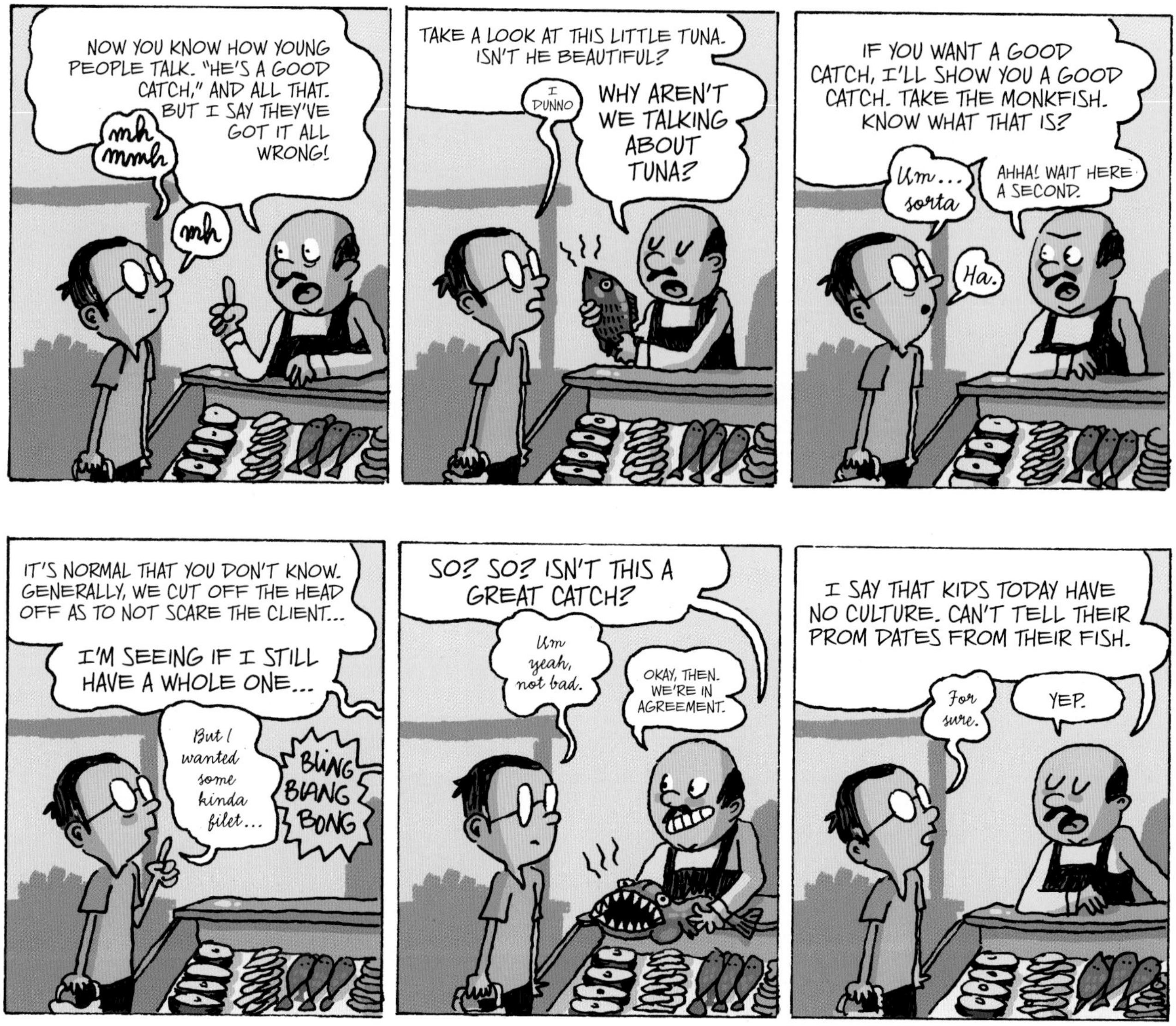
NOW YOU KNOW HOW YOUNG PEOPLE TALK. "HE'S A GOOD CATCH," AND ALL THAT. BUT I SAY THEY'VE GOT IT ALL WRONG!
mh mmh
mh
TAKE A LOOK AT THIS LITTLE TUNA. ISN'T HE BEAUTIFUL?
I DUNNO
WHY AREN'T WE TALKING ABOUT TUNA?
IF YOU WANT A GOOD CATCH, I'LL SHOW YOU A GOOD CATCH. TAKE THE MONKFISH. KNOW WHAT THAT IS?
Um... sorta
AHHA! WAIT HERE A SECOND.
Ha.
IT'S NORMAL THAT YOU DON'T KNOW. GENERALLY, WE CUT OFF THE HEAD OFF AS TO NOT SCARE THE CLIENT...
I'M SEEING IF I STILL HAVE A WHOLE ONE...
But I wanted some kinda filet...
BLING BLANG BONG
SO? SO? ISN'T THIS A GREAT CATCH?
Um yeah, not bad.
OKAY, THEN. WE'RE IN AGREEMENT.
I SAY THAT KIDS TODAY HAVE NO CULTURE. CAN'T TELL THEIR PROM DATES FROM THEIR FISH.
For sure.
YEP.

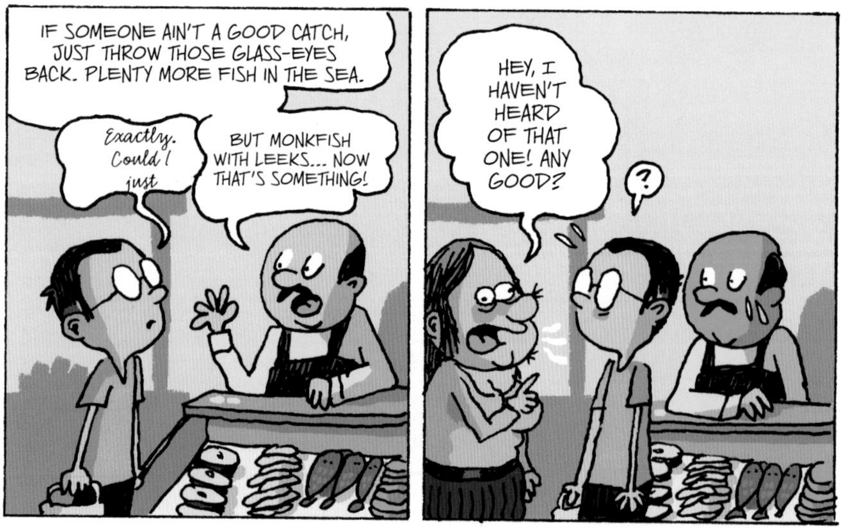
IF SOMEONE AIN'T A GOOD CATCH, JUST THROW THOSE GLASS-EYES BACK. PLENTY MORE FISH IN THE SEA.
Exactly. Could I just
BUT MONKFISH WITH LEEKS... NOW THAT'S SOMETHING!
HEY, I HAVEN'T HEARD OF THAT ONE! ANY GOOD?
?

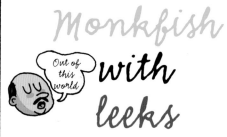

Monkfish with leeks

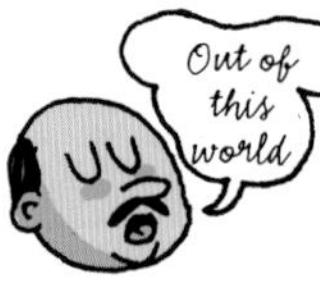
Out of this world

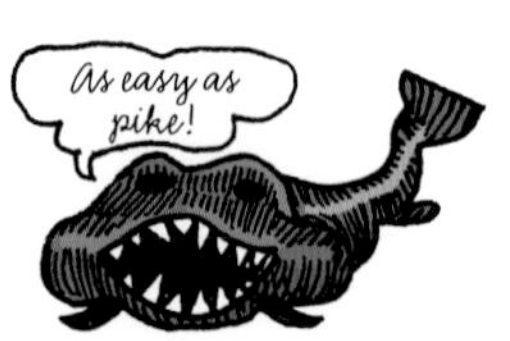
As easy as pike!

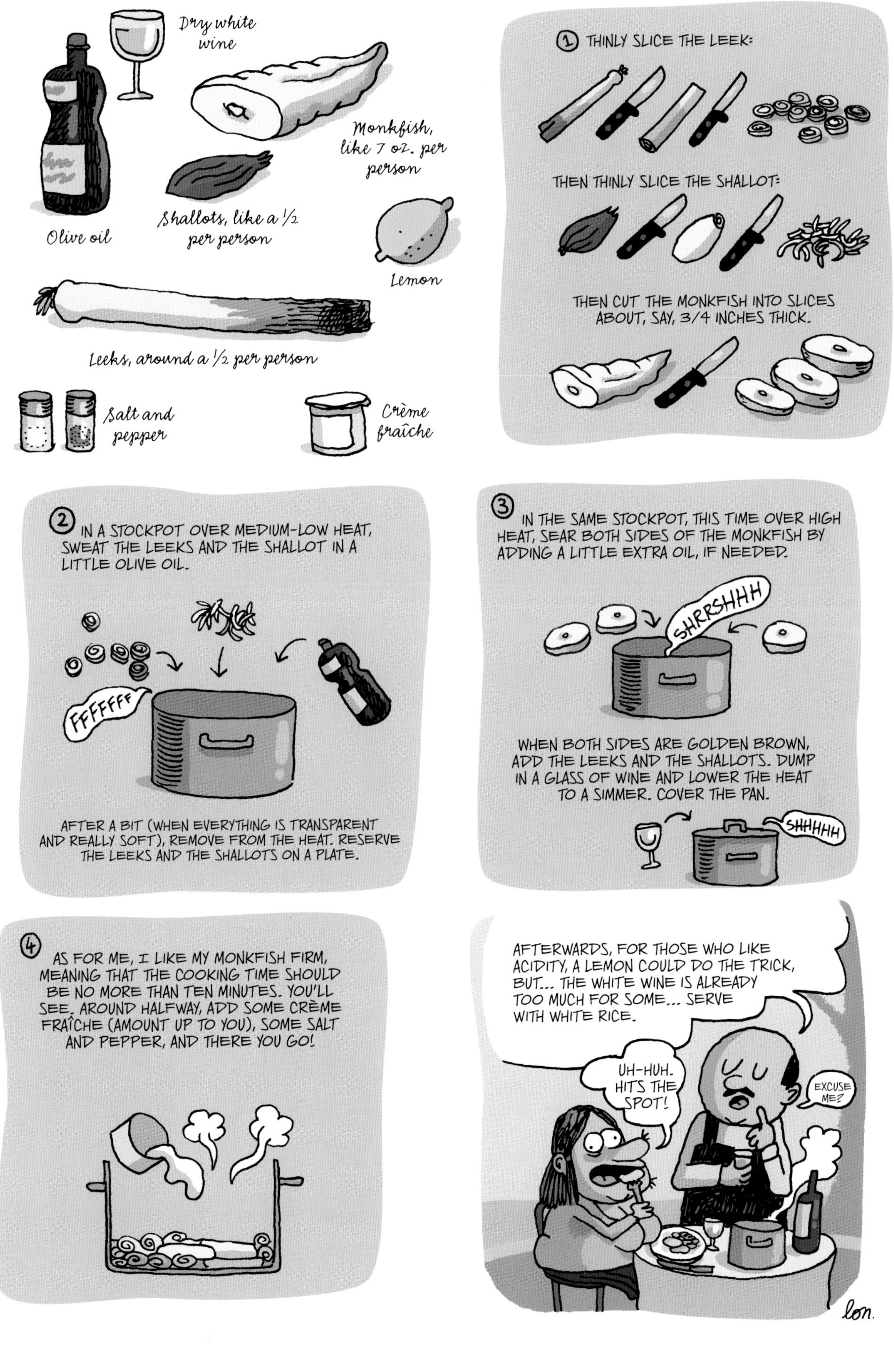
Dry white wine
Olive oil
Monkfish, like 7 oz. per person
Shallots, like a ½ per person
Lemon
Leeks, around a ½ per person
Salt and pepper
Crème fraîche
① THINLY SLICE THE LEEK:
THEN THINLY SLICE THE SHALLOT:
THEN CUT THE MONKFISH INTO SLICES ABOUT, SAY, 3/4 INCHES THICK.
② IN A STOCKPOT OVER MEDIUM-LOW HEAT, SWEAT THE LEEKS AND THE SHALLOT IN A LITTLE OLIVE OIL.
FFFFFFF
AFTER A BIT (WHEN EVERYTHING IS TRANSPARENT AND REALLY SOFT), REMOVE FROM THE HEAT. RESERVE THE LEEKS AND THE SHALLOTS ON A PLATE.
③ IN THE SAME STOCKPOT, THIS TIME OVER HIGH HEAT, SEAR BOTH SIDES OF THE MONKFISH BY ADDING A LITTLE EXTRA OIL, IF NEEDED.
SHRRSHHH
WHEN BOTH SIDES ARE GOLDEN BROWN, ADD THE LEEKS AND THE SHALLOTS. DUMP IN A GLASS OF WINE AND LOWER THE HEAT TO A SIMMER. COVER THE PAN.
SHHHHH
④ AS FOR ME, I LIKE MY MONKFISH FIRM, MEANING THAT THE COOKING TIME SHOULD BE NO MORE THAN TEN MINUTES. YOU'LL SEE. AROUND HALFWAY, ADD SOME CRÈME FRAÎCHE (AMOUNT UP TO YOU), SOME SALT AND PEPPER, AND THERE YOU GO!
AFTERWARDS, FOR THOSE WHO LIKE ACIDITY, A LEMON COULD DO THE TRICK, BUT... THE WHITE WINE IS ALREADY TOO MUCH FOR SOME... SERVE WITH WHITE RICE.
UH-HUH. HITS THE SPOT!
EXCUSE ME?
lon.

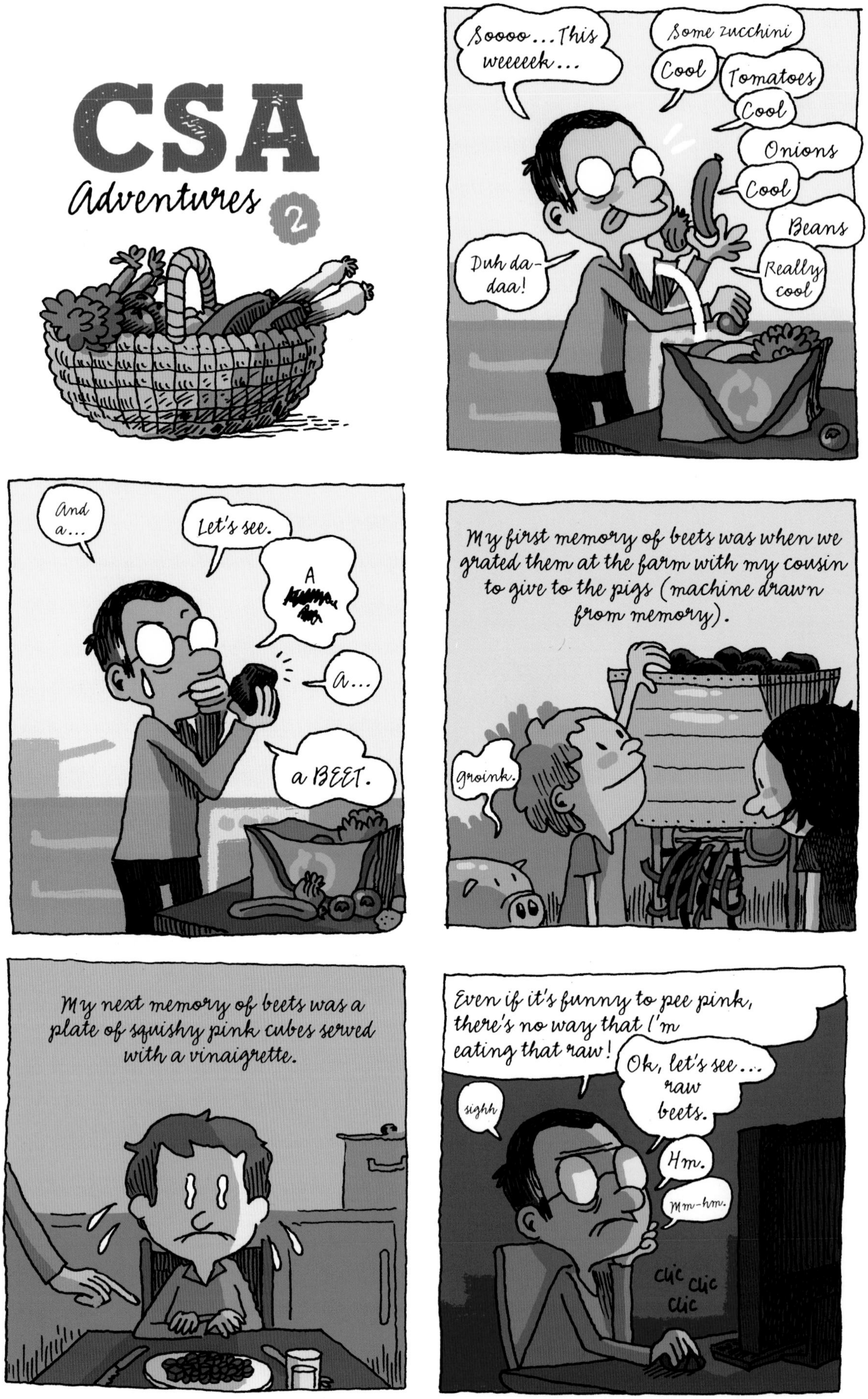
CSA
Adventures 2
Soooo... This weeeeek...
Some zucchini
Cool
Tomatoes
Cool
Onions
Cool
Beans
Really cool
Duh da-daa!
And a...
Let's see.
A
a...
a BEET.
My first memory of beets was when we grated them at the farm with my cousin to give to the pigs (machine drawn from memory).
Groink.
My next memory of beets was a plate of squishy pink cubes served with a vinaigrette.
Even if it's funny to pee pink, there's no way that I'm eating that raw!
sighh
Ok, let's see... raw beets.
Hm.
Mm-hm.
clic clic clic

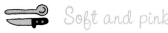

Hey! This doesn't seem too bad:

Tomato and beet carpaccio with ricotta

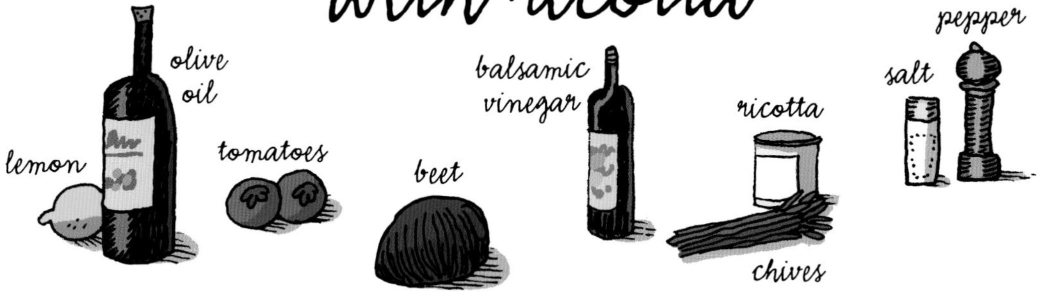
olive oil
lemon
tomatoes
beet
balsamic vinegar
ricotta
chives
salt
pepper

1. BEFORE COMMITTING TO ANYTHING, JUST KNOW THAT YOU'RE GONNA HAVE TO PEEL THE BEETS. AND IF YOU DON'T WANT RED FINGERS (WELL, IT IS KIND OF FUNNY), DO THE PEELING IN A BOWL OF WATER.

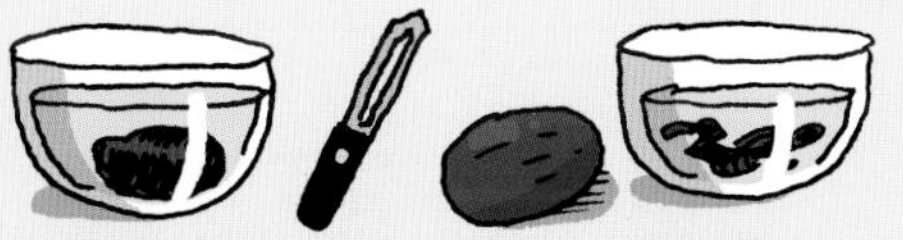

AND NEXT, CUT THE BEETS AND THE TOMATOES INTO VEEEERY THIIIIN SLICES (THE AMOUNT IS UP TO YOU).

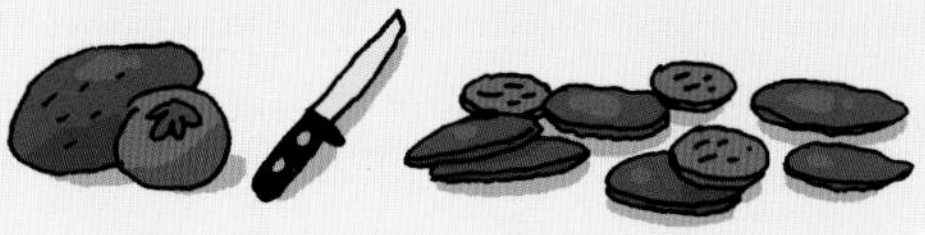

2. IN A BOWL, MIX THE RICOTTA WITH THE CHOPPED CHIVES.

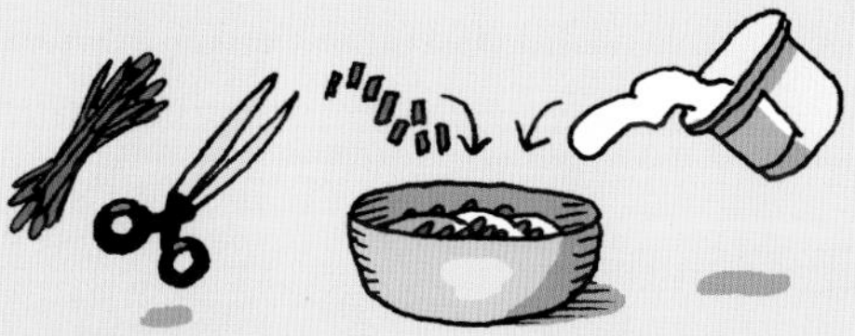

ADD A DRIZZLE OF OLIVE OIL AND A FEW DROPS OF LEMON JUICE TO TASTE.

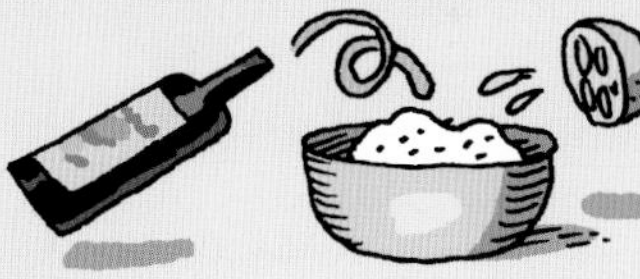

3. ON A PLATE, ARRANGE THE TOMATO AND BEET SLICES AS ARTFULLY AS YOU CAN MANAGE. SEASON WITH OLIVE OIL, BALSAMIC VINEGAR (IF IT'S WHITE BALSAMIC, IT WILL NOT STAIN THE TOMATOES), AND SALT AND PEPPER. FINALLY, TOP WITH YOUR RICOTTA MIXTURE, JUST AS ARTFULLY.

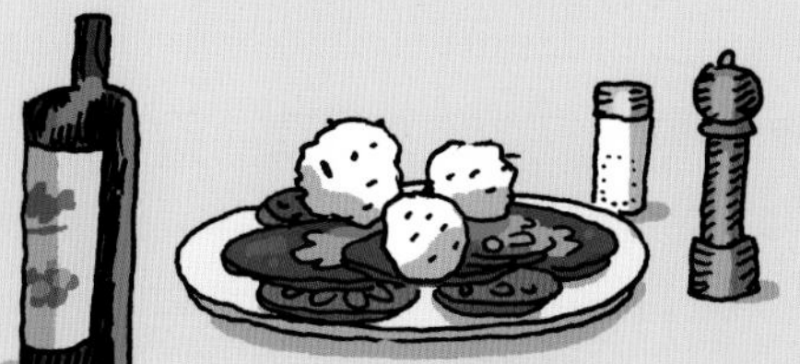

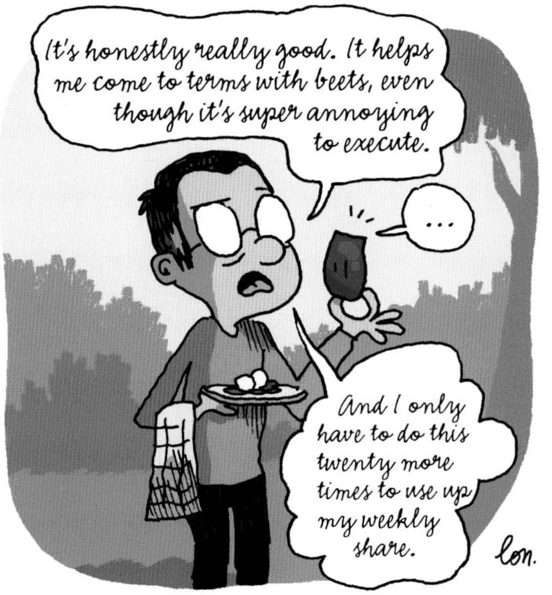
It's honestly really good. It helps me come to terms with beets, even though it's super annoying to execute.
...
And I only have to do this twenty more times to use up my weekly share.
Lon.

Sunny and cherry

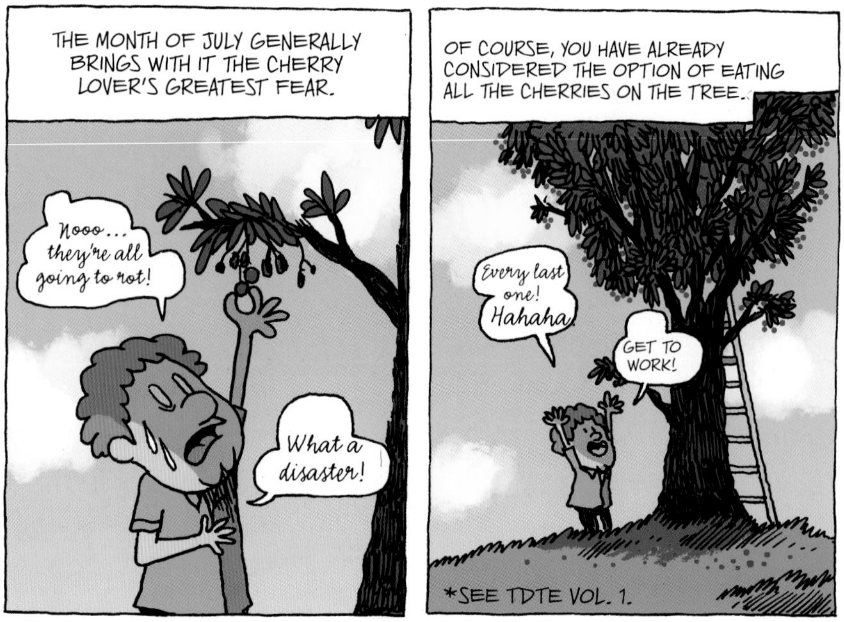
THE MONTH OF JULY GENERALLY BRINGS WITH IT THE CHERRY LOVER'S GREATEST FEAR.
Nooo... they're all going to rot!
What a disaster!
OF COURSE, YOU HAVE ALREADY CONSIDERED THE OPTION OF EATING ALL THE CHERRIES ON THE TREE.*
Every last one! Hahaha
GET TO WORK!
*SEE TDTE VOL. 1.

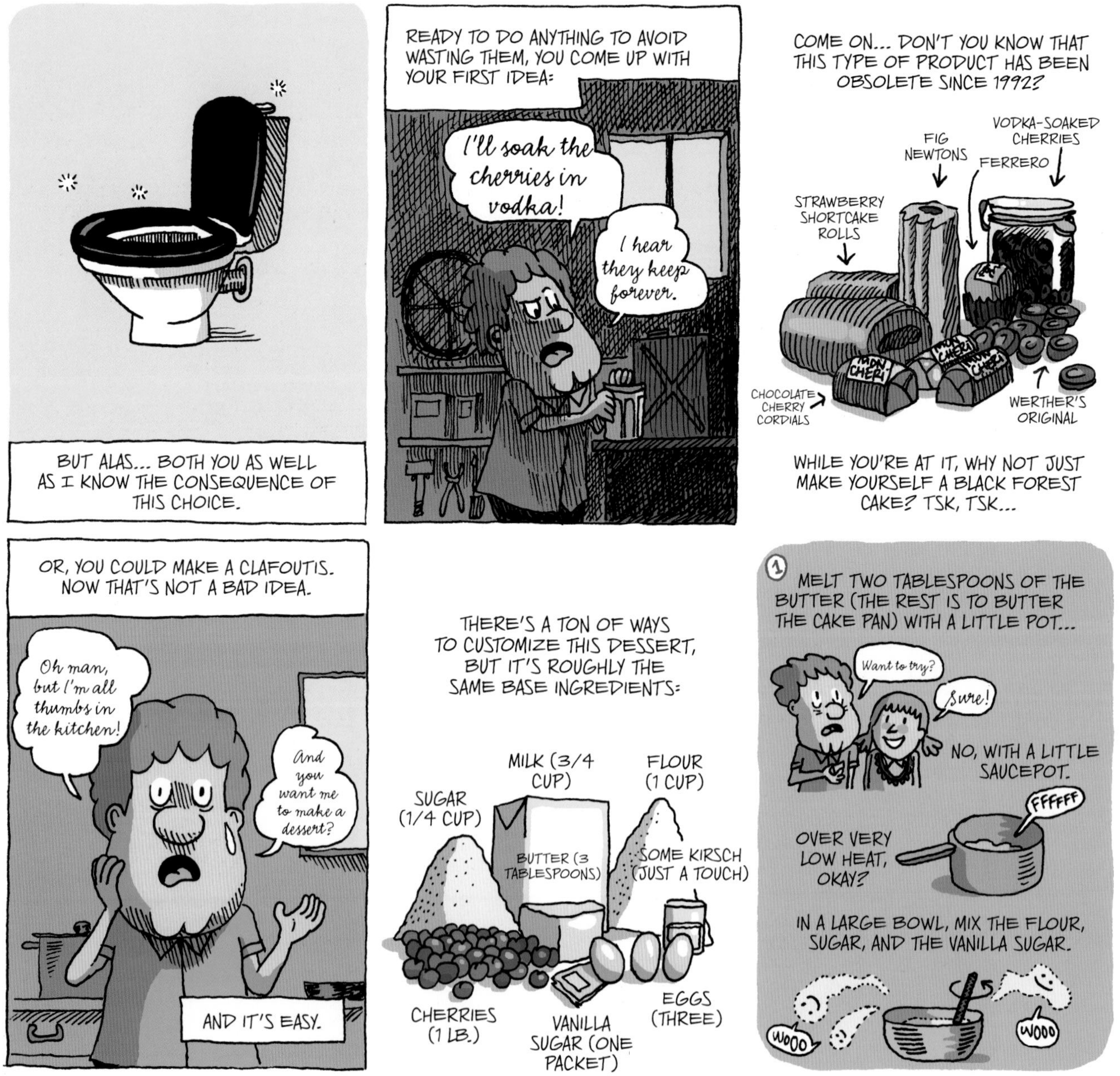
BUT ALAS... BOTH YOU AS WELL AS I KNOW THE CONSEQUENCE OF THIS CHOICE.
READY TO DO ANYTHING TO AVOID WASTING THEM, YOU COME UP WITH YOUR FIRST IDEA:
I'll soak the cherries in vodka!
I hear they keep forever.
COME ON... DON'T YOU KNOW THAT THIS TYPE OF PRODUCT HAS BEEN OBSOLETE SINCE 1992?
VODKA-SOAKED CHERRIES
FIG NEWTONS
FERRERO
STRAWBERRY SHORTCAKE ROLLS
CHOCOLATE CHERRY CORDIALS
WERTHER'S ORIGINAL
WHILE YOU'RE AT IT, WHY NOT JUST MAKE YOURSELF A BLACK FOREST CAKE? TSK, TSK...
OR, YOU COULD MAKE A CLAFOUTIS. NOW THAT'S NOT A BAD IDEA.
Oh man, but I'm all thumbs in the kitchen!
And you want me to make a dessert?
AND IT'S EASY.
THERE'S A TON OF WAYS TO CUSTOMIZE THIS DESSERT, BUT IT'S ROUGHLY THE SAME BASE INGREDIENTS:
MILK (3/4 CUP)
FLOUR (1 CUP)
SUGAR (1/4 CUP)
BUTTER (3 TABLESPOONS)
SOME KIRSCH (JUST A TOUCH)
CHERRIES (1 LB.)
VANILLA SUGAR (ONE PACKET)
EGGS (THREE)
1
MELT TWO TABLESPOONS OF THE BUTTER (THE REST IS TO BUTTER THE CAKE PAN) WITH A LITTLE POT...
Want to try?
Sure!
NO, WITH A LITTLE SAUCEPOT.
FFFFFF
OVER VERY LOW HEAT, OKAY?
IN A LARGE BOWL, MIX THE FLOUR, SUGAR, AND THE VANILLA SUGAR.
WOOO
WOOO

② ADD THE EGGS TO THE MIXTURE ONE AT A TIME:

Hey! *Ho!*

THEN THE MILK, AND FINALLY, THE MELTED BUTTER. TIP IN A TOUCH OF KIRSCH, OR RUM, OR COINTREAU, ETC.

Hey handle me gently!

?

← TOUCHY RUM

YOU'RE ALMOST THERE.

---

③ IN A BUTTERED 9-INCH CAKE PAN (WITH THE REST OF THE BUTTER, PLEASE TRY TO KEEP UP), ARRANGE THE CHERRIES:

POUR THE BATTER OVER THE CHERRIES, BAKE AT 400°F FOR A GOOD HALF HOUR. THAT'S IT.

Crap, I forgot to pit the cherries!!!

A CLAFOUTIS WITHOUT PITS? THAT'D BE LIKE A ROAST CHICKEN WITHOUT BONES, OR A SPRING ROLL WITHOUT SPRING!

Buuuut everyone will have to spit them out on their plaaaate...

THE PITS ADD FLAVOR

IF YOU MUST, SOAK THE PITS IN THE MILK OR BAKE THEM IN A SEPARATE DISH. BUT UNDER NO CIRCUMSTANCES MAY YOU NEGLECT THE PITS. THEY ARE THE HEART OF THE FLAVOR.

BUT ANYWAY... PITS OR NOT, THE CLAFOUTIS WON'T KEEP. AND IF YOUR GOAL IS TO GET RID OF YOUR STOCKPILE OF CHERRIES...

Is this some sort of running joke, or you just like drawing toilets?

BOTH YOU AS WELL AS I KNOW THE CONSEQUENCE OF THIS CHOICE.

NO... IF YOU REALLY HAVE AN OVERABUNDANCE OF CHERRIES, THE SECRET IS TO THINK **RACLETTE**

In this heat?

Meaning we're just gonna to let them rot on the tree?

NO, WE'LL CAN THEM.

PRESERVATION IN **VINEGAR** RATHER THAN ALCOHOL. IT'S EVEN EASIER THAN MAKING A CLAFOUTIS. YOU WILL NEED:

SUGAR (1 CUP)

VINEGAR OF YOUR CHOICE (1 QUART)

CLOVES CINNAMON

CHERRIES (2 1/2 LBS.)

WHATEVER SPICES MAKE YOU HAPPY

---

① WITH A LARGE POT... STOCKPOT... BOIL THE VINEGAR, THE SUGAR, A FEW CLOVES, AND A STICK OF CINNAMON OVER MEDIUM-HIGH HEAT:

This kills my eyes! Can't watch!

YOU'LL OBTAIN A SYRUPY MIXTURE.

---

② FILL (CLEAN) GLASS JARS WITH THE CHERRIES, ADD THE SPICES THAT MAKE YOU HAPPY, THE SYRUPY MIXTURE, AND ALLOW IT TO COOL.

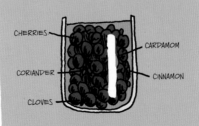

CHERRIES

CARDAMOM

CORIANDER

CINNAMON

CLOVES

WHEN COOLED, SCREW ON LIDS AND KEEP IN A COOL DARK PLACE BLAHBLAHBLAHBLAH UNTIL NEXT WINTER. OR THE FOLLOWING ONE, IF YOU WANT.

PICKLED CHERRIES ARE EXCELLENT WITH RACLETTES, FONDUES, COLD MEATS, ETC.

Thare ak-tully reery good!

I cud eat them all!

Sluurp

COME ON NOW... DO YOU NEED ME TO DRAW YOU ANOTHER TOILET?

lon.

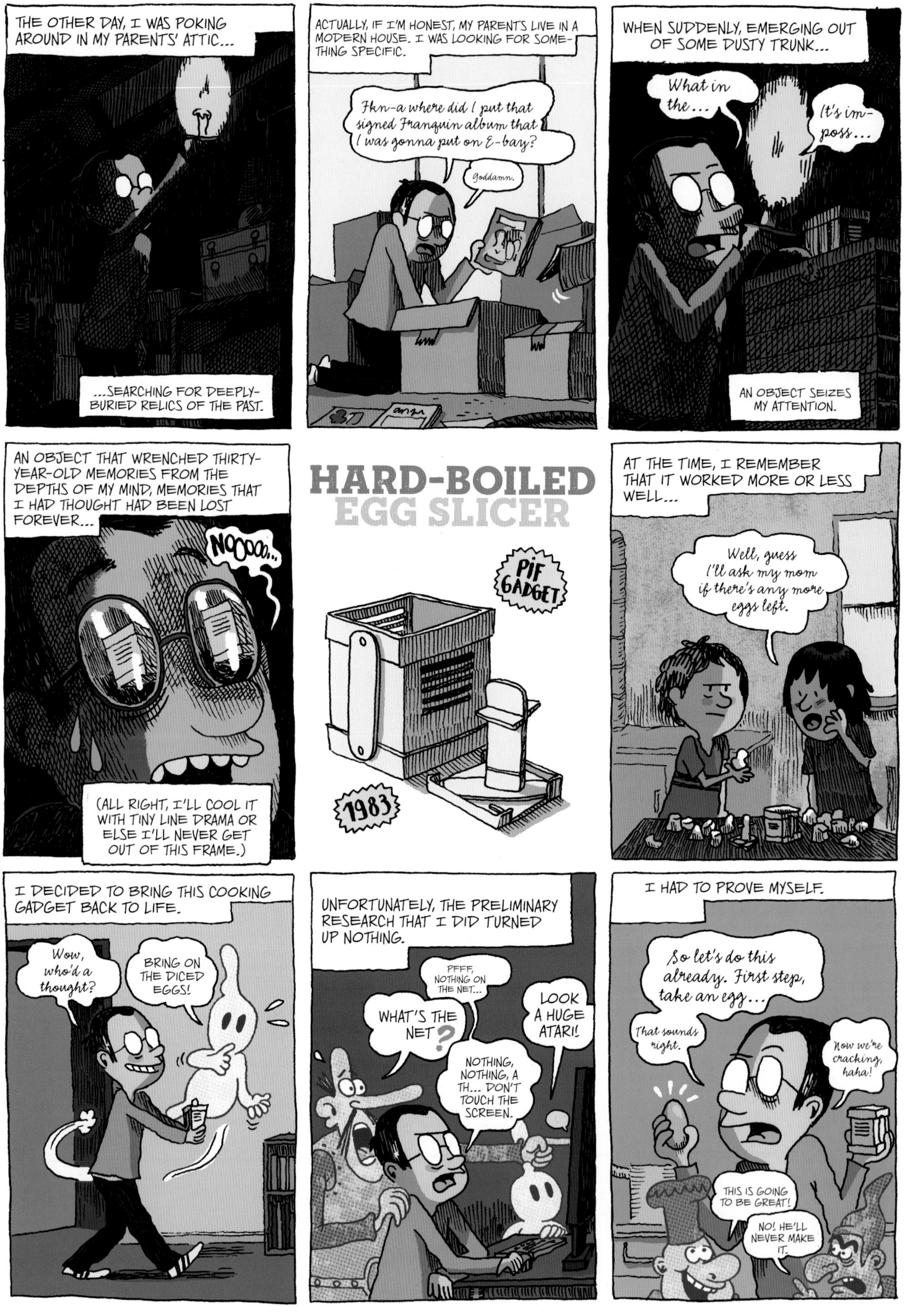
THE OTHER DAY, I WAS POKING AROUND IN MY PARENTS' ATTIC...
...SEARCHING FOR DEEPLY-BURIED RELICS OF THE PAST.
ACTUALLY, IF I'M HONEST, MY PARENTS LIVE IN A MODERN HOUSE. I WAS LOOKING FOR SOMETHING SPECIFIC.
Hrn-a where did I put that signed Franquin album that I was gonna put on E-bay?
Goddamn.
WHEN SUDDENLY, EMERGING OUT OF SOME DUSTY TRUNK...
What in the...
It's im-poss...
AN OBJECT SEIZES MY ATTENTION.
AN OBJECT THAT WRENCHED THIRTY-YEAR-OLD MEMORIES FROM THE DEPTHS OF MY MIND, MEMORIES THAT I HAD THOUGHT HAD BEEN LOST FOREVER...
NOOOOO...
(ALL RIGHT, I'LL COOL IT WITH TINY LINE DRAMA OR ELSE I'LL NEVER GET OUT OF THIS FRAME.)
HARD-BOILED
EGG SLICER
PIF GADGET
1983
AT THE TIME, I REMEMBER THAT IT WORKED MORE OR LESS WELL...
Well, guess I'll ask my mom if there's any more eggs left.
I DECIDED TO BRING THIS COOKING GADGET BACK TO LIFE.
Wow, who'd a thought?
BRING ON THE DICED EGGS!
UNFORTUNATELY, THE PRELIMINARY RESEARCH THAT I DID TURNED UP NOTHING.
PFFF, NOTHING ON THE NET...
WHAT'S THE NET?
LOOK A HUGE ATARI!
NOTHING, NOTHING, A TH... DON'T TOUCH THE SCREEN.
I HAD TO PROVE MYSELF.
So let's do this already. First step, take an egg...
That sounds right.
Now we're cracking, haha!
THIS IS GOING TO BE GREAT!
NO! HE'LL NEVER MAKE IT.

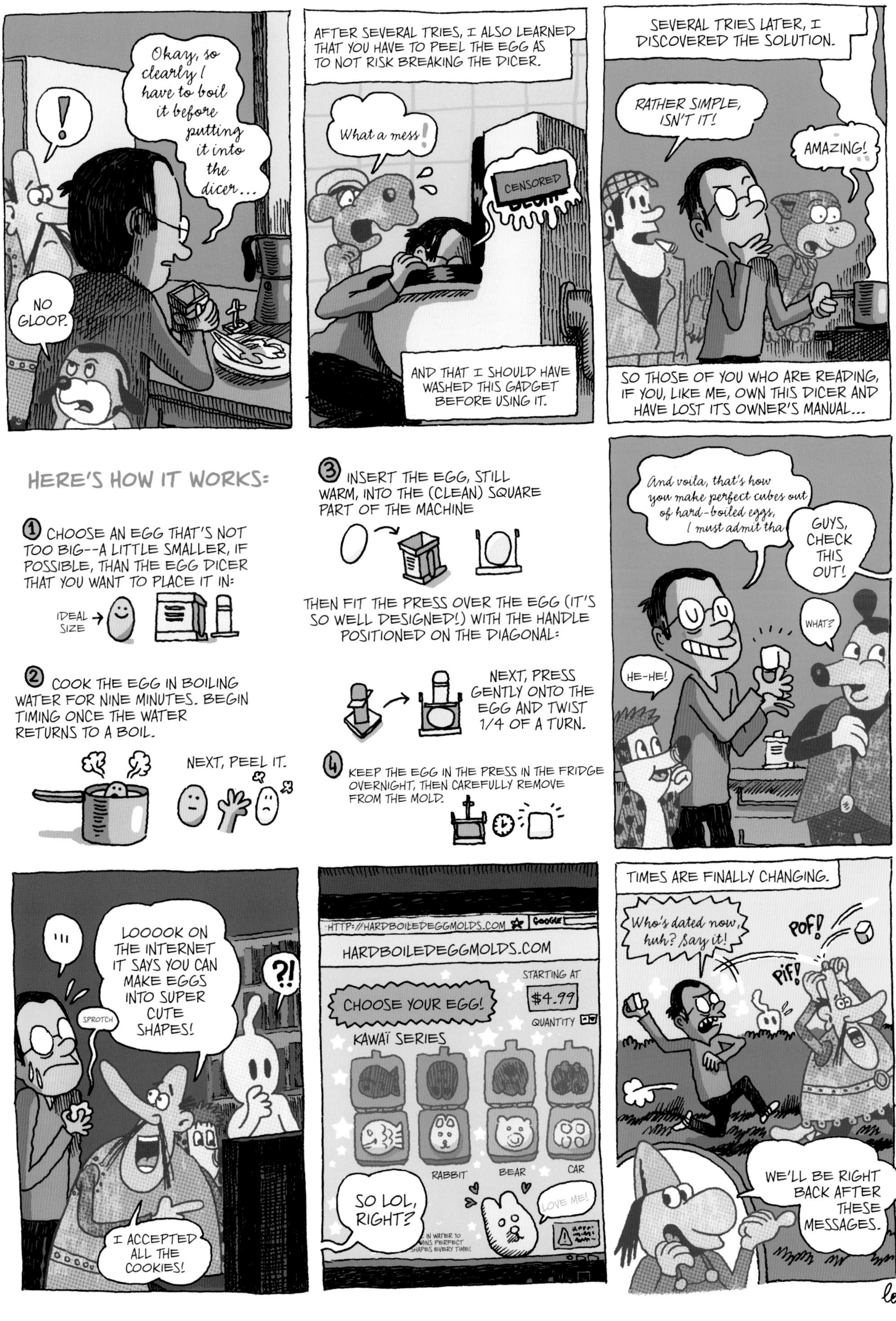
!
Okay, so clearly I have to boil it before putting it into the dicer...
NO GLOOP.
AFTER SEVERAL TRIES, I ALSO LEARNED THAT YOU HAVE TO PEEL THE EGG AS TO NOT RISK BREAKING THE DICER.
What a mess!
CENSORED
AND THAT I SHOULD HAVE WASHED THIS GADGET BEFORE USING IT.
SEVERAL TRIES LATER, I DISCOVERED THE SOLUTION.
RATHER SIMPLE, ISN'T IT!
AMAZING!
SO THOSE OF YOU WHO ARE READING, IF YOU, LIKE ME, OWN THIS DICER AND HAVE LOST ITS OWNER'S MANUAL...
HERE'S HOW IT WORKS:
1 CHOOSE AN EGG THAT'S NOT TOO BIG--A LITTLE SMALLER, IF POSSIBLE, THAN THE EGG DICER THAT YOU WANT TO PLACE IT IN:
IDEAL SIZE
2 COOK THE EGG IN BOILING WATER FOR NINE MINUTES. BEGIN TIMING ONCE THE WATER RETURNS TO A BOIL.
NEXT, PEEL IT.
3 INSERT THE EGG, STILL WARM, INTO THE (CLEAN) SQUARE PART OF THE MACHINE
THEN FIT THE PRESS OVER THE EGG (IT'S SO WELL DESIGNED!) WITH THE HANDLE POSITIONED ON THE DIAGONAL:
NEXT, PRESS GENTLY ONTO THE EGG AND TWIST 1/4 OF A TURN.
4 KEEP THE EGG IN THE PRESS IN THE FRIDGE OVERNIGHT, THEN CAREFULLY REMOVE FROM THE MOLD.
And voila, that's how you make perfect cubes out of hard-boiled eggs, I must admit tha
GUYS, CHECK THIS OUT!
WHAT?
HE-HE!
...
SPROTCH
LOOOOK ON THE INTERNET IT SAYS YOU CAN MAKE EGGS INTO SUPER CUTE SHAPES!
?!
I ACCEPTED ALL THE COOKIES!
HTTP://HARDBOILEDEGGMOLDS.COM
GOOGLE
HARDBOILEDEGGMOLDS.COM
STARTING AT
$4.99
CHOOSE YOUR EGG!
QUANTITY
KAWAÏ SERIES
RABBIT
BEAR
CAR
SO LOL, RIGHT?
LOVE ME!
TIMES ARE FINALLY CHANGING.
Who's dated now, huh? Say it!
POF!
PIF!
WE'LL BE RIGHT BACK AFTER THESE MESSAGES.
lon.

Cannelloni WITH BROUTCHIO

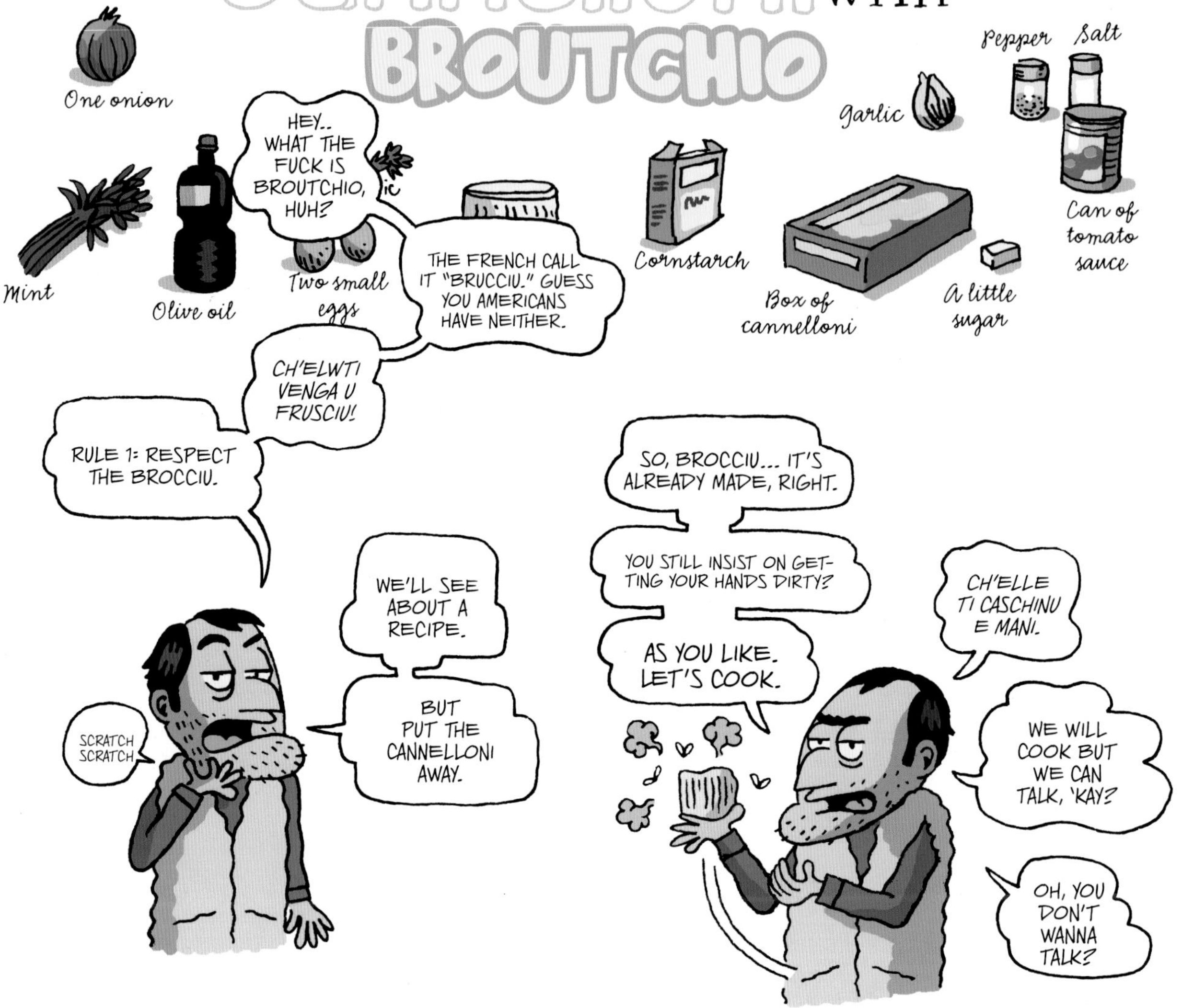
One onion
Mint
Olive oil
Two small eggs
Cornstarch
Box of cannelloni
A little sugar
Garlic
Pepper
Salt
Can of tomato sauce
HEY.. WHAT THE FUCK IS BROUTCHIO, HUH?
THE FRENCH CALL IT "BRUCCIU." GUESS YOU AMERICANS HAVE NEITHER.
CH'ELWTI VENGA U FRUSCIU!
RULE 1: RESPECT THE BROCCIU.
SO, BROCCIU... IT'S ALREADY MADE, RIGHT.
YOU STILL INSIST ON GETTING YOUR HANDS DIRTY?
AS YOU LIKE. LET'S COOK.
WE'LL SEE ABOUT A RECIPE.
BUT PUT THE CANNELLONI AWAY.
SCRATCH SCRATCH
CH'ELLE TI CASCHINU E MANI.
WE WILL COOK BUT WE CAN TALK, 'KAY?
OH, YOU DON'T WANNA TALK?

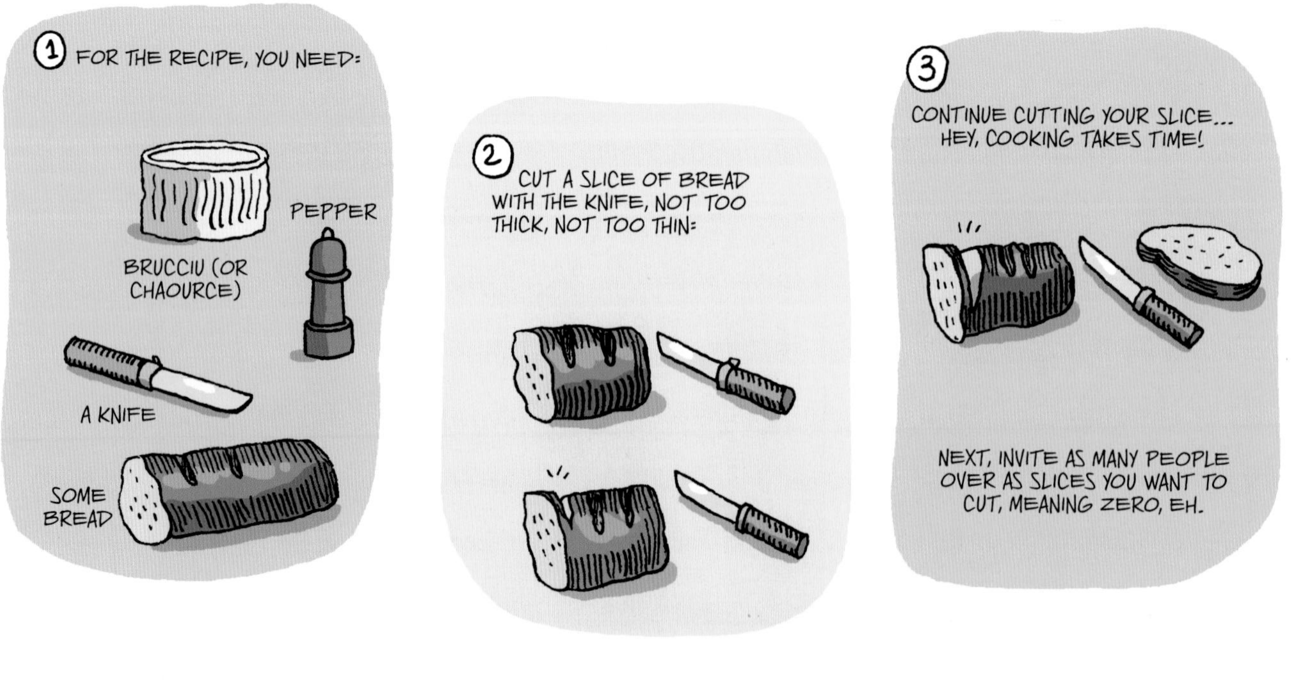
1 FOR THE RECIPE, YOU NEED:
BRUCCIU (OR CHAOURCE)
PEPPER
A KNIFE
SOME BREAD
2 CUT A SLICE OF BREAD WITH THE KNIFE, NOT TOO THICK, NOT TOO THIN:
3 CONTINUE CUTTING YOUR SLICE... HEY, COOKING TAKES TIME!
NEXT, INVITE AS MANY PEOPLE OVER AS SLICES YOU WANT TO CUT, MEANING ZERO, EH.

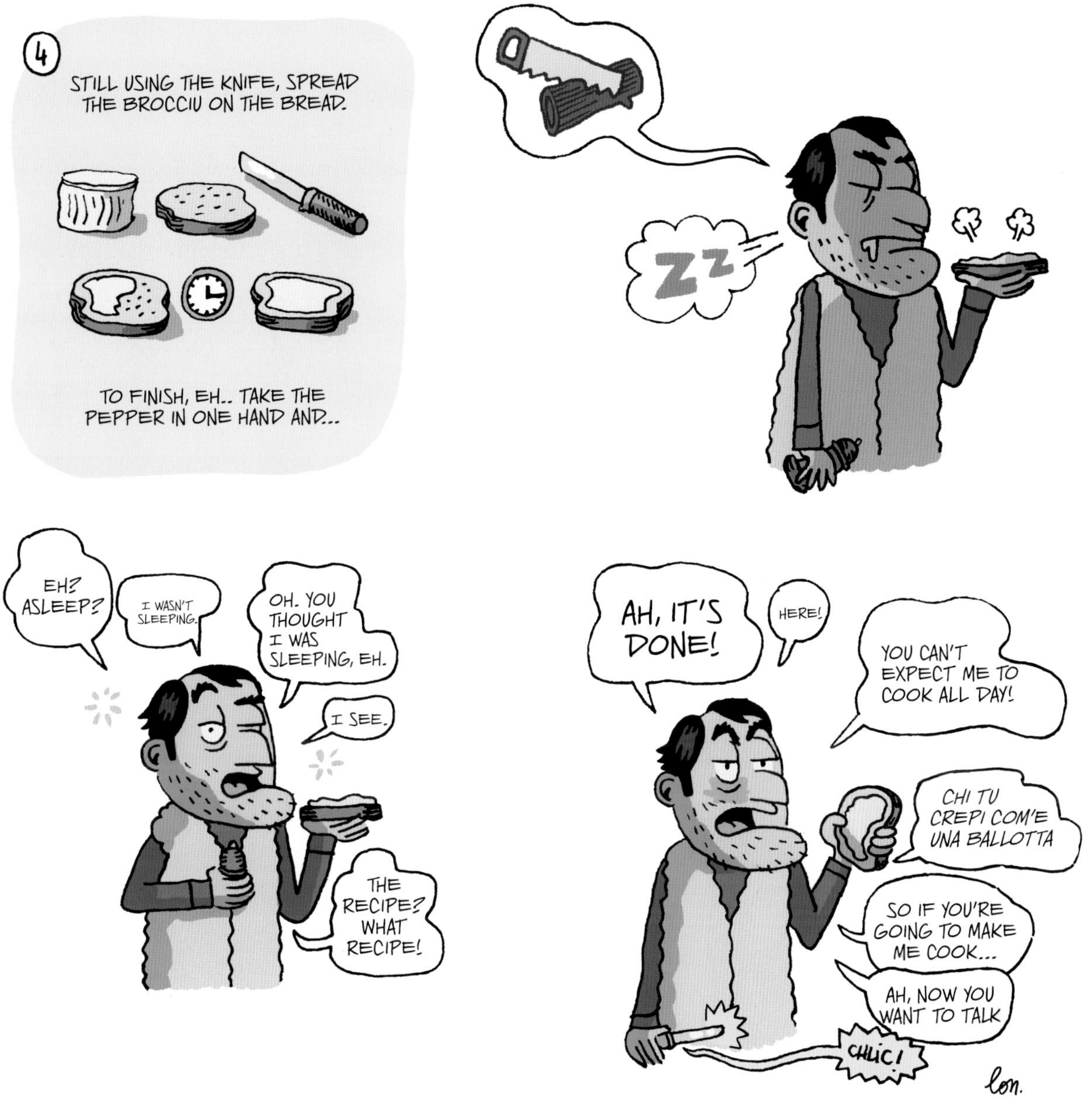
4
STILL USING THE KNIFE, SPREAD THE BROCCIU ON THE BREAD.
TO FINISH, EH.. TAKE THE PEPPER IN ONE HAND AND...
ZZ
EH? ASLEEP?
I WASN'T SLEEPING.
OH. YOU THOUGHT I WAS SLEEPING, EH.
I SEE.
THE RECIPE? WHAT RECIPE!
AH, IT'S DONE!
HERE!
YOU CAN'T EXPECT ME TO COOK ALL DAY!
CHI TU CREPI COM'E UNA BALLOTTA
SO IF YOU'RE GOING TO MAKE ME COOK...
AH, NOW YOU WANT TO TALK
CHLIC!
lon.

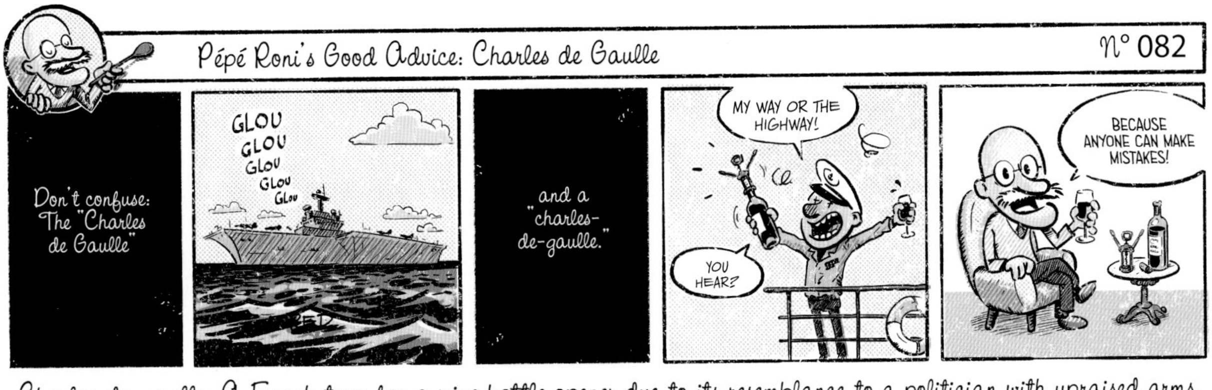
Pépé Roni's Good Advice: Charles de Gaulle
N° 082
Don't confuse: The "Charles de Gaulle"
GLOU
GLOU
GLOU
GLOU
GLOU
...and a "charles-de-gaulle."
MY WAY OR THE HIGHWAY!
YOU HEAR?
BECAUSE ANYONE CAN MAKE MISTAKES!

Charles-de-gaulle: A French term for a wine bottle opener due to its resemblance to a politician with upraised arms.

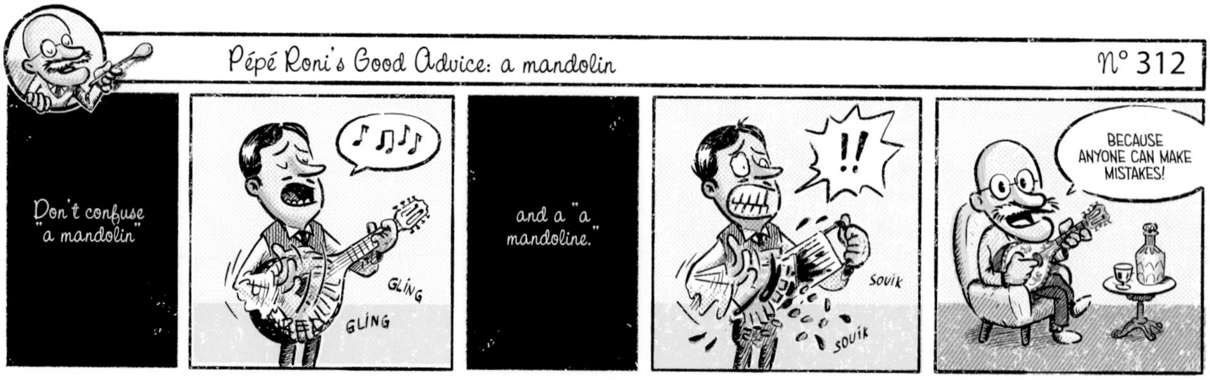
Pépé Roni's Good Advice: a mandolin
N° 312
Don't confuse "a mandolin"
GLING
GLING
and a "a mandoline."
!!
SOUIK
SOUIK
BECAUSE ANYONE CAN MAKE MISTAKES!

Mandoline: A kitchen utensil often made out of stainless steel used to slice vegetables of even widths.

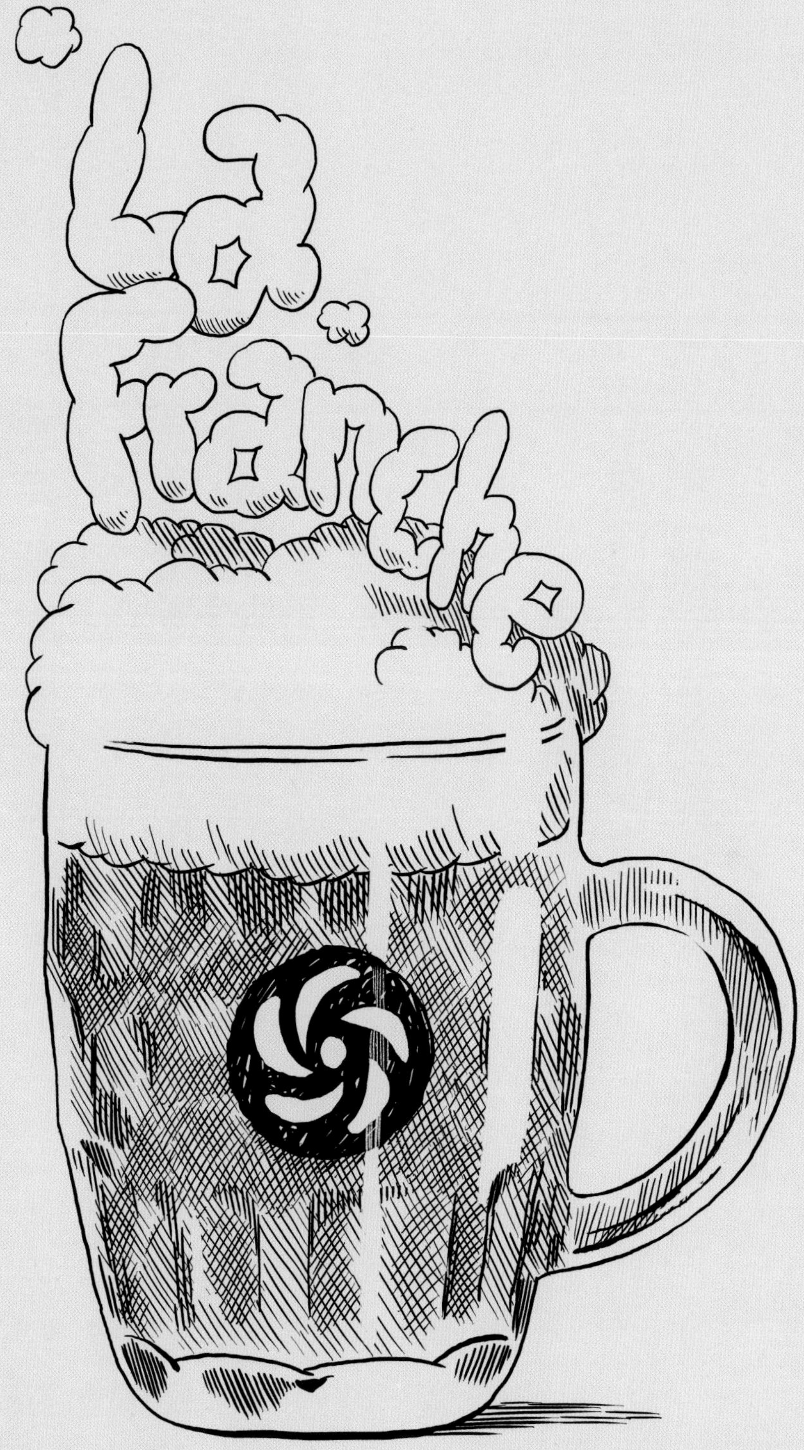
La Franche

I DON'T LIKE BEER. I DRINK IT FROM TIME TO TIME, BUT HAVE NEVER BEEN LOYAL TO A PARTICULAR BRAND OR STYLE. WHAT'S FUNNY IS THAT I EVENTUALLY LEARNED TO LIKE MOST THINGS THAT I FOUND REALLY DISGUSTING AS A KID, LIKE WINE, ENDIVES, OR FRISÉE LETTUCE. BUT BEER--NOT REALLY.

(THIS IS BECAUSE, AS KIDS, OUR PALATES DEVELOP TO FAVOR SWEETNESS AND ACIDITY (SOUR PATCH KIDS = JACKPOT). IN CONTRAST, AS ADULTS, OUR PALATES ADJUST TO BITTERNESS AND SALT.)

I THINK MEN PROBABLY BEGAN DRINKING BEER TO BOND AS WARRIORS OR WHATEVER, AND AFTERWARDS, THEY ACTUALLY BEGAN TO LIKE IT...

So gross, right?

Yeah!

But no women are nearby... so.

To you, friend!

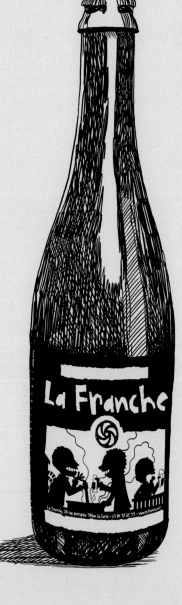

WELL, THAT'S ONLY ONE THEORY.

ALL OF THAT TO SAY THAT SOMETIMES, LIFE'S A CURIOUS BEAST. I JUST RECEIVED A REQUEST TO DESIGN A BEER LABEL FOR A BREWERY NOT FAR FROM MY HOME IN FRANCE, AND THE GUYS SUGGESTED THAT I COME TAKE A...

COKE

TOUR OF THE LA FRANCHE BREWERY

LA FERTÉ, FRANCE

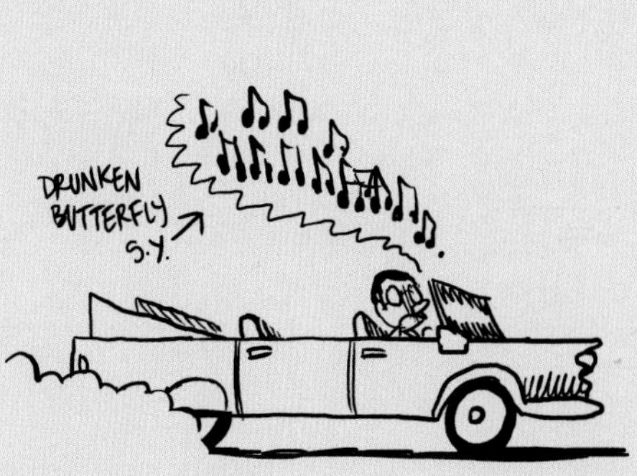
DRUNKEN BUTTERFLY
S.Y.

I'M WELCOMED AT THE BREWERY BY RÉGIS. THE BREWING STUFF IS INSTALLED NEARBY IN A FULLY RESTORED BARN.

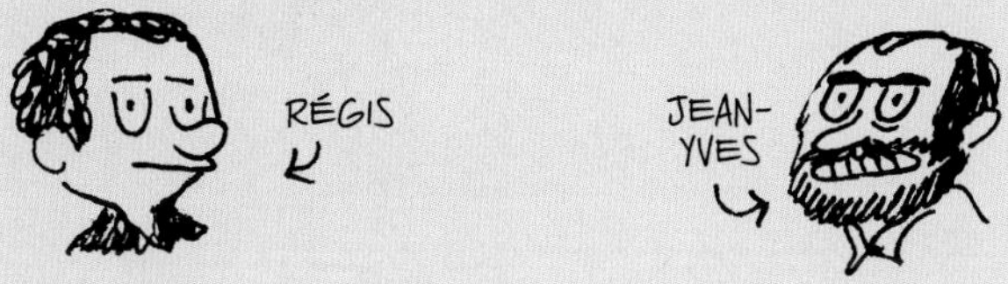
RÉGIS
JEAN-YVES

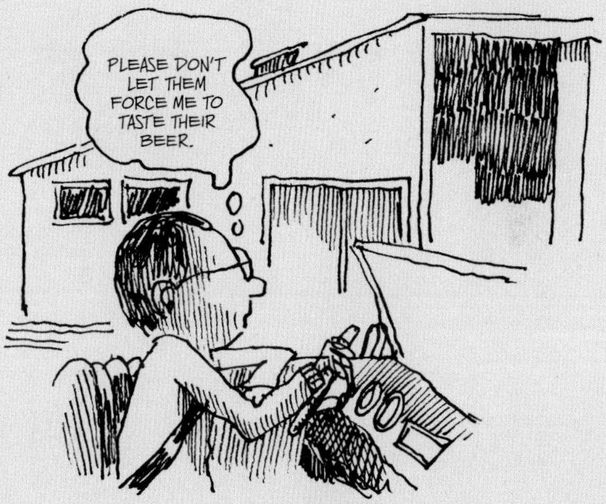
PLEASE DON'T LET THEM FORCE ME TO TASTE THEIR BEER.

HE TELLS ME THAT IN THE BEGINNING OF LA FRANCHE, HE WORKED WITH HIS BUDDY JEAN-YVES. TO GRIND THE MALT, THEY HAD INSTALLED A KIND OF UNICYCLE (WELL, I DON'T KNOW HOW TO DO A PERSPECTIVE DRAWING OF A BIKE) BUT IT LOOKS A LITTLE LIKE THIS:

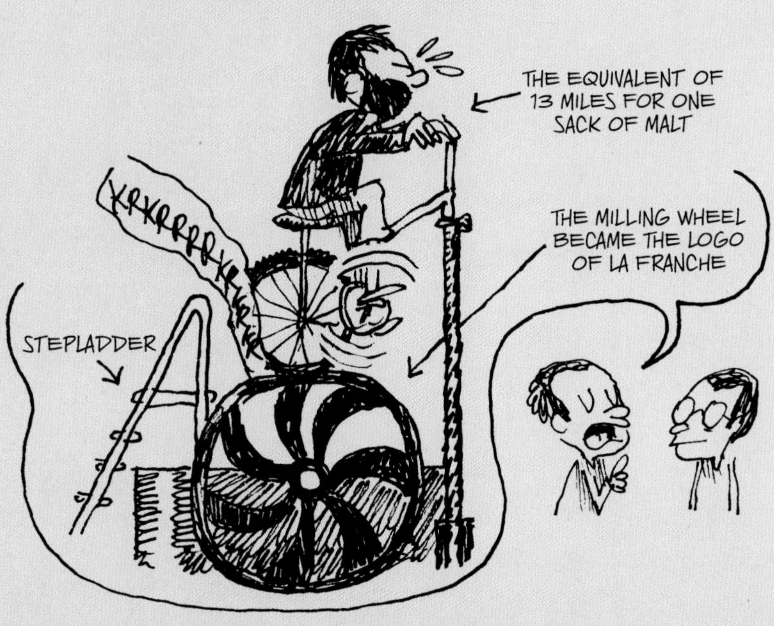
THE EQUIVALENT OF 13 MILES FOR ONE SACK OF MALT
THE MILLING WHEEL BECAME THE LOGO OF LA FRANCHE
STEPLADDER

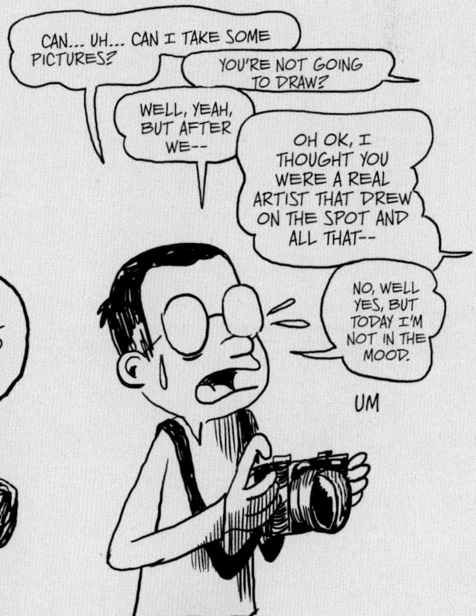
CAN... UH... CAN I TAKE SOME PICTURES?
YOU'RE NOT GOING TO DRAW?
WELL, YEAH, BUT AFTER WE--
OH OK, I THOUGHT YOU WERE A REAL ARTIST THAT DREW ON THE SPOT AND ALL THAT--
NO, WELL YES, BUT TODAY I'M NOT IN THE MOOD.
UM

HOW IS BEER MADE?

(In broad strokes)

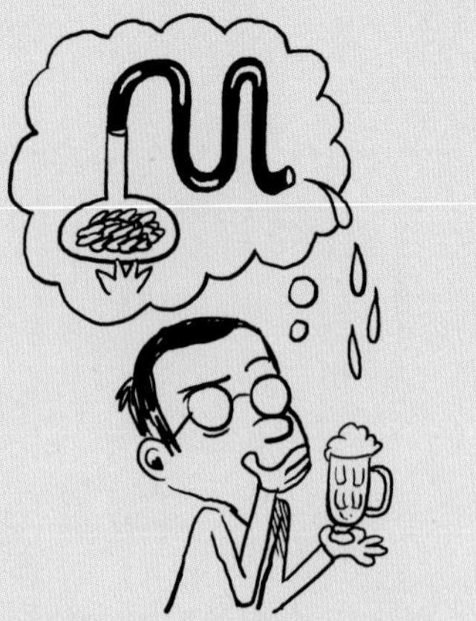

① IT ALL BEGINS WITH GOOD QUALITY WATER AND MALT.

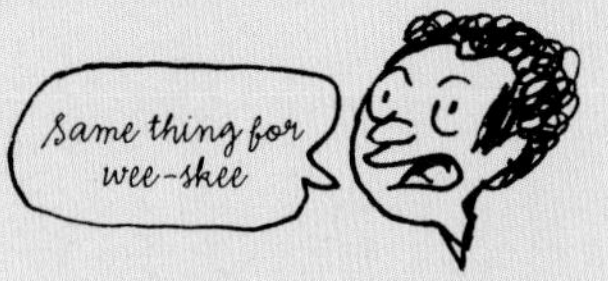
Same thing for wee-skee

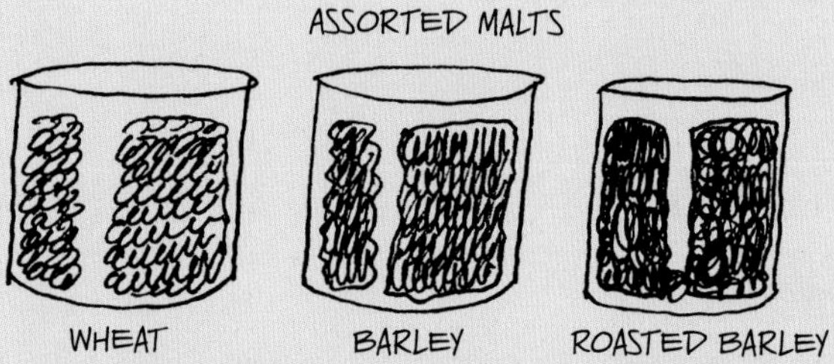
ASSORTED MALTS
WHEAT
BARLEY
ROASTED BARLEY

AND MALT IS A GRAIN (BARLEY OR WHEAT) THAT HAS SPROUTED, BEEN DRIED, AND THEN ROASTED AT DIFFERENT TEMPERATURES

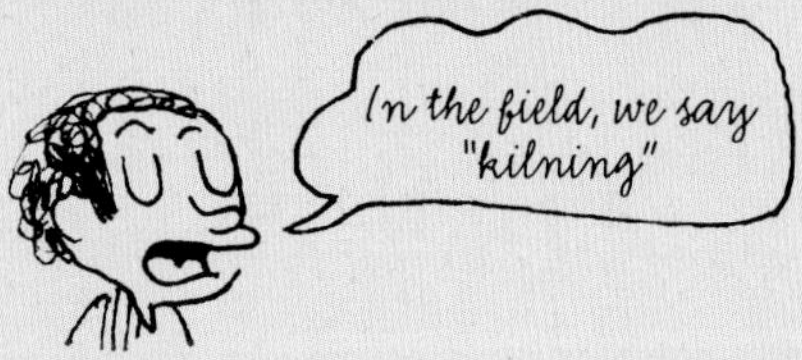
In the field, we say "kilning"

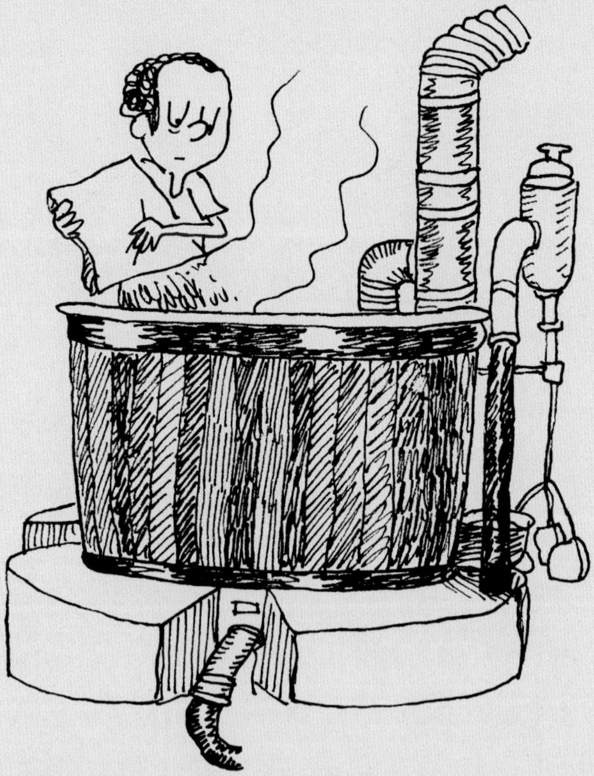

② NEXT, THE MALT IS MILLED (TODAY, LA FRANCHE HAS A MACHINE THAT DOES THAT). THE MALT CONTAINS STARCH THAT WILL TRANSFORM INTO SUGAR AFTER BEING SOAKED IN HOT WATER.

(THE WATER IS HEATED TO 150°F)

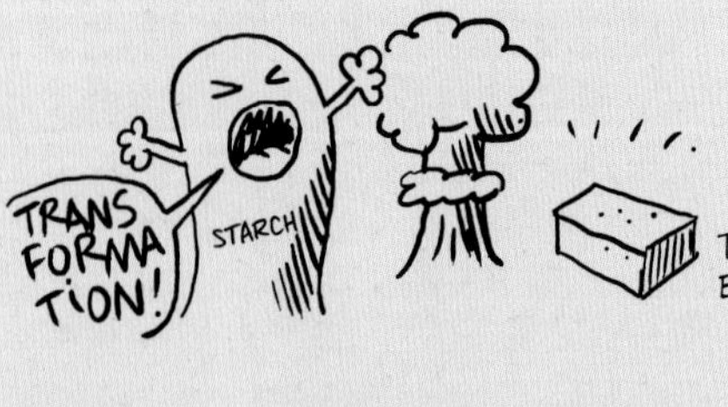
TRANSFORMATION!
STARCH

THE MIXTURE IS BREWED THEN FILTERED

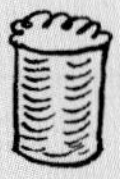
White ale (franche galle) barley + wheat

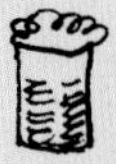
Blond ale (franche d'en bas) barley + lightly-toasted malt

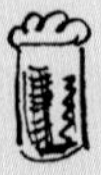
Amber ale (franche de vie) lightly-toasted malt + caramel or crystal malts

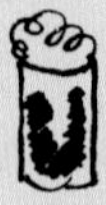
Belgian-style brown ale (franche ipane): Mixture of toasted malts

③ NEXT,* THE BREWER ADDS THE HOPS. HOPS WORK LIKE TEA DOES, MEANING YOU HAVE TO SOAK THEM FOR A SPECIFIC LENGTH OF TIME (THE LONGER THE TIME, THE MORE BITTER THE BEER). THIS IS WHAT ADDS AROMA.

*WHEN THERE'S ONLY SUGAR REMAINING AND AFTER IT'S BEEN FILTERED

HOPS

FILTERING

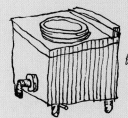

(Drawing of their first tank from when they were making beer in their house. It's still in use.)

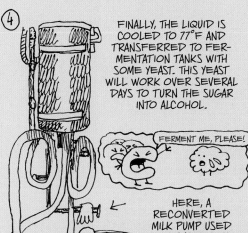

④ FINALLY, THE LIQUID IS COOLED TO 77°F AND TRANSFERRED TO FERMENTATION TANKS WITH SOME YEAST. THIS YEAST WILL WORK OVER SEVERAL DAYS TO TURN THE SUGAR INTO ALCOHOL.

FERMENT ME, PLEASE!

HERE, A RECONVERTED MILK PUMP USED TO TRANSFER THE BEER BETWEEN THE TANKS (EVERYTHING'S A LITTLE DIY AT LA FRANCHE).

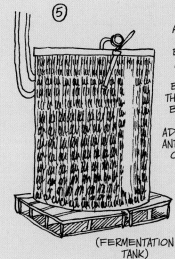

⑤ AFTER THE FERMENTATION, THE YEAST IS DECANTED FROM THE BOTTOM OF THE TANK, CHILLED, AND RESERVED FOR THE NEXT BATCH. (THIS IS THE OLDEST BEER-MAKING TECHNIQUE.) BUT THE LIQUID IN THE TANK IS NOT YET BEER. IT WILL NEXT BE SEALED INTO BOTTLES OR KEGS, SOME ADDITIONAL SUGAR WILL BE ADDED, AND THE SUGAR WILL MAKE CO_2 OUT OF ANY RESIDUAL YEAST, MEANING BUBBLES, MEANING BEER!

(FERMENTATION TANK)

CARRY ON THE GOOD WORK!

TURN ME INTO BUBBLES!

previously, I worked for the state, but I let all of that go for the brewery.

Why did you choose to enter this field?

Well, our generation was basically raised on beer, wasn't it?

Uh, not me.

For me, it seemed like a natural choice. I liked beer when I was young, and now I brew exactly what I want to drink.

(kinda like if I ever became an engineer at Lego...)

I've finally corrected the fatal error of the pirate ship of '92: it now floats.

VIDUNDERLIG!

BEER ISN'T A LOCAL PRODUCT IN THE CLASSICAL SENSE OF TERROIR, BUT RÉGIS AND JEAN-YVES WORK TO STRENGTHEN LOCAL FOOD SYSTEMS THROUGH LA FRANCHE. BECAUSE OF THIS COMMITMENT, THEIR NEXT HOPE IS TO BEGIN GROWING THEIR OWN BARLEY. OH YEAH, AND, MOST IMPORTANTLY, THEIR BEERS ARE:

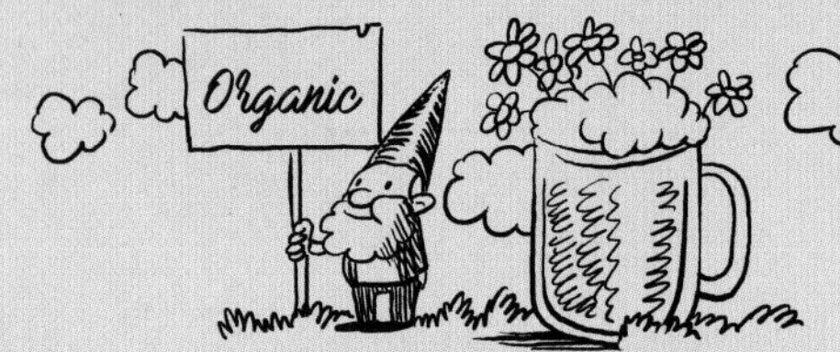
Organic

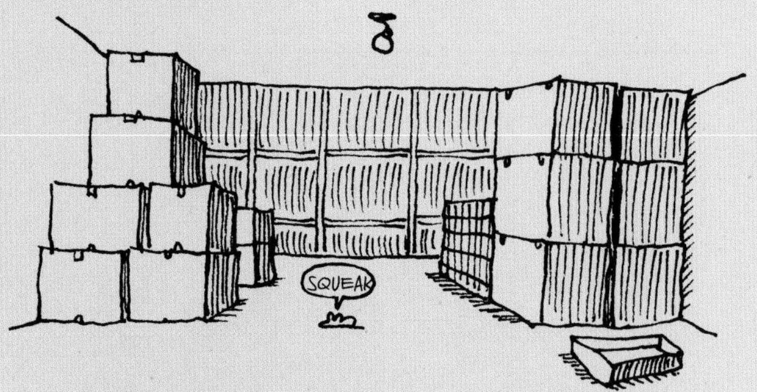
SQUEAK

THERE ARE MICE IN THE WARM ROOM FOR THE BOTTLE CONDITIONING (77°F), SO THEY DECIDED TO MAKE AN OCCASIONAL LABEL WITH A MOUSE HIDDEN ON IT. IF YOU FIND IT, YOU WIN CASE OF BEER!

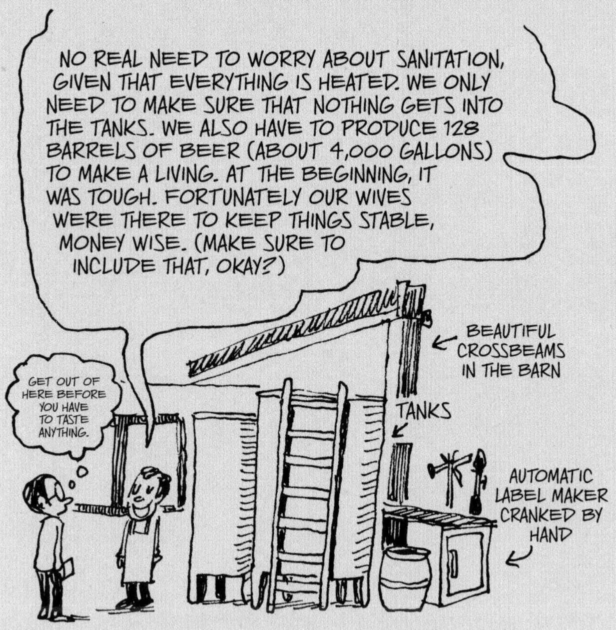
NO REAL NEED TO WORRY ABOUT SANITATION, GIVEN THAT EVERYTHING IS HEATED. WE ONLY NEED TO MAKE SURE THAT NOTHING GETS INTO THE TANKS. WE ALSO HAVE TO PRODUCE 128 BARRELS OF BEER (ABOUT 4,000 GALLONS) TO MAKE A LIVING. AT THE BEGINNING, IT WAS TOUGH. FORTUNATELY OUR WIVES WERE THERE TO KEEP THINGS STABLE, MONEY WISE. (MAKE SURE TO INCLUDE THAT, OKAY?)
GET OUT OF HERE BEFORE YOU HAVE TO TASTE ANYTHING.
BEAUTIFUL CROSSBEAMS IN THE BARN
TANKS
AUTOMATIC LABEL MAKER CRANKED BY HAND

THEY LIKE TO EXPERIMENT AT LA FRANCHE, AND THEY DREAM UP CONCEPTS LIKE:

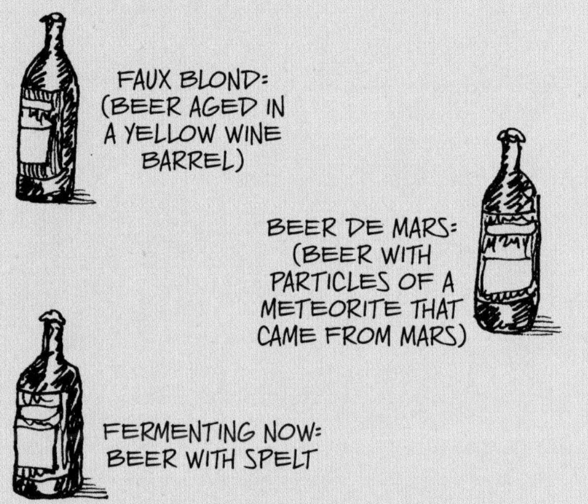
FAUX BLOND: (BEER AGED IN A YELLOW WINE BARREL)
BEER DE MARS: (BEER WITH PARTICLES OF A METEORITE THAT CAME FROM MARS)
FERMENTING NOW: BEER WITH SPELT

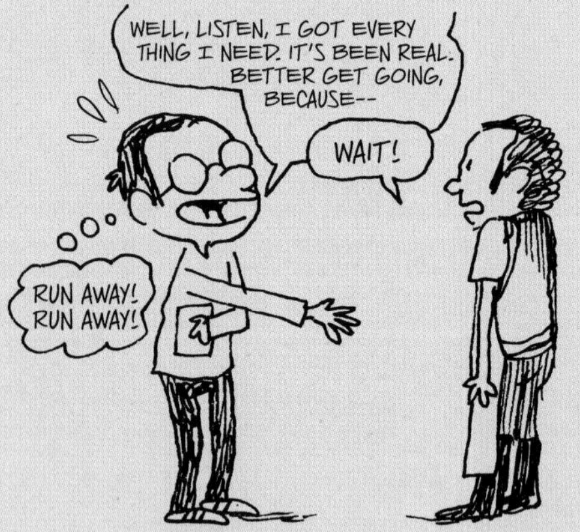
WELL, LISTEN, I GOT EVERY THING I NEED. IT'S BEEN REAL. BETTER GET GOING, BECAUSE--
WAIT!
RUN AWAY! RUN AWAY!

THERE'S NO WAY OUT. I'M GOING TO HAVE TO DRINK THE BEER AND SAY THAT I LIKE IT.

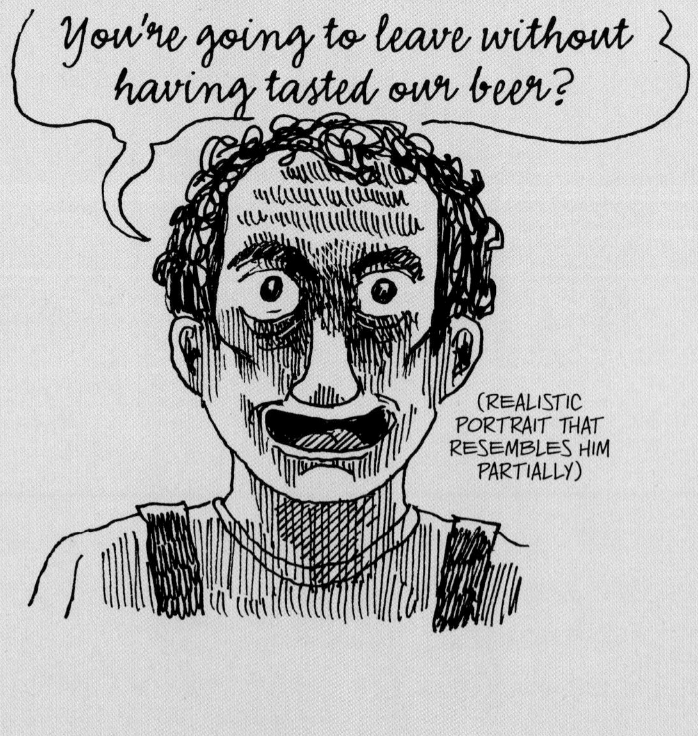
You're going to leave without having tasted our beer?
(REALISTIC PORTRAIT THAT RESEMBLES HIM PARTIALLY)

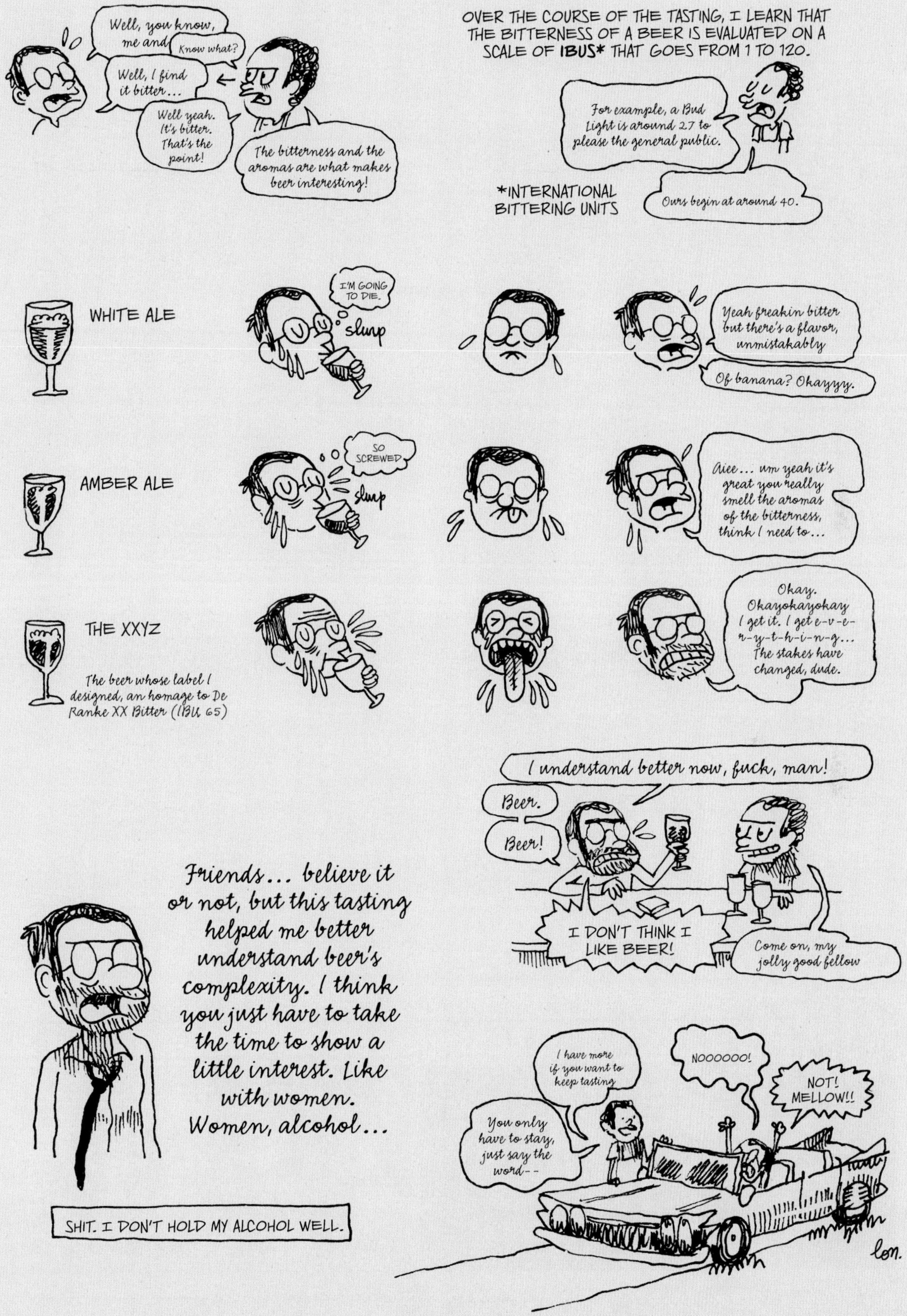
Well, you know, me and
Know what?
Well, I find it bitter...
Well yeah. It's bitter. That's the point!
The bitterness and the aromas are what makes beer interesting!
OVER THE COURSE OF THE TASTING, I LEARN THAT THE BITTERNESS OF A BEER IS EVALUATED ON A SCALE OF IBUS* THAT GOES FROM 1 TO 120.
For example, a Bud Light is around 27 to please the general public.
Ours begin at around 40.
*INTERNATIONAL BITTERING UNITS
WHITE ALE
I'M GOING TO DIE.
slurp
Yeah freakin bitter but there's a flavor, unmistakably
Of banana? Okayyy.
AMBER ALE
SO SCREWED
slurp
Aiee... um yeah it's great you really smell the aromas of the bitterness, think I need to...
THE XXYZ
The beer whose label I designed, an homage to De Ranke XX Bitter (IBU 65)
Okay. Okayokayokay I get it. I get e-v-e-r-y-t-h-i-n-g... The stakes have changed, dude.
I understand better now, fuck, man!
Beer.
Beer!
I DON'T THINK I LIKE BEER!
Come on, my jolly good fellow
Friends... believe it or not, but this tasting helped me better understand beer's complexity. I think you just have to take the time to show a little interest. Like with women. Women, alcohol...
SHIT. I DON'T HOLD MY ALCOHOL WELL.
I have more if you want to keep tasting
NOOOOOO!
NOT! MELLOW!!
You only have to stay, just say the word--
lon.

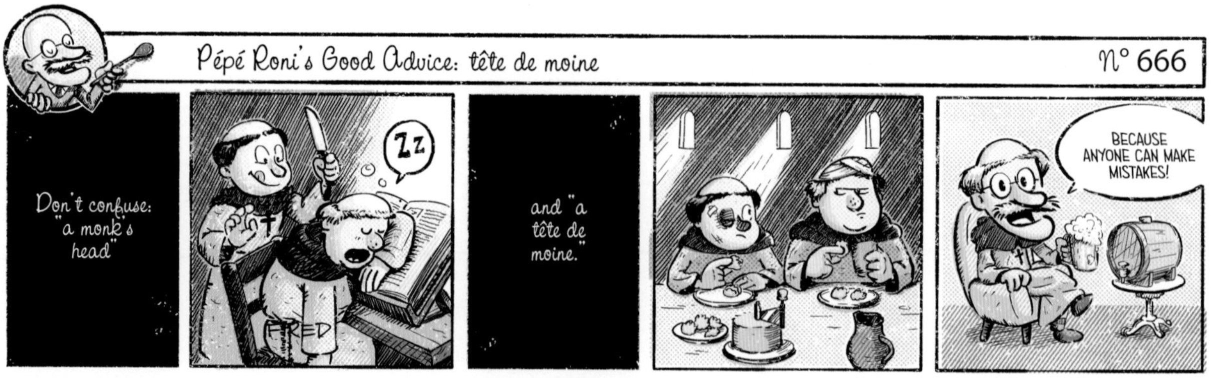
Pépé Roni's Good Advice: tête de moine
N° 666
Don't confuse: "a monk's head"
Zz
FRED
and "a tête de moine."
BECAUSE ANYONE CAN MAKE MISTAKES!

Tête de moine: Literally French for "monk's head," a specialty AOC cheese from Switzerland eaten in thin shavings carved by special device with a circular blade.

Fall

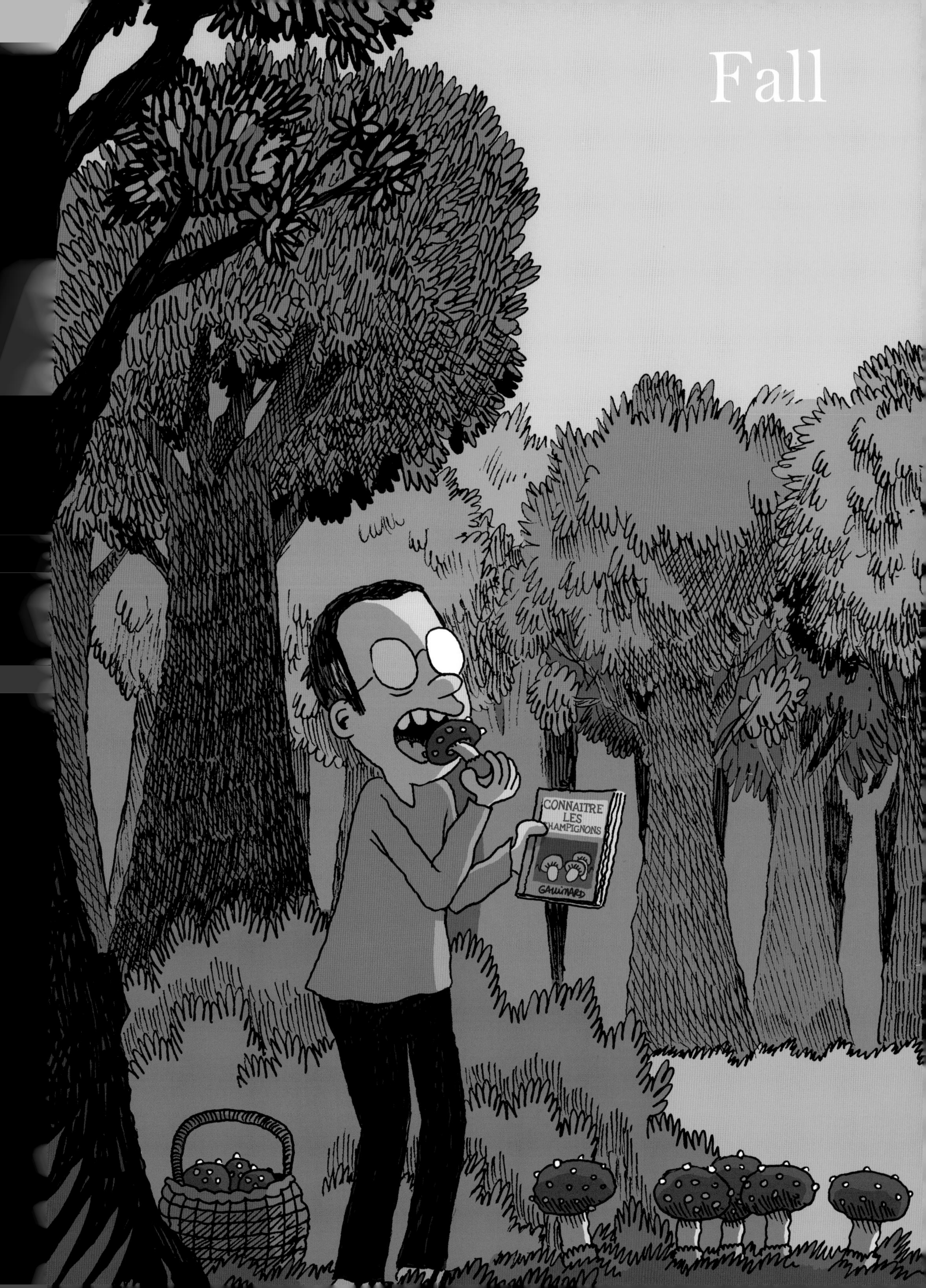
CONNAITRE
LES
GALLIMARD

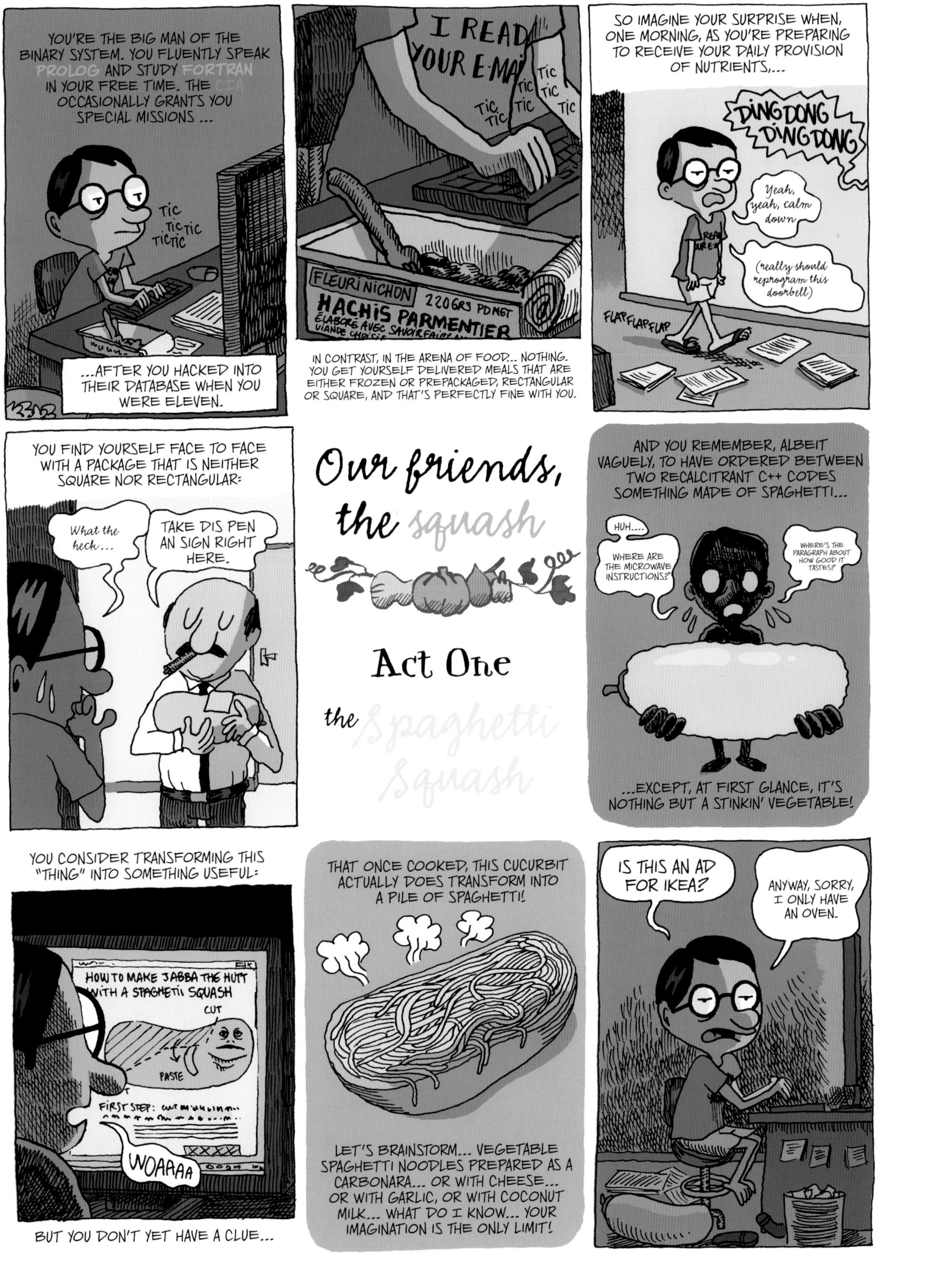
YOU'RE THE BIG MAN OF THE BINARY SYSTEM. YOU FLUENTLY SPEAK PROLOG AND STUDY FORTRAN IN YOUR FREE TIME. THE CIA OCCASIONALLY GRANTS YOU SPECIAL MISSIONS ...
TIC TIC TIC TIC TIC
...AFTER YOU HACKED INTO THEIR DATABASE WHEN YOU WERE ELEVEN.
I READ YOUR E-MA
TIC TIC TIC TIC TIC TIC TIC
FLEURI NICHON
220GRS PDNET
HACHIS PARMENTIER
ÉLABORÉ AVEC SAVOIR-FAIRE
VIANDE CHOISIE
IN CONTRAST, IN THE ARENA OF FOOD... NOTHING. YOU GET YOURSELF DELIVERED MEALS THAT ARE EITHER FROZEN OR PREPACKAGED, RECTANGULAR OR SQUARE, AND THAT'S PERFECTLY FINE WITH YOU.
SO IMAGINE YOUR SURPRISE WHEN, ONE MORNING, AS YOU'RE PREPARING TO RECEIVE YOUR DAILY PROVISION OF NUTRIENTS,...
DING DONG DING DONG
Yeah, yeah, calm down
(really should reprogram this doorbell)
FLAP FLAP FLAP
YOU FIND YOURSELF FACE TO FACE WITH A PACKAGE THAT IS NEITHER SQUARE NOR RECTANGULAR:
What the heck...
TAKE DIS PEN AN SIGN RIGHT HERE.
Our friends, the squash
Act One
the Spaghetti Squash
AND YOU REMEMBER, ALBEIT VAGUELY, TO HAVE ORDERED BETWEEN TWO RECALCITRANT C++ CODES SOMETHING MADE OF SPAGHETTI...
HUH....
WHERE ARE THE MICROWAVE INSTRUCTIONS?
WHERE'S THE PARAGRAPH ABOUT HOW GOOD IT TASTES?
...EXCEPT, AT FIRST GLANCE, IT'S NOTHING BUT A STINKIN' VEGETABLE!
YOU CONSIDER TRANSFORMING THIS "THING" INTO SOMETHING USEFUL:
HOW TO MAKE JABBA THE HUTT WITH A SPAGHETTI SQUASH
CUT
PASTE
FIRST STEP:
WOAAAA
BUT YOU DON'T YET HAVE A CLUE...
THAT ONCE COOKED, THIS CUCURBIT ACTUALLY DOES TRANSFORM INTO A PILE OF SPAGHETTI!
LET'S BRAINSTORM... VEGETABLE SPAGHETTI NOODLES PREPARED AS A CARBONARA... OR WITH CHEESE... OR WITH GARLIC, OR WITH COCONUT MILK... WHAT DO I KNOW... YOUR IMAGINATION IS THE ONLY LIMIT!
IS THIS AN AD FOR IKEA?
ANYWAY, SORRY, I ONLY HAVE AN OVEN.

Jabba the squash

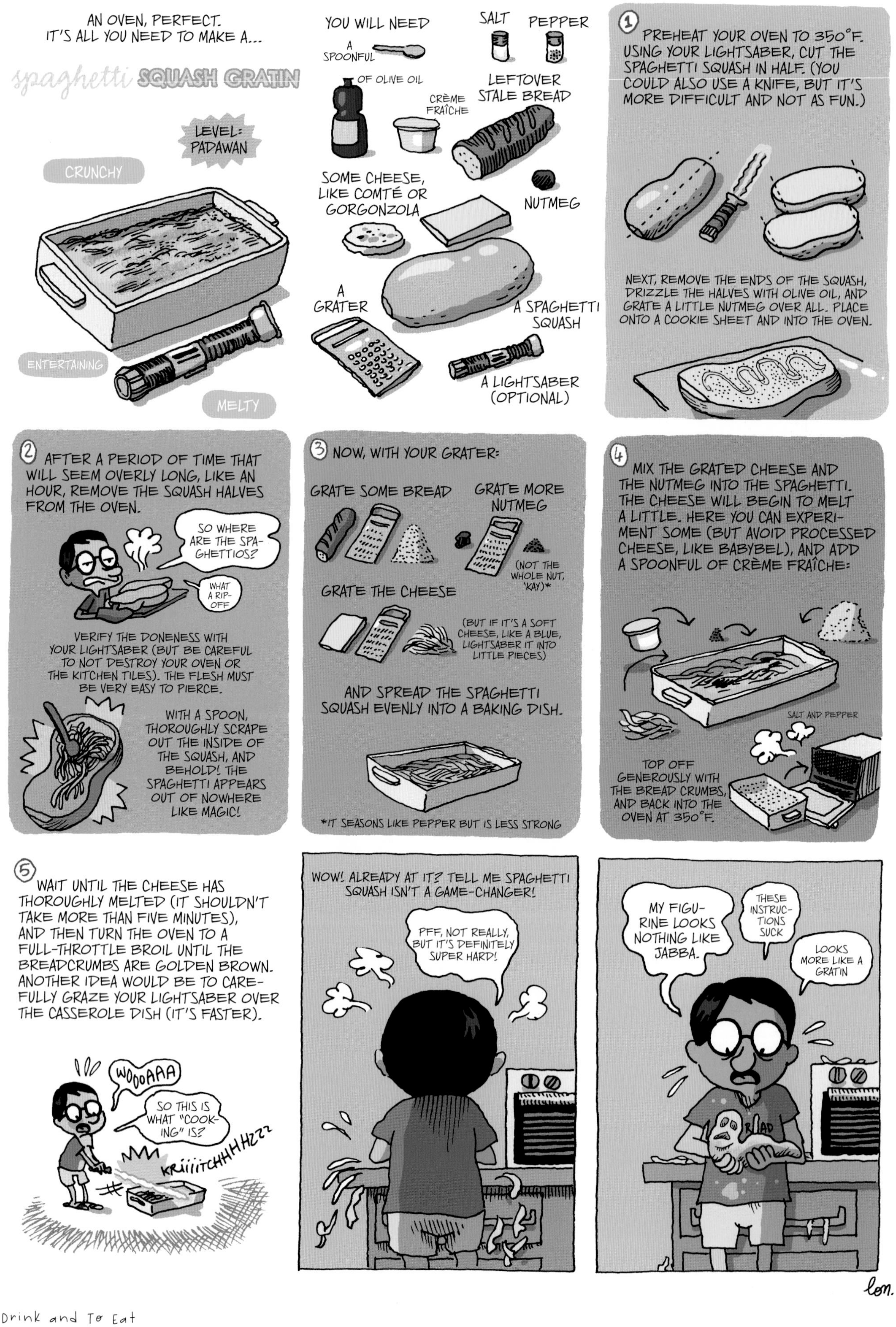

AN OVEN, PERFECT. IT'S ALL YOU NEED TO MAKE A...
spaghetti SQUASH GRATIN
LEVEL: PADAWAN
CRUNCHY
ENTERTAINING
MELTY
YOU WILL NEED
A SPOONFUL
OF OLIVE OIL
SALT
PEPPER
CRÈME FRAÎCHE
LEFTOVER STALE BREAD
SOME CHEESE, LIKE COMTÉ OR GORGONZOLA
NUTMEG
A GRATER
A SPAGHETTI SQUASH
A LIGHTSABER (OPTIONAL)
1 PREHEAT YOUR OVEN TO 350°F. USING YOUR LIGHTSABER, CUT THE SPAGHETTI SQUASH IN HALF. (YOU COULD ALSO USE A KNIFE, BUT IT'S MORE DIFFICULT AND NOT AS FUN.)
NEXT, REMOVE THE ENDS OF THE SQUASH, DRIZZLE THE HALVES WITH OLIVE OIL, AND GRATE A LITTLE NUTMEG OVER ALL. PLACE ONTO A COOKIE SHEET AND INTO THE OVEN.
2 AFTER A PERIOD OF TIME THAT WILL SEEM OVERLY LONG, LIKE AN HOUR, REMOVE THE SQUASH HALVES FROM THE OVEN.
SO WHERE ARE THE SPAGHETTIOS?
WHAT A RIP-OFF
VERIFY THE DONENESS WITH YOUR LIGHTSABER (BUT BE CAREFUL TO NOT DESTROY YOUR OVEN OR THE KITCHEN TILES). THE FLESH MUST BE VERY EASY TO PIERCE.
WITH A SPOON, THOROUGHLY SCRAPE OUT THE INSIDE OF THE SQUASH, AND BEHOLD! THE SPAGHETTI APPEARS OUT OF NOWHERE LIKE MAGIC!
3 NOW, WITH YOUR GRATER:
GRATE SOME BREAD
GRATE MORE NUTMEG
(NOT THE WHOLE NUT, 'KAY)*
GRATE THE CHEESE
(BUT IF IT'S A SOFT CHEESE, LIKE A BLUE, LIGHTSABER IT INTO LITTLE PIECES)
AND SPREAD THE SPAGHETTI SQUASH EVENLY INTO A BAKING DISH.
*IT SEASONS LIKE PEPPER BUT IS LESS STRONG
4 MIX THE GRATED CHEESE AND THE NUTMEG INTO THE SPAGHETTI. THE CHEESE WILL BEGIN TO MELT A LITTLE. HERE YOU CAN EXPERIMENT SOME (BUT AVOID PROCESSED CHEESE, LIKE BABYBEL), AND ADD A SPOONFUL OF CRÈME FRAÎCHE:
SALT AND PEPPER
TOP OFF GENEROUSLY WITH THE BREAD CRUMBS, AND BACK INTO THE OVEN AT 350°F.
5 WAIT UNTIL THE CHEESE HAS THOROUGHLY MELTED (IT SHOULDN'T TAKE MORE THAN FIVE MINUTES), AND THEN TURN THE OVEN TO A FULL-THROTTLE BROIL UNTIL THE BREADCRUMBS ARE GOLDEN BROWN. ANOTHER IDEA WOULD BE TO CAREFULLY GRAZE YOUR LIGHTSABER OVER THE CASSEROLE DISH (IT'S FASTER).
WOOOAAAA
SO THIS IS WHAT "COOKING" IS?
KRiiiiTCHHHHZZZ
WOW! ALREADY AT IT? TELL ME SPAGHETTI SQUASH ISN'T A GAME-CHANGER!
PFF, NOT REALLY, BUT IT'S DEFINITELY SUPER HARD!
MY FIGURINE LOOKS NOTHING LIKE JABBA.
THESE INSTRUCTIONS SUCK
LOOKS MORE LIKE A GRATIN
len.

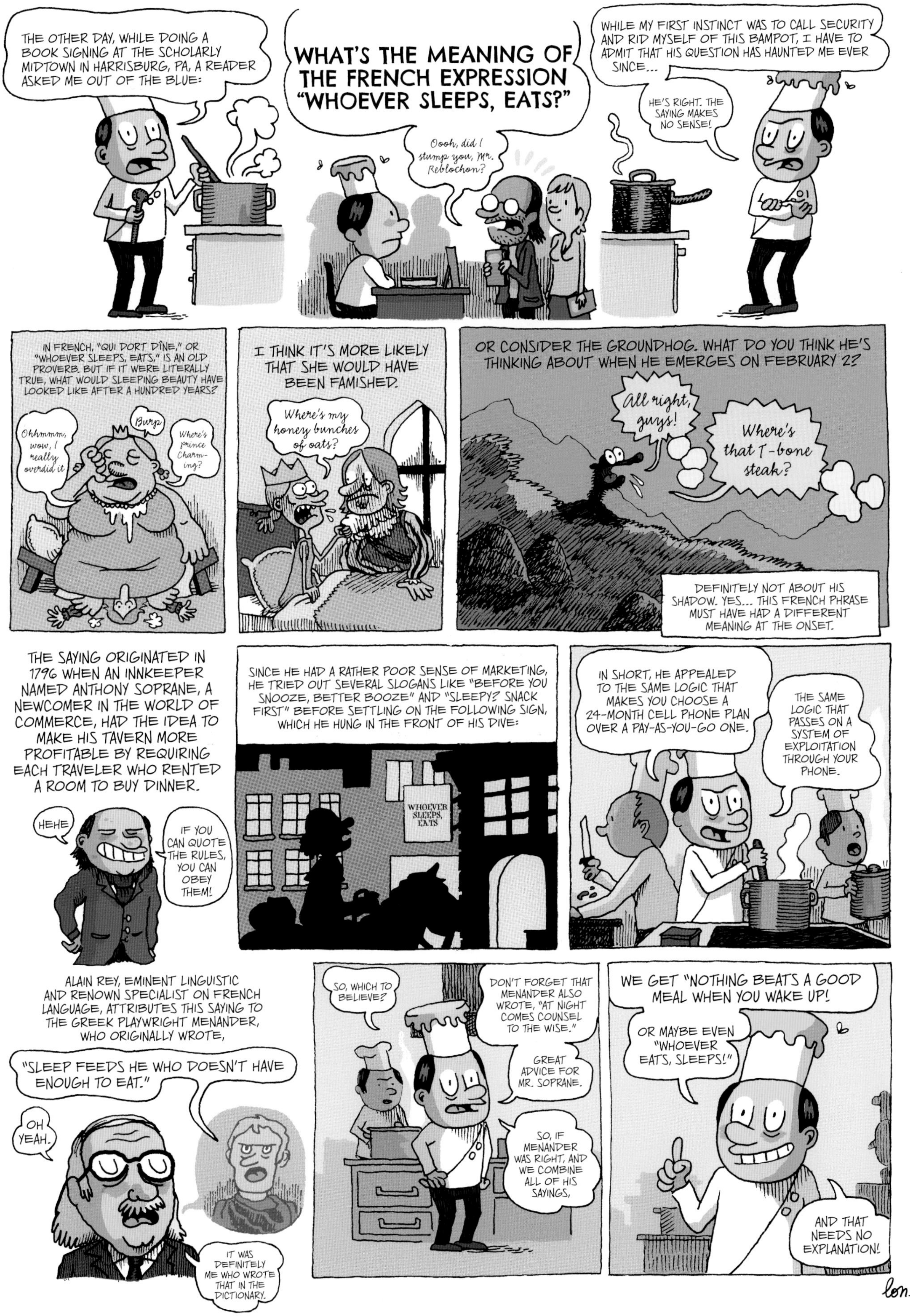
THE OTHER DAY, WHILE DOING A BOOK SIGNING AT THE SCHOLARLY MIDTOWN IN HARRISBURG, PA, A READER ASKED ME OUT OF THE BLUE:
WHAT'S THE MEANING OF THE FRENCH EXPRESSION "WHOEVER SLEEPS, EATS?"
Oooh, did I stump you, Mr. Reblochon?
WHILE MY FIRST INSTINCT WAS TO CALL SECURITY AND RID MYSELF OF THIS BAMPOT, I HAVE TO ADMIT THAT HIS QUESTION HAS HAUNTED ME EVER SINCE...
HE'S RIGHT. THE SAYING MAKES NO SENSE!
IN FRENCH, "QUI DORT DÎNE," OR "WHOEVER SLEEPS, EATS," IS AN OLD PROVERB. BUT IF IT WERE LITERALLY TRUE, WHAT WOULD SLEEPING BEAUTY HAVE LOOKED LIKE AFTER A HUNDRED YEARS?
Ohhmmm, wow, I really overdid it
Burp
Where's prince Charming?
I THINK IT'S MORE LIKELY THAT SHE WOULD HAVE BEEN FAMISHED.
Where's my honey bunches of oats?
OR CONSIDER THE GROUNDHOG. WHAT DO YOU THINK HE'S THINKING ABOUT WHEN HE EMERGES ON FEBRUARY 2?
All right, guys!
Where's that T-bone steak?
DEFINITELY NOT ABOUT HIS SHADOW. YES... THIS FRENCH PHRASE MUST HAVE HAD A DIFFERENT MEANING AT THE ONSET.
THE SAYING ORIGINATED IN 1796 WHEN AN INNKEEPER NAMED ANTHONY SOPRANE, A NEWCOMER IN THE WORLD OF COMMERCE, HAD THE IDEA TO MAKE HIS TAVERN MORE PROFITABLE BY REQUIRING EACH TRAVELER WHO RENTED A ROOM TO BUY DINNER.
HEHE
IF YOU CAN QUOTE THE RULES, YOU CAN OBEY THEM!
SINCE HE HAD A RATHER POOR SENSE OF MARKETING, HE TRIED OUT SEVERAL SLOGANS LIKE "BEFORE YOU SNOOZE, BETTER BOOZE" AND "SLEEPY? SNACK FIRST" BEFORE SETTLING ON THE FOLLOWING SIGN, WHICH HE HUNG IN THE FRONT OF HIS DIVE:
WHOEVER SLEEPS, EATS
IN SHORT, HE APPEALED TO THE SAME LOGIC THAT MAKES YOU CHOOSE A 24-MONTH CELL PHONE PLAN OVER A PAY-AS-YOU-GO ONE.
THE SAME LOGIC THAT PASSES ON A SYSTEM OF EXPLOITATION THROUGH YOUR PHONE.
ALAIN REY, EMINENT LINGUISTIC AND RENOWN SPECIALIST ON FRENCH LANGUAGE, ATTRIBUTES THIS SAYING TO THE GREEK PLAYWRIGHT MENANDER, WHO ORIGINALLY WROTE,
"SLEEP FEEDS HE WHO DOESN'T HAVE ENOUGH TO EAT."
OH YEAH.
IT WAS DEFINITELY ME WHO WROTE THAT IN THE DICTIONARY.
SO, WHICH TO BELIEVE?
DON'T FORGET THAT MENANDER ALSO WROTE, "AT NIGHT COMES COUNSEL TO THE WISE."
GREAT ADVICE FOR MR. SOPRANE.
SO, IF MENANDER WAS RIGHT, AND WE COMBINE ALL OF HIS SAYINGS,
WE GET "NOTHING BEATS A GOOD MEAL WHEN YOU WAKE UP!
OR MAYBE EVEN "WHOEVER EATS, SLEEPS!"
AND THAT NEEDS NO EXPLANATION!
lon.

Guinea fowl on a bed of toast

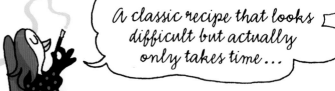

A classic recipe that looks difficult but actually only takes time...

ON THE PHONE WITH MY NEW FRIEND!

YOU'RE WRITING THIS DOWN, I HOPE?

FOR FOUR TO SIX PEOPLE

ABOUT A POUND OF CHICKEN LIVERS

STRIPS OF BACON

OIL

BUTTER

DUCK FAT, GOOSE FAT, OR LARD

SO PHAT

I'LL HELP, BUT AFTERWARDS, WE'RE GOING TO THE POOL

AN UNSLICED LOAF OF BREAD

A DECEASED GUINEA FOWL (BUT NOT OF NATURAL CAUSES), AROUND 3 1/2 LBS

A SMALL GLASS OF COGNAC

SALT

TWO SHALLOTS

PEPPER

THYME

 1 'MKAY, SO, A GUINEA FOWL COOKS JUST LIKE A CHICKEN. IT'S A LOT BETTER BUT IT ALSO DRIES OUT QUICKER... SO YOU HAVE TO OIL THE THIGHS, FIRST OF ALL... SURE, LIKE A MAGAZINE COVER, IF THAT HELPS. NEXT, WITH SOME BUTTER, YOU... YEAH, LIKE A PIECE OF BREAD. OR ANY OTHER KIND OF OIL YOU'D LIKE. WHAT? YEAH, LIKE

A... WAIT A SECOND, YOU WRITING THIS DOWN? DON'T TELL ME YOU'RE ACTUALLY COOKI... WHAT? BUT THIS WILL TAKE THREE HOURS ON THE PHONE!

2 TOO LATE! YEAH, SORRY 'BOUT THAT... YEAH... OKAY, WHAT TEMPERATURE SHOULD THE OVEN BE AT? BETWEEN 350° OR 400°F, OKAY... NEXT, I SHOULD SEASON THE OLD BIRD WITH SALT AND PEPPER... YES... A SPRIG OR TWO OF THYME IN THE CAVITY, SUPER EAS... WHAT? I SHOULD ALSO PUT SALT AND PEPPER INSIDE? WEIRD YEAH, BUT OKAY... AND THEN I SHOULD SHAKE THE GUINEA FOWL LIKE A MARACA?

HANG ON, I HAVE BUTTER EVERYWHERE

OKAY, DONE.

3 YOU HAVE BUTTER ON YOUR FINGERS? TYPICAL, YOU SHOULD HAVE SALTED AND PEPPERED THE CAVITY FIRS... HUH? THINK FOR YOURSELF FOR ONCE! YEAH... WELL NO... OKAY, MOVING ON: YOU'RE GOING TO ROAST THE GUINEA FOWL FOR ABOUT FORTY-FIVE MINUTES BY DOING EXACTLY THIS: FIFTEEN MINUTES ON ONE THIGH, ANOTHER FIFTEEN ON THE OTHER THIGH, AND A FINAL FIFTEEN ON THE BACK... WHAT? YEAH, YEAH, PUT THE GUINEA FOWL IN A ROASTING DISH, NOT DIRECTLY ON THE GRATES!

AND THEN YOU BASTE THE FOWL FROM TIME TO TIME.

HAVE YOU NEVER ROASTED A CHICKEN BEFORE?

YEAH, PUT IT IN.

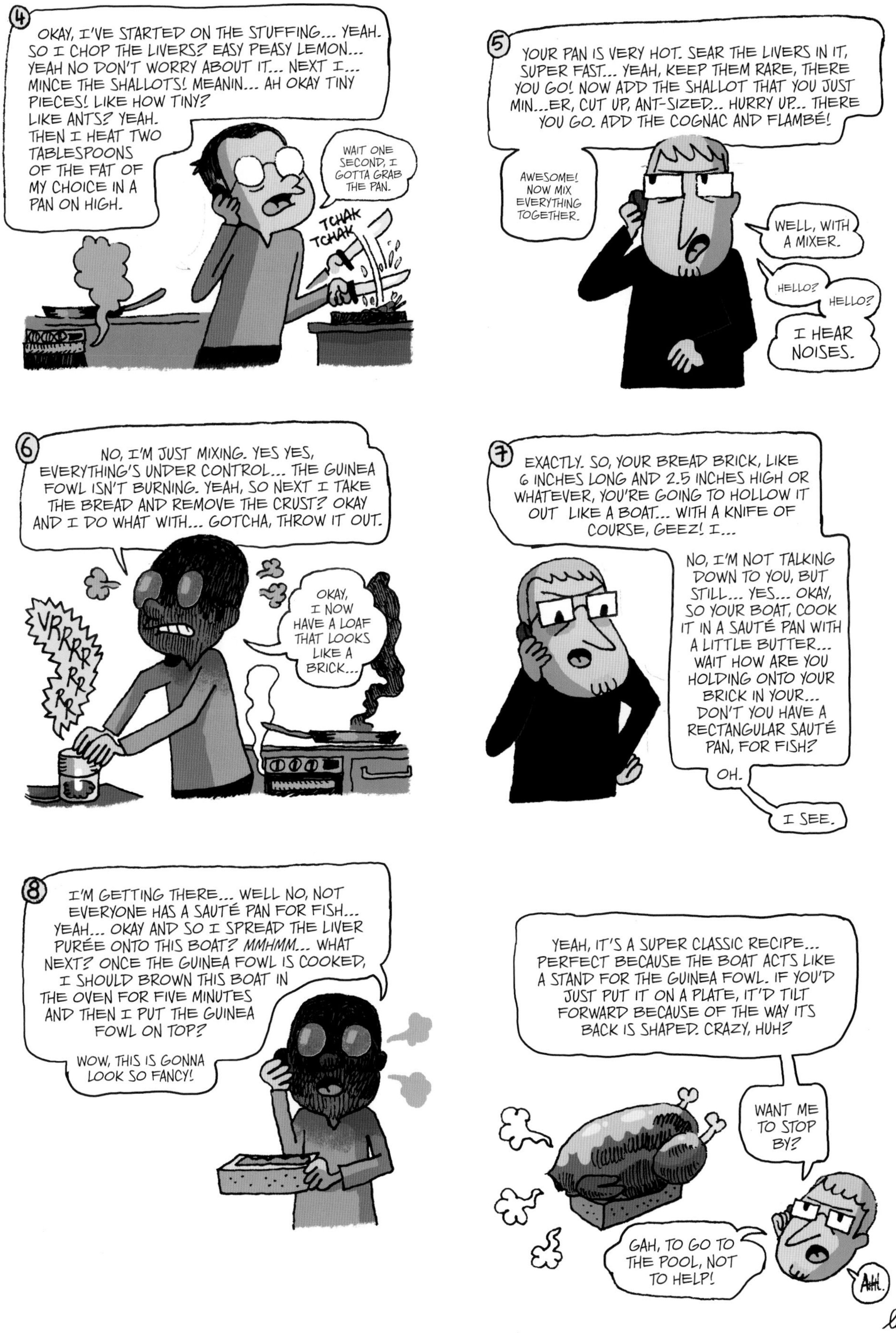

4
OKAY, I'VE STARTED ON THE STUFFING... YEAH. SO I CHOP THE LIVERS? EASY PEASY LEMON... YEAH NO DON'T WORRY ABOUT IT... NEXT I... MINCE THE SHALLOTS! MEANIN... AH OKAY TINY PIECES! LIKE HOW TINY? LIKE ANTS? YEAH. THEN I HEAT TWO TABLESPOONS OF THE FAT OF MY CHOICE IN A PAN ON HIGH.
WAIT ONE SECOND, I GOTTA GRAB THE PAN.
TCHAK TCHAK
5
YOUR PAN IS VERY HOT. SEAR THE LIVERS IN IT, SUPER FAST... YEAH, KEEP THEM RARE, THERE YOU GO! NOW ADD THE SHALLOT THAT YOU JUST MIN...ER, CUT UP, ANT-SIZED.. HURRY UP.. THERE YOU GO. ADD THE COGNAC AND FLAMBÉ!
AWESOME! NOW MIX EVERYTHING TOGETHER.
WELL, WITH A MIXER.
HELLO?
HELLO?
I HEAR NOISES.
6
NO, I'M JUST MIXING. YES YES, EVERYTHING'S UNDER CONTROL... THE GUINEA FOWL ISN'T BURNING. YEAH, SO NEXT I TAKE THE BREAD AND REMOVE THE CRUST? OKAY AND I DO WHAT WITH... GOTCHA, THROW IT OUT.
VRRRRRRR
OKAY, I NOW HAVE A LOAF THAT LOOKS LIKE A BRICK...
7
EXACTLY. SO, YOUR BREAD BRICK, LIKE 6 INCHES LONG AND 2.5 INCHES HIGH OR WHATEVER, YOU'RE GOING TO HOLLOW IT OUT LIKE A BOAT... WITH A KNIFE OF COURSE, GEEZ! I...
NO, I'M NOT TALKING DOWN TO YOU, BUT STILL... YES... OKAY, SO YOUR BOAT, COOK IT IN A SAUTÉ PAN WITH A LITTLE BUTTER... WAIT HOW ARE YOU HOLDING ONTO YOUR BRICK IN YOUR... DON'T YOU HAVE A RECTANGULAR SAUTÉ PAN, FOR FISH?
OH.
I SEE.
8
I'M GETTING THERE... WELL NO, NOT EVERYONE HAS A SAUTÉ PAN FOR FISH... YEAH... OKAY AND SO I SPREAD THE LIVER PURÉE ONTO THIS BOAT? MMHMM... WHAT NEXT? ONCE THE GUINEA FOWL IS COOKED, I SHOULD BROWN THIS BOAT IN THE OVEN FOR FIVE MINUTES AND THEN I PUT THE GUINEA FOWL ON TOP?
WOW, THIS IS GONNA LOOK SO FANCY!
YEAH, IT'S A SUPER CLASSIC RECIPE... PERFECT BECAUSE THE BOAT ACTS LIKE A STAND FOR THE GUINEA FOWL. IF YOU'D JUST PUT IT ON A PLATE, IT'D TILT FORWARD BECAUSE OF THE WAY ITS BACK IS SHAPED. CRAZY, HUH?
WANT ME TO STOP BY?
GAH, TO GO TO THE POOL, NOT TO HELP!
AHH.
len.

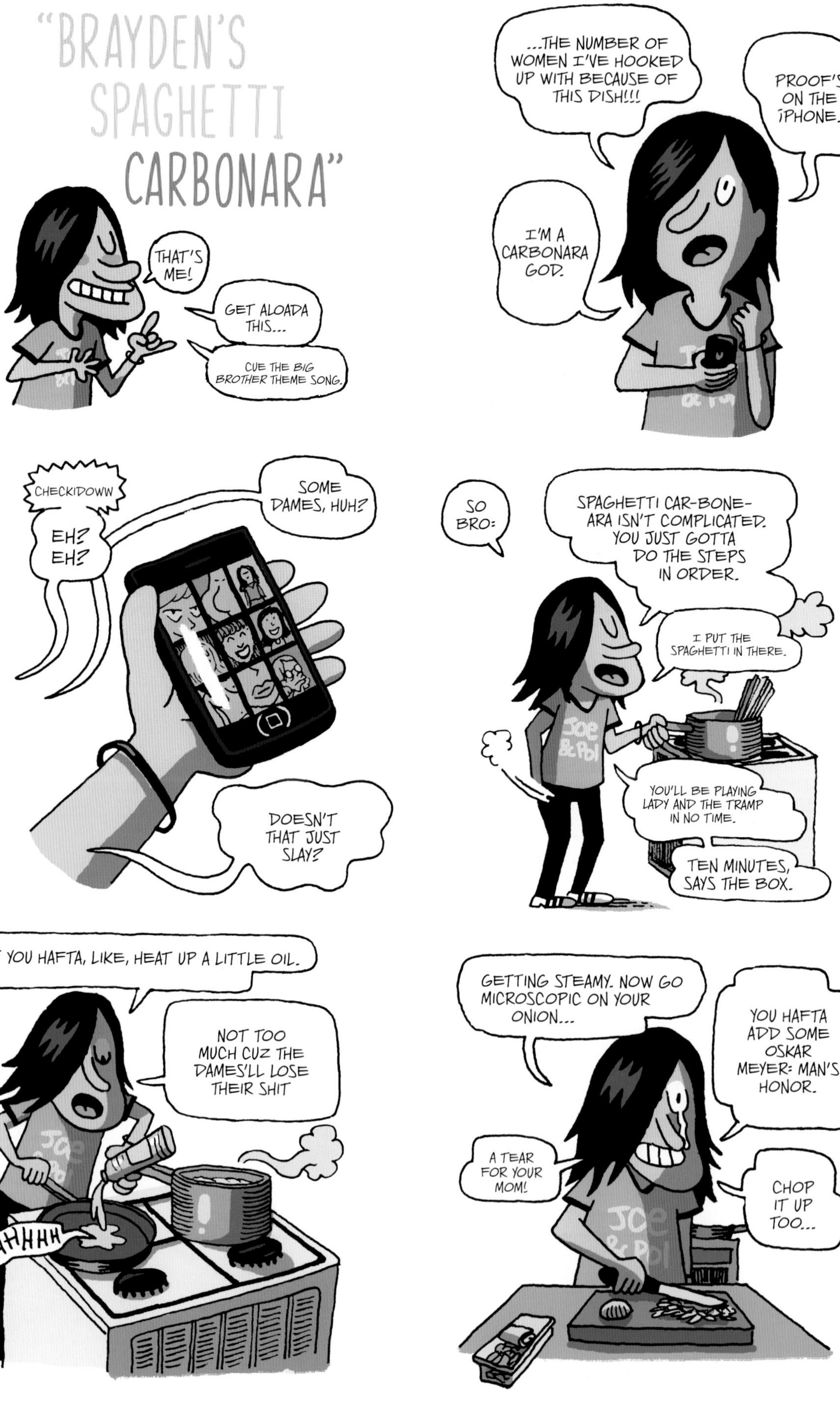
"BRAYDEN'S SPAGHETTI CARBONARA"
THAT'S ME!
GET ALOADA THIS...
CUE THE BIG BROTHER THEME SONG.
...THE NUMBER OF WOMEN I'VE HOOKED UP WITH BECAUSE OF THIS DISH!!!
PROOF'S ON THE iPHONE.
I'M A CARBONARA GOD.
CHECKIDOWW
EH? EH?
SOME DAMES, HUH?
DOESN'T THAT JUST SLAY?
SO BRO:
SPAGHETTI CAR-BONE-ARA ISN'T COMPLICATED. YOU JUST GOTTA DO THE STEPS IN ORDER.
I PUT THE SPAGHETTI IN THERE.
YOU'LL BE PLAYING LADY AND THE TRAMP IN NO TIME.
TEN MINUTES, SAYS THE BOX.
NEXT YOU HAFTA, LIKE, HEAT UP A LITTLE OIL.
NOT TOO MUCH CUZ THE DAMES'LL LOSE THEIR SHIT
TSHHHHH
GETTING STEAMY. NOW GO MICROSCOPIC ON YOUR ONION...
YOU HAFTA ADD SOME OSKAR MEYER: MAN'S HONOR.
A TEAR FOR YOUR MOM!
CHOP IT UP TOO...

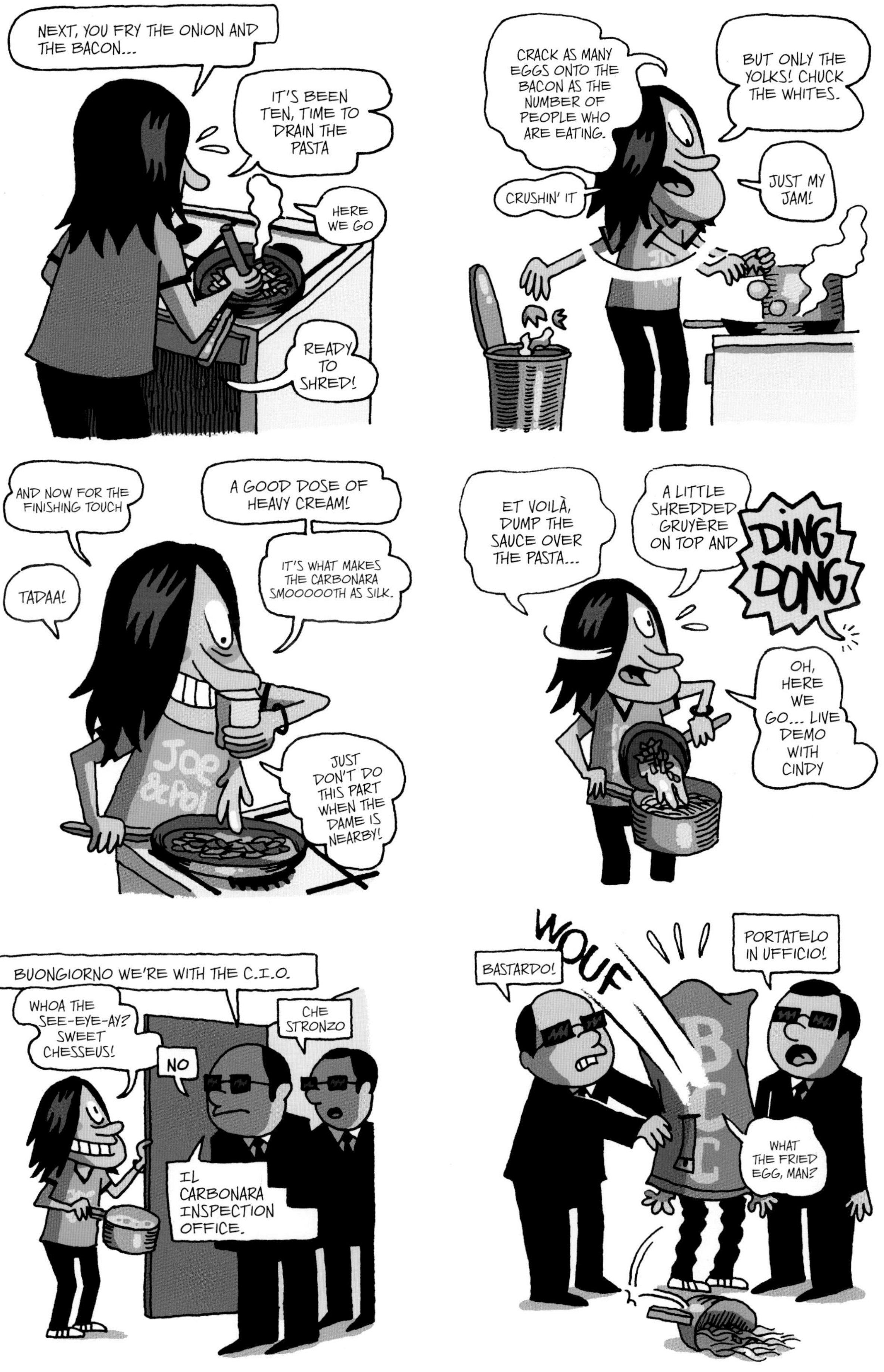
NEXT, YOU FRY THE ONION AND THE BACON...
IT'S BEEN TEN, TIME TO DRAIN THE PASTA
HERE WE GO
READY TO SHRED!
CRACK AS MANY EGGS ONTO THE BACON AS THE NUMBER OF PEOPLE WHO ARE EATING.
BUT ONLY THE YOLKS! CHUCK THE WHITES.
CRUSHIN' IT
JUST MY JAM!
AND NOW FOR THE FINISHING TOUCH
A GOOD DOSE OF HEAVY CREAM!
IT'S WHAT MAKES THE CARBONARA SMOOOOOTH AS SILK.
TADAA!
JUST DON'T DO THIS PART WHEN THE DAME IS NEARBY!
ET VOILÀ, DUMP THE SAUCE OVER THE PASTA...
A LITTLE SHREDDED GRUYÈRE ON TOP AND
DING DONG
OH, HERE WE GO... LIVE DEMO WITH CINDY
BUONGIORNO WE'RE WITH THE C.I.O.
WHOA THE SEE-EYE-AY? SWEET CHESSEUS!
CHE STRONZO
NO
IL CARBONARA INSPECTION OFFICE.
BASTARDO!
WOUF
PORTATELO IN UFFICIO!
WHAT THE FRIED EGG, MAN?

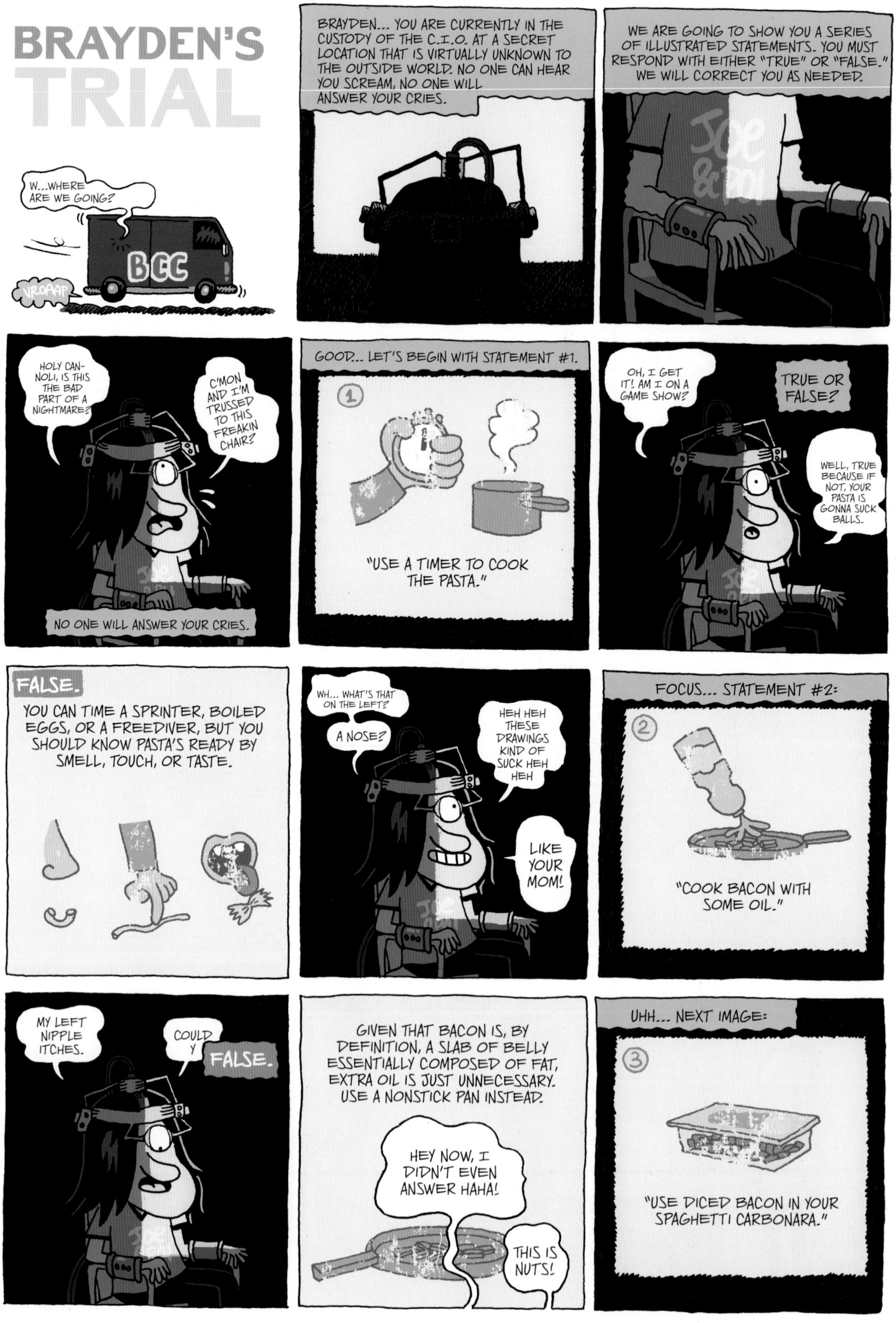
BRAYDEN'S TRIAL
W... WHERE ARE WE GOING?
BCC
VROAAP
BRAYDEN... YOU ARE CURRENTLY IN THE CUSTODY OF THE C.I.O. AT A SECRET LOCATION THAT IS VIRTUALLY UNKNOWN TO THE OUTSIDE WORLD. NO ONE CAN HEAR YOU SCREAM, NO ONE WILL ANSWER YOUR CRIES.
WE ARE GOING TO SHOW YOU A SERIES OF ILLUSTRATED STATEMENTS. YOU MUST RESPOND WITH EITHER "TRUE" OR "FALSE." WE WILL CORRECT YOU AS NEEDED.
HOLY CANNOLI, IS THIS THE BAD PART OF A NIGHTMARE?
C'MON AND I'M TRUSSED TO THIS FREAKIN CHAIR?
NO ONE WILL ANSWER YOUR CRIES.
GOOD... LET'S BEGIN WITH STATEMENT #1.
1
"USE A TIMER TO COOK THE PASTA."
OH, I GET IT! AM I ON A GAME SHOW?
TRUE OR FALSE?
WELL, TRUE BECAUSE IF NOT, YOUR PASTA IS GONNA SUCK BALLS.
FALSE.
YOU CAN TIME A SPRINTER, BOILED EGGS, OR A FREEDIVER, BUT YOU SHOULD KNOW PASTA'S READY BY SMELL, TOUCH, OR TASTE.
WH... WHAT'S THAT ON THE LEFT?
A NOSE?
HEH HEH THESE DRAWINGS KIND OF SUCK HEH HEH
LIKE YOUR MOM!
FOCUS... STATEMENT #2:
2
"COOK BACON WITH SOME OIL."
MY LEFT NIPPLE ITCHES.
COULD Y
FALSE.
GIVEN THAT BACON IS, BY DEFINITION, A SLAB OF BELLY ESSENTIALLY COMPOSED OF FAT, EXTRA OIL IS JUST UNNECESSARY. USE A NONSTICK PAN INSTEAD.
HEY NOW, I DIDN'T EVEN ANSWER HAHA!
THIS IS NUTS!
UHH... NEXT IMAGE:
3
"USE DICED BACON IN YOUR SPAGHETTI CARBONARA."

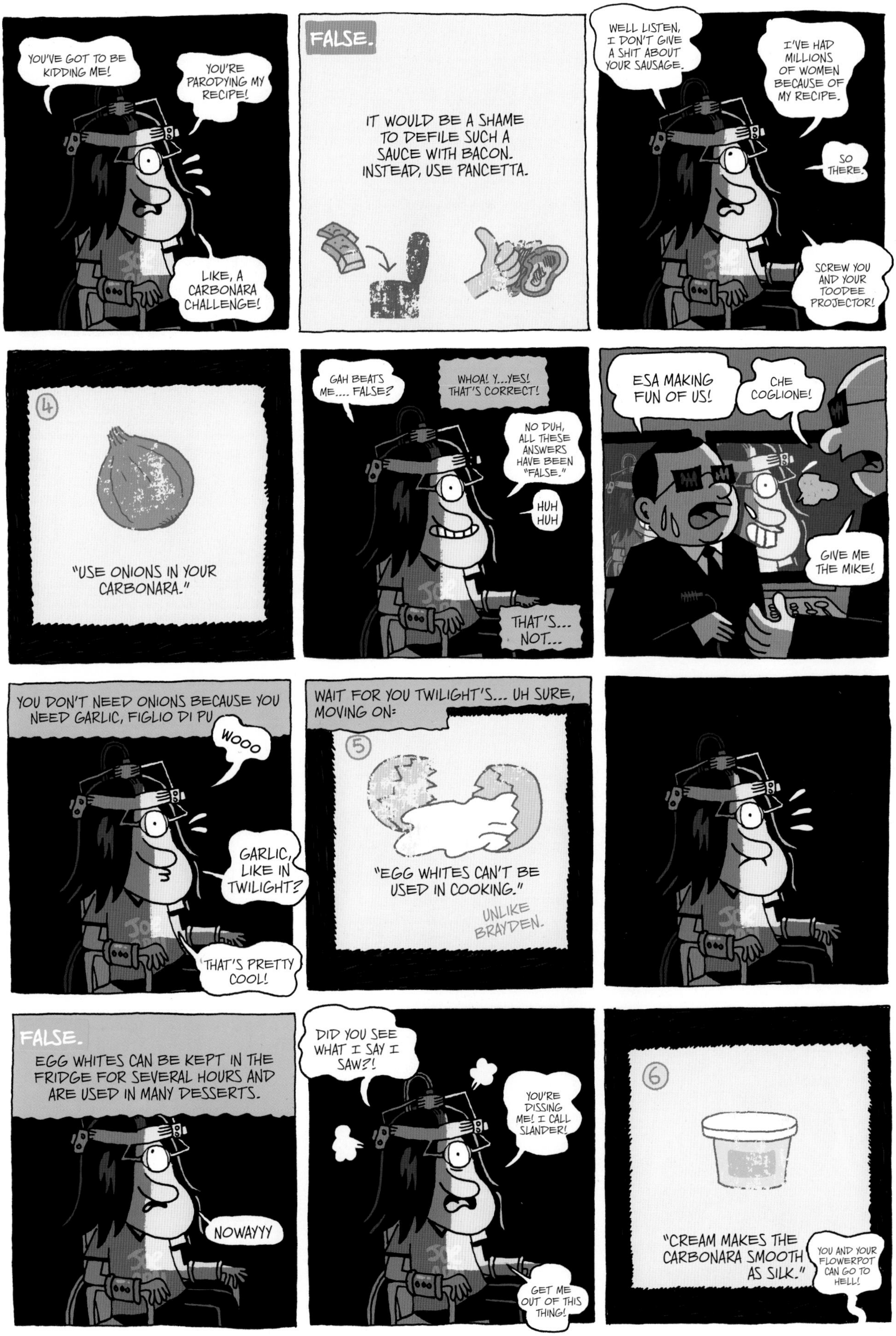
YOU'VE GOT TO BE KIDDING ME!
YOU'RE PARODYING MY RECIPE!
LIKE, A CARBONARA CHALLENGE!
FALSE.
IT WOULD BE A SHAME TO DEFILE SUCH A SAUCE WITH BACON. INSTEAD, USE PANCETTA.
WELL LISTEN, I DON'T GIVE A SHIT ABOUT YOUR SAUSAGE.
I'VE HAD MILLIONS OF WOMEN BECAUSE OF MY RECIPE.
SO THERE.
SCREW YOU AND YOUR TOODEE PROJECTOR!
4
"USE ONIONS IN YOUR CARBONARA."
GAH BEATS ME.... FALSE?
WHOA! Y...YES! THAT'S CORRECT!
NO DUH, ALL THESE ANSWERS HAVE BEEN "FALSE."
HUH HUH
THAT'S... NOT...
ESA MAKING FUN OF US!
CHE COGLIONE!
GIVE ME THE MIKE!
YOU DON'T NEED ONIONS BECAUSE YOU NEED GARLIC, FIGLIO DI PU
WOOO
GARLIC, LIKE IN TWILIGHT?
THAT'S PRETTY COOL!
WAIT FOR YOU TWILIGHT'S... UH SURE, MOVING ON:
5
"EGG WHITES CAN'T BE USED IN COOKING."
UNLIKE BRAYDEN.
FALSE.
EGG WHITES CAN BE KEPT IN THE FRIDGE FOR SEVERAL HOURS AND ARE USED IN MANY DESSERTS.
NOWAYYY
DID YOU SEE WHAT I SAY I SAW?!
YOU'RE DISSING ME! I CALL SLANDER!
GET ME OUT OF THIS THING!
6
"CREAM MAKES THE CARBONARA SMOOTH AS SILK."
YOU AND YOUR FLOWERPOT CAN GO TO HELL!

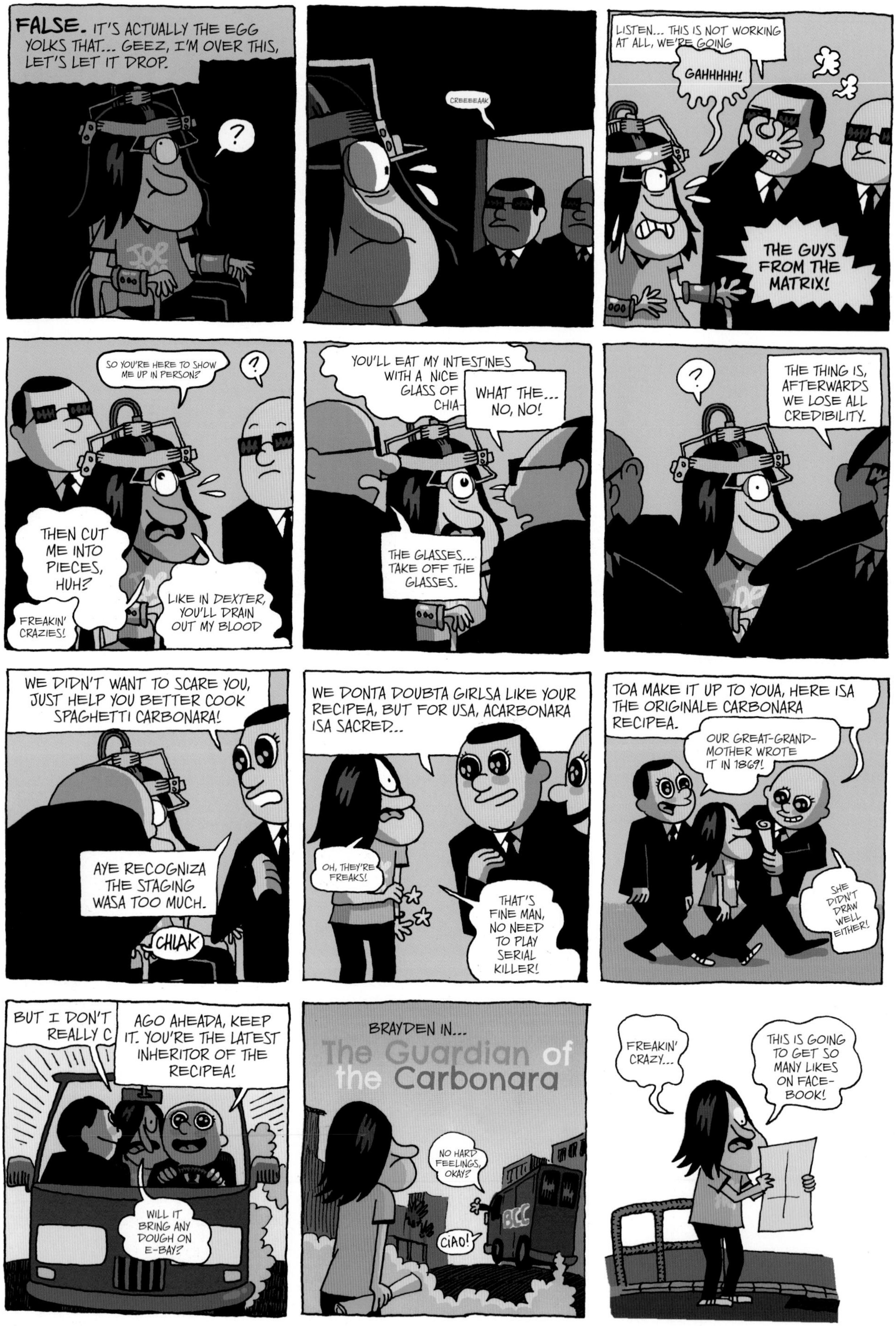
FALSE. IT'S ACTUALLY THE EGG YOLKS THAT... GEEZ, I'M OVER THIS, LET'S LET IT DROP.
?
CREEEEAAK
LISTEN... THIS IS NOT WORKING AT ALL, WE'RE GOING
GAHHHHH!
THE GUYS FROM THE MATRIX!
SO YOU'RE HERE TO SHOW ME UP IN PERSON?
?
THEN CUT ME INTO PIECES, HUH?
FREAKIN' CRAZIES!
LIKE IN DEXTER, YOU'LL DRAIN OUT MY BLOOD
YOU'LL EAT MY INTESTINES WITH A NICE GLASS OF CHIA-
WHAT THE... NO, NO!
THE GLASSES... TAKE OFF THE GLASSES.
?
THE THING IS, AFTERWARDS WE LOSE ALL CREDIBILITY.
WE DIDN'T WANT TO SCARE YOU, JUST HELP YOU BETTER COOK SPAGHETTI CARBONARA!
AYE RECOGNIZA THE STAGING WASA TOO MUCH.
CHLAK
WE DONTA DOUBTA GIRLSA LIKE YOUR RECIPEA, BUT FOR USA, ACARBONARA ISA SACRED...
OH, THEY'RE FREAKS!
THAT'S FINE MAN, NO NEED TO PLAY SERIAL KILLER!
TOA MAKE IT UP TO YOUA, HERE ISA THE ORIGINALE CARBONARA RECIPEA.
OUR GREAT-GRAND-MOTHER WROTE IT IN 1869!
SHE DIDN'T DRAW WELL EITHER!
BUT I DON'T REALLY C
AGO AHEADA, KEEP IT. YOU'RE THE LATEST INHERITOR OF THE RECIPEA!
WILL IT BRING ANY DOUGH ON E-BAY?
BRAYDEN IN...
The Guardian of the Carbonara
NO HARD FEELINGS, OKAY?
CIAO!
BCC
FREAKIN' CRAZY...
THIS IS GOING TO GET SO MANY LIKES ON FACE-BOOK!

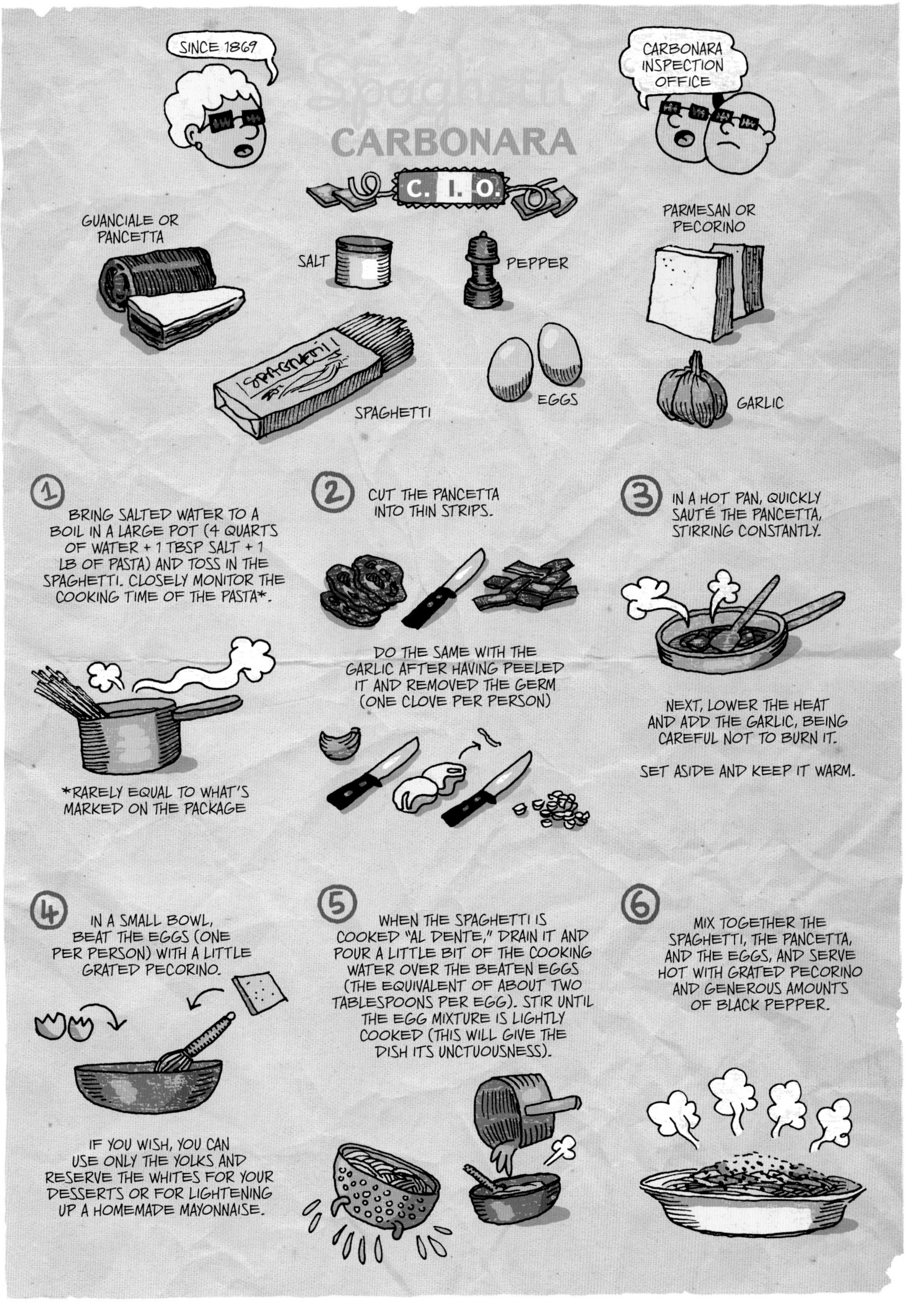
SINCE 1869
CARBONARA INSPECTION OFFICE
Spaghetti
CARBONARA
C. I. O.
GUANCIALE OR PANCETTA
SALT
PEPPER
PARMESAN OR PECORINO
SPAGHETTI
SPAGHETTI
EGGS
GARLIC
1
BRING SALTED WATER TO A BOIL IN A LARGE POT (4 QUARTS OF WATER + 1 TBSP SALT + 1 LB OF PASTA) AND TOSS IN THE SPAGHETTI. CLOSELY MONITOR THE COOKING TIME OF THE PASTA*.
*RARELY EQUAL TO WHAT'S MARKED ON THE PACKAGE
2
CUT THE PANCETTA INTO THIN STRIPS.
DO THE SAME WITH THE GARLIC AFTER HAVING PEELED IT AND REMOVED THE GERM (ONE CLOVE PER PERSON)
3
IN A HOT PAN, QUICKLY SAUTÉ THE PANCETTA, STIRRING CONSTANTLY.
NEXT, LOWER THE HEAT AND ADD THE GARLIC, BEING CAREFUL NOT TO BURN IT.
SET ASIDE AND KEEP IT WARM.
4
IN A SMALL BOWL, BEAT THE EGGS (ONE PER PERSON) WITH A LITTLE GRATED PECORINO.
IF YOU WISH, YOU CAN USE ONLY THE YOLKS AND RESERVE THE WHITES FOR YOUR DESSERTS OR FOR LIGHTENING UP A HOMEMADE MAYONNAISE.
5
WHEN THE SPAGHETTI IS COOKED "AL DENTE," DRAIN IT AND POUR A LITTLE BIT OF THE COOKING WATER OVER THE BEATEN EGGS (THE EQUIVALENT OF ABOUT TWO TABLESPOONS PER EGG). STIR UNTIL THE EGG MIXTURE IS LIGHTLY COOKED (THIS WILL GIVE THE DISH ITS UNCTUOUSNESS).
6
MIX TOGETHER THE SPAGHETTI, THE PANCETTA, AND THE EGGS, AND SERVE HOT WITH GRATED PECORINO AND GENEROUS AMOUNTS OF BLACK PEPPER.

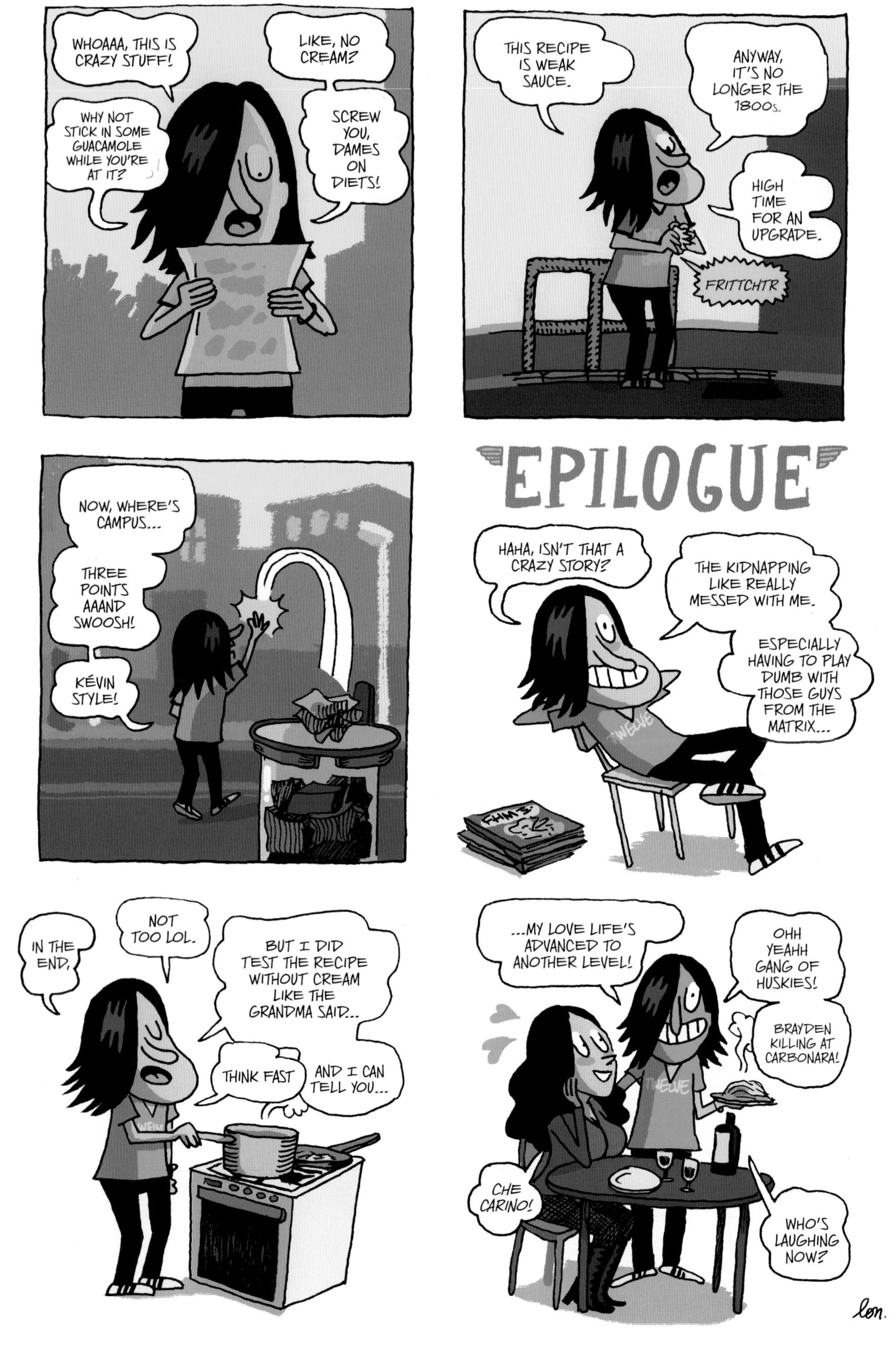
WHOAAA, THIS IS CRAZY STUFF!
LIKE, NO CREAM?
WHY NOT STICK IN SOME GUACAMOLE WHILE YOU'RE AT IT?
SCREW YOU, DAMES ON DIETS!
THIS RECIPE IS WEAK SAUCE.
ANYWAY, IT'S NO LONGER THE 1800s.
HIGH TIME FOR AN UPGRADE.
FRITTCHTR
NOW, WHERE'S CAMPUS...
THREE POINTS AAAND SWOOSH!
KÉVIN STYLE!
EPILOGUE
HAHA, ISN'T THAT A CRAZY STORY?
THE KIDNAPPING LIKE REALLY MESSED WITH ME.
ESPECIALLY HAVING TO PLAY DUMB WITH THOSE GUYS FROM THE MATRIX...
IN THE END,
NOT TOO LOL.
BUT I DID TEST THE RECIPE WITHOUT CREAM LIKE THE GRANDMA SAID...
THINK FAST
AND I CAN TELL YOU...
...MY LOVE LIFE'S ADVANCED TO ANOTHER LEVEL!
OHH YEAHH GANG OF HUSKIES!
BRAYDEN KILLING AT CARBONARA!
CHE CARINO!
WHO'S LAUGHING NOW?
lon.

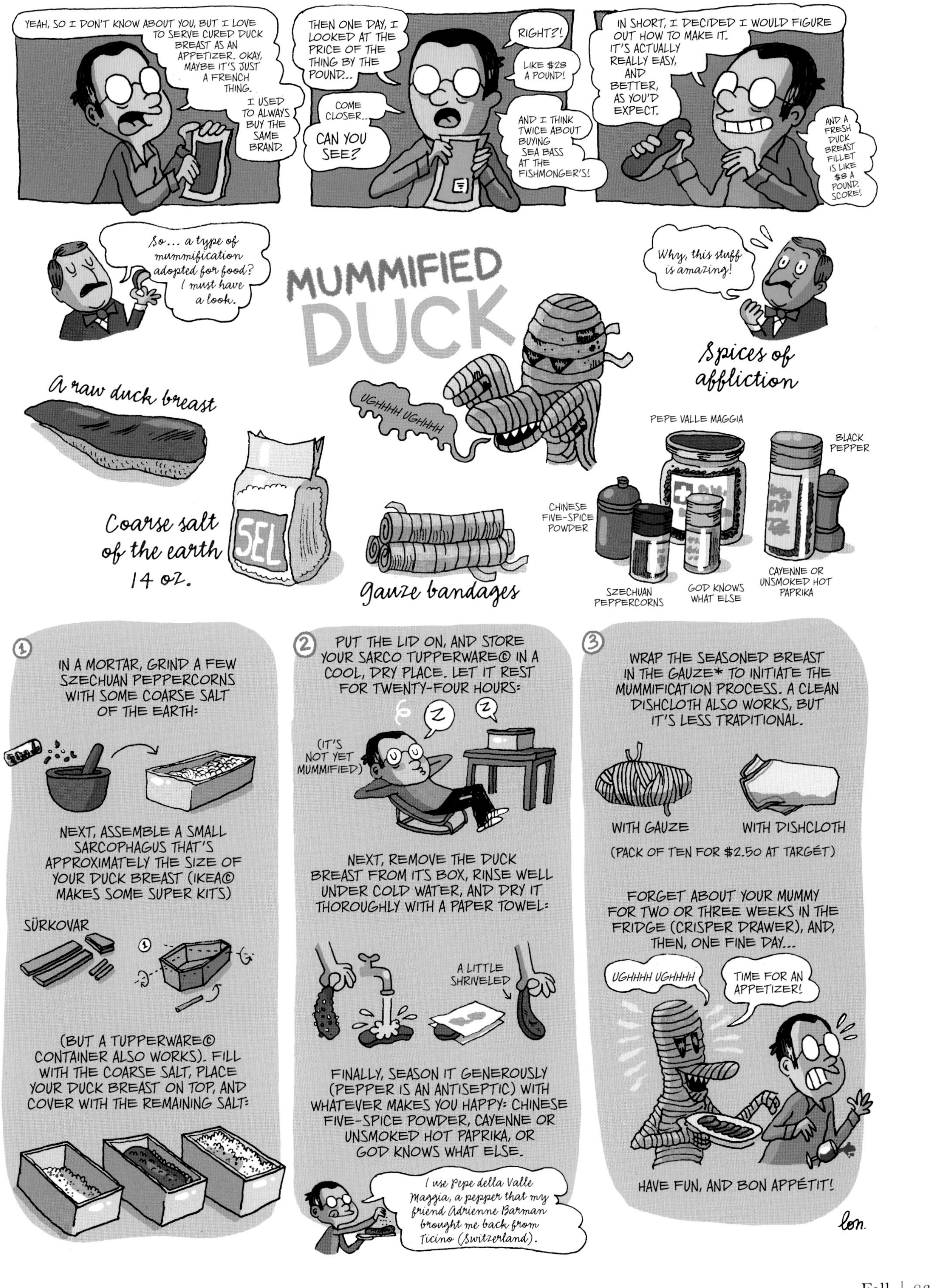
YEAH, SO I DON'T KNOW ABOUT YOU, BUT I LOVE TO SERVE CURED DUCK BREAST AS AN APPETIZER. OKAY, MAYBE IT'S JUST A FRENCH THING.
I USED TO ALWAYS BUY THE SAME BRAND.
THEN ONE DAY, I LOOKED AT THE PRICE OF THE THING BY THE POUND...
RIGHT?!
LIKE $28 A POUND!
COME CLOSER...
CAN YOU SEE?
AND I THINK TWICE ABOUT BUYING SEA BASS AT THE FISHMONGER'S!
IN SHORT, I DECIDED I WOULD FIGURE OUT HOW TO MAKE IT. IT'S ACTUALLY REALLY EASY, AND BETTER, AS YOU'D EXPECT.
AND A FRESH DUCK BREAST FILLET IS LIKE $8 A POUND. SCORE!
So... a type of mummification adopted for food? I must have a look.
MUMMIFIED DUCK
Why, this stuff is amazing!
Spices of affliction
A raw duck breast
UGHHHH UGHHHH
PEPE VALLE MAGGIA
BLACK PEPPER
CHINESE FIVE-SPICE POWDER
SEL
Coarse salt of the earth 14 oz.
Gauze bandages
SZECHUAN PEPPERCORNS
GOD KNOWS WHAT ELSE
CAYENNE OR UNSMOKED HOT PAPRIKA
1
IN A MORTAR, GRIND A FEW SZECHUAN PEPPERCORNS WITH SOME COARSE SALT OF THE EARTH:
NEXT, ASSEMBLE A SMALL SARCOPHAGUS THAT'S APPROXIMATELY THE SIZE OF YOUR DUCK BREAST (IKEA© MAKES SOME SUPER KITS)
SÜRKOVAR
(BUT A TUPPERWARE© CONTAINER ALSO WORKS). FILL WITH THE COARSE SALT, PLACE YOUR DUCK BREAST ON TOP, AND COVER WITH THE REMAINING SALT:
2
PUT THE LID ON, AND STORE YOUR SARCO TUPPERWARE© IN A COOL, DRY PLACE. LET IT REST FOR TWENTY-FOUR HOURS:
(IT'S NOT YET MUMMIFIED)
NEXT, REMOVE THE DUCK BREAST FROM ITS BOX, RINSE WELL UNDER COLD WATER, AND DRY IT THOROUGHLY WITH A PAPER TOWEL:
A LITTLE SHRIVELED
FINALLY, SEASON IT GENEROUSLY (PEPPER IS AN ANTISEPTIC) WITH WHATEVER MAKES YOU HAPPY: CHINESE FIVE-SPICE POWDER, CAYENNE OR UNSMOKED HOT PAPRIKA, OR GOD KNOWS WHAT ELSE.
I use Pepe della Valle Maggia, a pepper that my friend Adrienne Barman brought me back from Ticino (Switzerland).
3
WRAP THE SEASONED BREAST IN THE GAUZE* TO INITIATE THE MUMMIFICATION PROCESS. A CLEAN DISHCLOTH ALSO WORKS, BUT IT'S LESS TRADITIONAL.
WITH GAUZE
WITH DISHCLOTH
(PACK OF TEN FOR $2.50 AT TARGÉT)
FORGET ABOUT YOUR MUMMY FOR TWO OR THREE WEEKS IN THE FRIDGE (CRISPER DRAWER), AND, THEN, ONE FINE DAY...
UGHHHH UGHHHH
TIME FOR AN APPETIZER!
HAVE FUN, AND BON APPÉTIT!
lon.

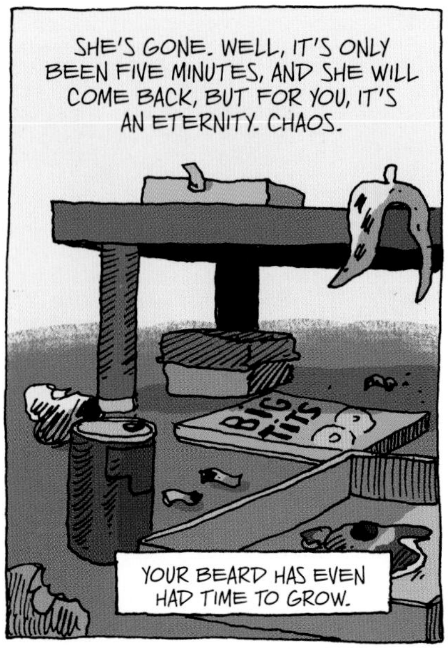
SHE'S GONE. WELL, IT'S ONLY BEEN FIVE MINUTES, AND SHE WILL COME BACK, BUT FOR YOU, IT'S AN ETERNITY. CHAOS.
BIG TITS
YOUR BEARD HAS EVEN HAD TIME TO GROW.

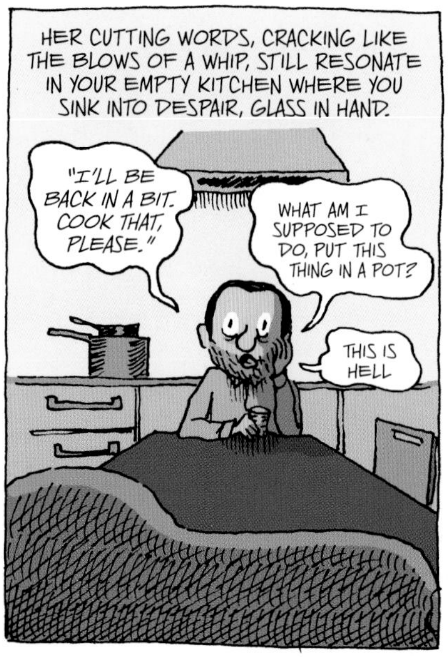
HER CUTTING WORDS, CRACKING LIKE THE BLOWS OF A WHIP, STILL RESONATE IN YOUR EMPTY KITCHEN WHERE YOU SINK INTO DESPAIR, GLASS IN HAND.
"I'LL BE BACK IN A BIT. COOK THAT, PLEASE."
WHAT AM I SUPPOSED TO DO, PUT THIS THING IN A POT?
THIS IS HELL

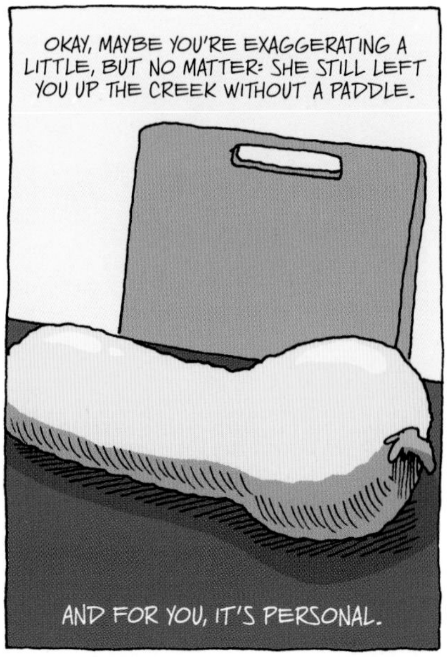
OKAY, MAYBE YOU'RE EXAGGERATING A LITTLE, BUT NO MATTER: SHE STILL LEFT YOU UP THE CREEK WITHOUT A PADDLE.
AND FOR YOU, IT'S PERSONAL.

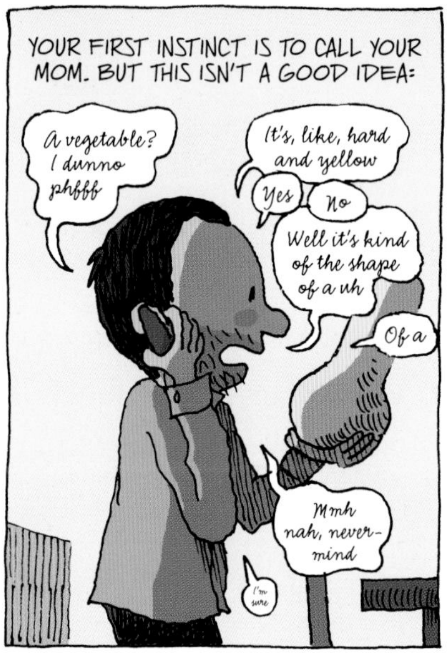
YOUR FIRST INSTINCT IS TO CALL YOUR MOM. BUT THIS ISN'T A GOOD IDEA:
A vegetable? I dunno phfff
It's, like, hard and yellow
Yes
No
Well it's kind of the shape of a uh
Of a
Mmh nah, never-mind
I'm sure

Our friends, the squash

Act Two

the butternut squash

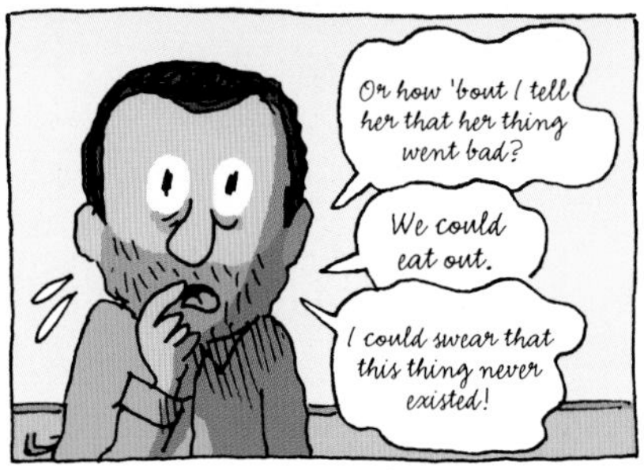
Or how 'bout I tell her that her thing went bad?
We could eat out.
I could swear that this thing never existed!

COME NOW... DON'T PANIC SO EASILY! IT'S JUST A HARMLESS LITTLE SQUASH THAT ACTUALLY TASTES REALLY GOOD. YOU COULD COOK IT A THOUSAND WAYS: IN A GRATIN, STUFFED, IN A SOUP, AS A CRUMBLE, ETC. BUT SINCE WE'RE A LITTLE SHORT ON TIME, WE'RE GOING TO GO FOR A QUICK, SIMPLIFIED RISOTTO.

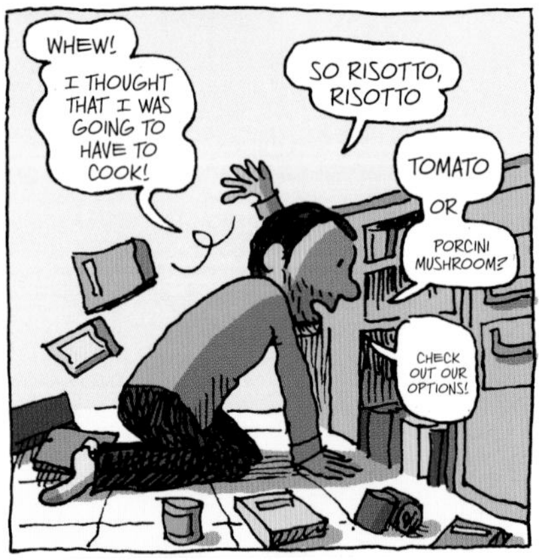
WHEW! I THOUGHT THAT I WAS GOING TO HAVE TO COOK!
SO RISOTTO, RISOTTO
TOMATO
OR
PORCINI MUSHROOM?
CHECK OUT OUR OPTIONS!

HAHA! WELL, NO. WE'RE NOT GOING TO JUST OPEN A BOX OF INSTANT RISOTTO. MAINTAIN AT LEAST A SHRED OF DIGNITY! WE'RE GOING TO MAKE A REAL RISOTTO WITH REAL FLAVOR, AND WE'RE GOING TO DO THAT BY USING THIS BUTTERNUT SQUASH!

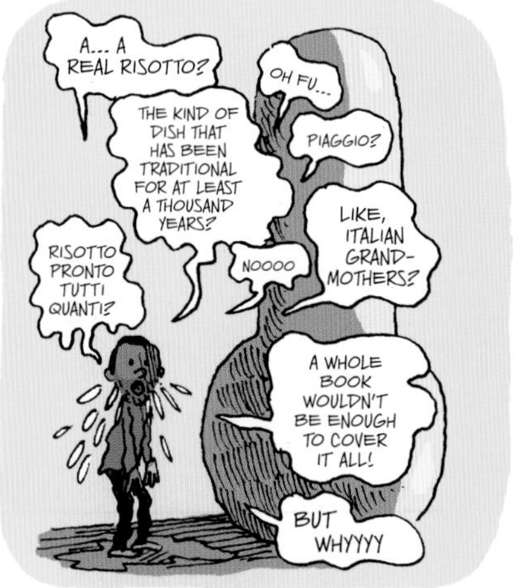
A... A REAL RISOTTO?
OH FU...
THE KIND OF DISH THAT HAS BEEN TRADITIONAL FOR AT LEAST A THOUSAND YEARS?
PIAGGIO?
RISOTTO PRONTO TUTTI QUANTI?
NOOOO
LIKE, ITALIAN GRAND-MOTHERS?
A WHOLE BOOK WOULDN'T BE ENOUGH TO COVER IT ALL!
BUT WHYYYY

WELL, THAT'S A GOOD START. IT'S ALWAYS IMPORTANT TO KNOW WHAT YOU'RE GETTING YOURSELF INTO, ESPECIALLY WITH A RISOTTO. THE SECOND-MOST IMPORTANT THING TO KNOW BEFORE YOU BEGIN IS THE INGREDIENTS!

FOR TWO HEARTY EATERS, YOU WILL NEED:

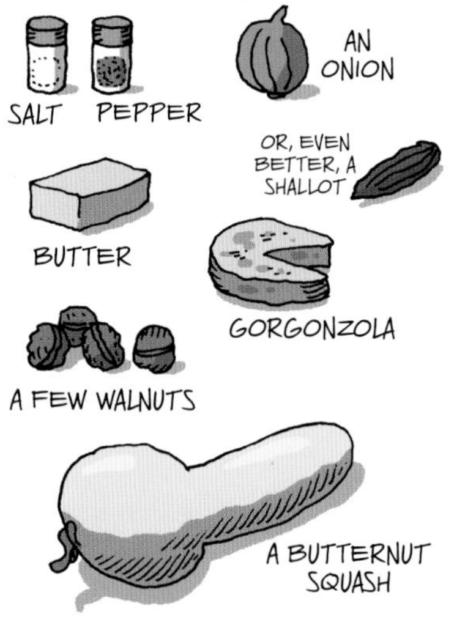
SALT
PEPPER
AN ONION
OR, EVEN BETTER, A SHALLOT
BUTTER
GORGONZOLA
A FEW WALNUTS
A BUTTERNUT SQUASH

AND SOME RISOTTO, OF COURSE:

ADVICE FROM FLORIANA

Use carnaroli, capisci? If you don't, you're a shame to all of Italy. Since I'm sure you're already making lasagna with béchamel, hahahahaha!

Go on, hurry! In bocca al lupo!

AND LASTLY, SOME BEEF STOCK:

WHETHER SOME HOMEMADE FROM YOUR FREEZER

TSHHHH

HOT SHOT

OR A BOUILLON CUBE IN A QUART OF WATER

TOTALLY FINE TOO

① AS YOUR STOCK (A GENEROUS QUART) SLOWLY COMES TO A SIMMER, CUT THE SQUASH IN HALF, REMOVE THE SEEDS, AND PEEL IT (GRUELING.)

THEN CUT A GOOD CHUNK INTO 1-INCH CUBES (DON'T BOTHER WITH A RULER, BUT BE UNIFORM.)

NEXT, PEEL THE ONION (OR THE SHALLOT) AND MINCE IT FINELY, AVOIDING YOUR FINGERS:

② HEAT A NOB OF BUTTER IN A MEDIUM SAUCEPAN AND ADD THE RICE (14 OZ. FOR ME. I WANT LEFTOVERS!) AS WELL AS THE MINCED ONION

TSHHHH

(HERE, THE RICE IS SUPPOSED TO BECOMING TRANSLUCENT, BUT IT'S NEVER THE CASE FOR ME. AT BEST, IT TAKES ON A LITTLE COLOR.)

AFTER A COUPLE OF MINUTES, ADD THE SQUASH CUBES AND STIR CAREFULLY, MAKING SURE THAT THE RICE DOESN'T STICK TO THE BOTTOM OF THE POT.

Oh shit

I can't believe I'm actually making risotto!

③ NOW'S WHEN THE FUN'S OVER: YOU HAVE TO COOK THE RISOTTO. IN THEORY, YOU ADD LADLE AFTER LADLE OF HOT BROTH TO THE RICE AND THE SQUASH, STIRRING TO MAKE THE LIQUID ABSORB (NOT BOIL OFF), AND REPEAT UNTIL READY...

IN THEORY, YEAH.

IN REALITY, I DUMP THE BROTH INTO THE RICE, TRYING NOT TO GET IT EVERYWHERE, AND I ADD MORE STOCK WHEN IT REDUCES A LITTLE TOO MUCH:

TSHHHH

a.   b.

WATCH OUT FOR THE STEAM

④ TO GAUGE WHEN IT'S DONE, KNOW THAT THE RICE WILL COOK IN ABOUT TWENTY MINUTES. THE TEXTURE SHOULD STILL BE FIRM, AND THE SAUCE SHOULD BE MOSTLY LIQUID.

REMEMBER TO:

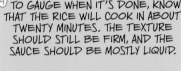

STIR

PAY ATTENTION

NOT LET THE RICE STICK TO THE BOTTOM

TASTE

⑤ WHEN THE RICE ISN'T TOO FAR FROM BEING DONE (DON'T WORRY ABOUT THE SQUASH, IT WILL BE FINE), CRUMBLE UP A LITTLE GORGONZOLA ALONG WITH A FEW CHOPPED WALNUTS:

AT THE LAST MINUTE, ADD THEM TO THE RISOTTO AND SEASON WITH SALT AND PEPPER.

POUR IN A LITTLE EXTRA BROTH IF IT'S TOO DRY

I...I... I made risotto!

DING DONG

Oh! She's here!

JUST IN TIME!

SHHHHHH

Oh no what the

Crap the

no noo nooo!

DING DONG

DING DONG

BLING

DON'T MISS OUR NEXT EPISODE:
HOW TO MAKE YOUR APARTMENT GIRLFRIEND-READY IN FIVE MINUTES FLAT

lon.

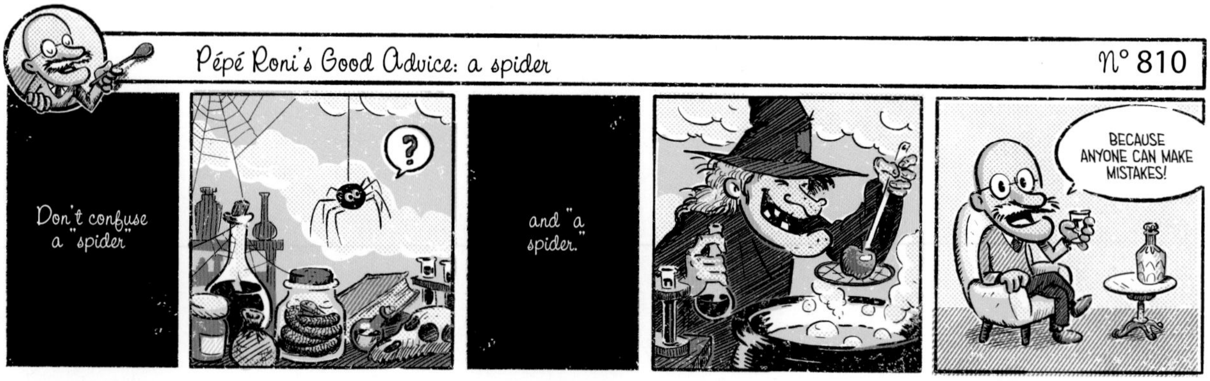
Pépé Roni's Good Advice: a spider
N° 810
Don't confuse a "spider"
?
and "a spider."
BECAUSE ANYONE CAN MAKE MISTAKES!

A spider: A shallow, stainless steel strainer used to remove fried foods from hot grease.

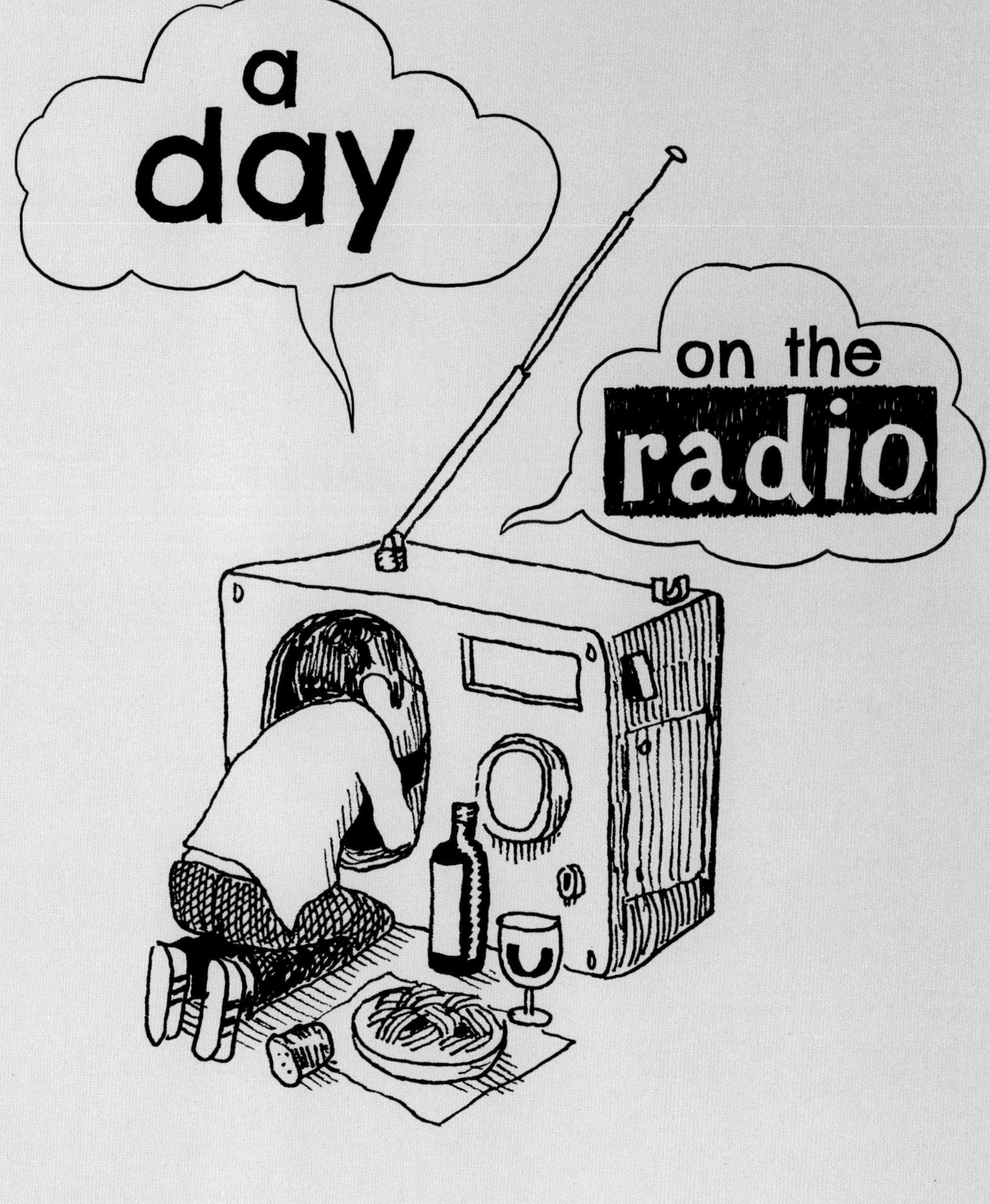
a day
on the radio

To mark the French release of the first volume of To Drink and To Eat, I am invited to the broadcast of François-Régis Gaudry's "On va déguster" on Sunday, January 22, 2012.

IN THE PREP KITCHEN OF

france inter*

*AKA THE FRENCH NPR

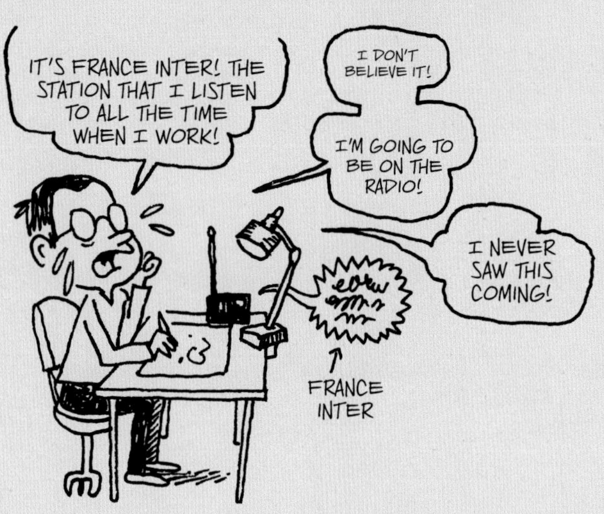
IT'S FRANCE INTER! THE STATION THAT I LISTEN TO ALL THE TIME WHEN I WORK!
I DON'T BELIEVE IT!
I'M GOING TO BE ON THE RADIO!
I NEVER SAW THIS COMING!
FRANCE INTER

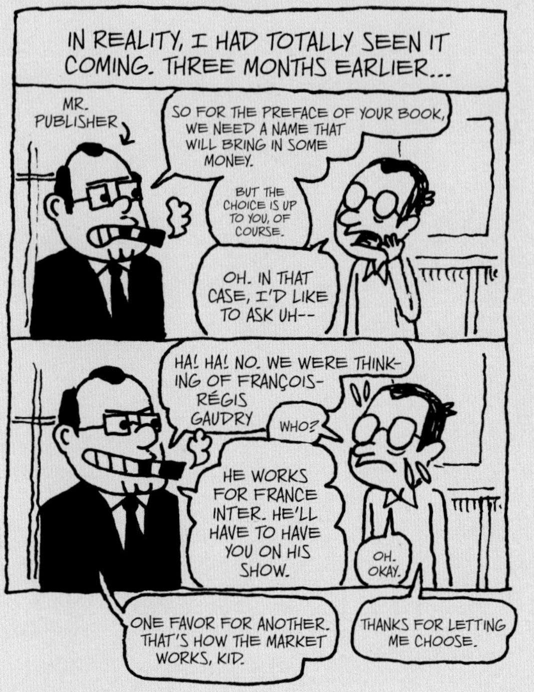
IN REALITY, I HAD TOTALLY SEEN IT COMING. THREE MONTHS EARLIER...
MR. PUBLISHER
SO FOR THE PREFACE OF YOUR BOOK, WE NEED A NAME THAT WILL BRING IN SOME MONEY.
BUT THE CHOICE IS UP TO YOU, OF COURSE.
OH. IN THAT CASE, I'D LIKE TO ASK UH--
HA! HA! NO. WE WERE THINKING OF FRANÇOIS-RÉGIS GAUDRY
WHO?
HE WORKS FOR FRANCE INTER. HE'LL HAVE TO HAVE YOU ON HIS SHOW.
OH. OKAY.
ONE FAVOR FOR ANOTHER. THAT'S HOW THE MARKET WORKS, KID.
THANKS FOR LETTING ME CHOOSE.

So that's how it happened. I am invited to the show by the guy who wrote the preface of my book, and I'm really happy. So is Mr. Publisher.

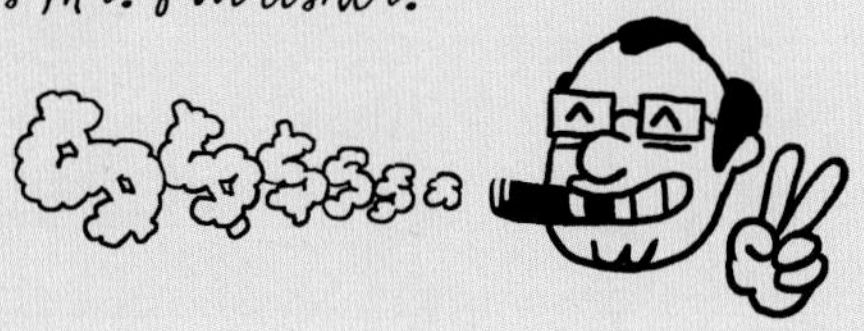

FRANÇOIS-RÉGIS AND I PREP FOR THE INTERVIEW ON THE PHONE. HE HAS THE VOICE OF A 45-YEAR-OLD, BUT ACTUALLY, HE'S ONLY TWO YEARS OLDER THAN ME!

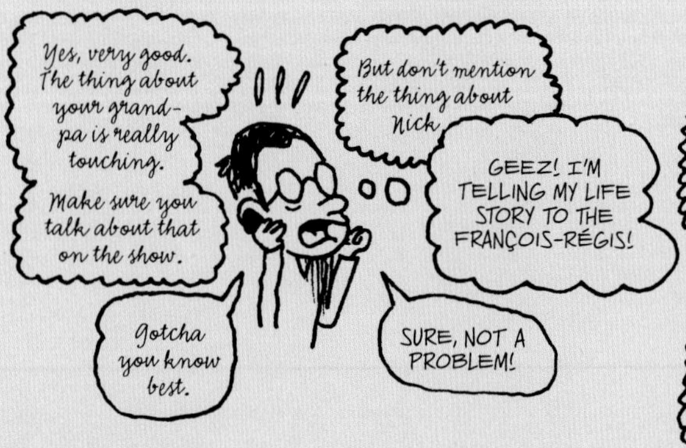
Yes, very good. The thing about your grand-pa is really touching. Make sure you talk about that on the show.
But don't mention the thing about Nick.
GEEZ! I'M TELLING MY LIFE STORY TO THE FRANÇOIS-RÉGIS!
Gotcha you know best.
SURE, NOT A PROBLEM!

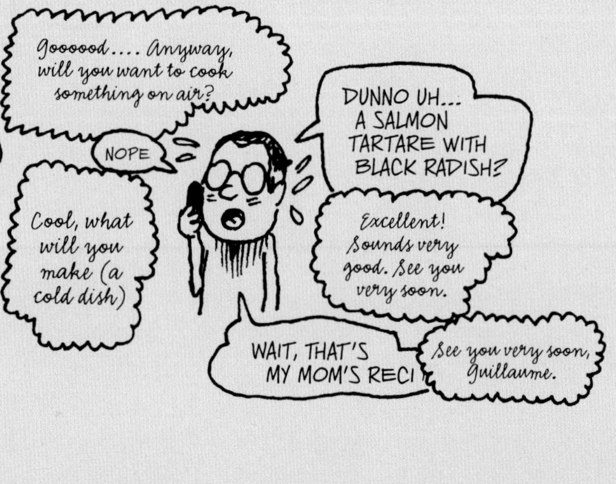
Goooood.... Anyway, will you want to cook something on air?
NOPE
DUNNO UH... A SALMON TARTARE WITH BLACK RADISH?
Cool, what will you make (a cold dish)
Excellent! Sounds very good. See you very soon.
WAIT, THAT'S MY MOM'S RECI
See you very soon, Guillaume.

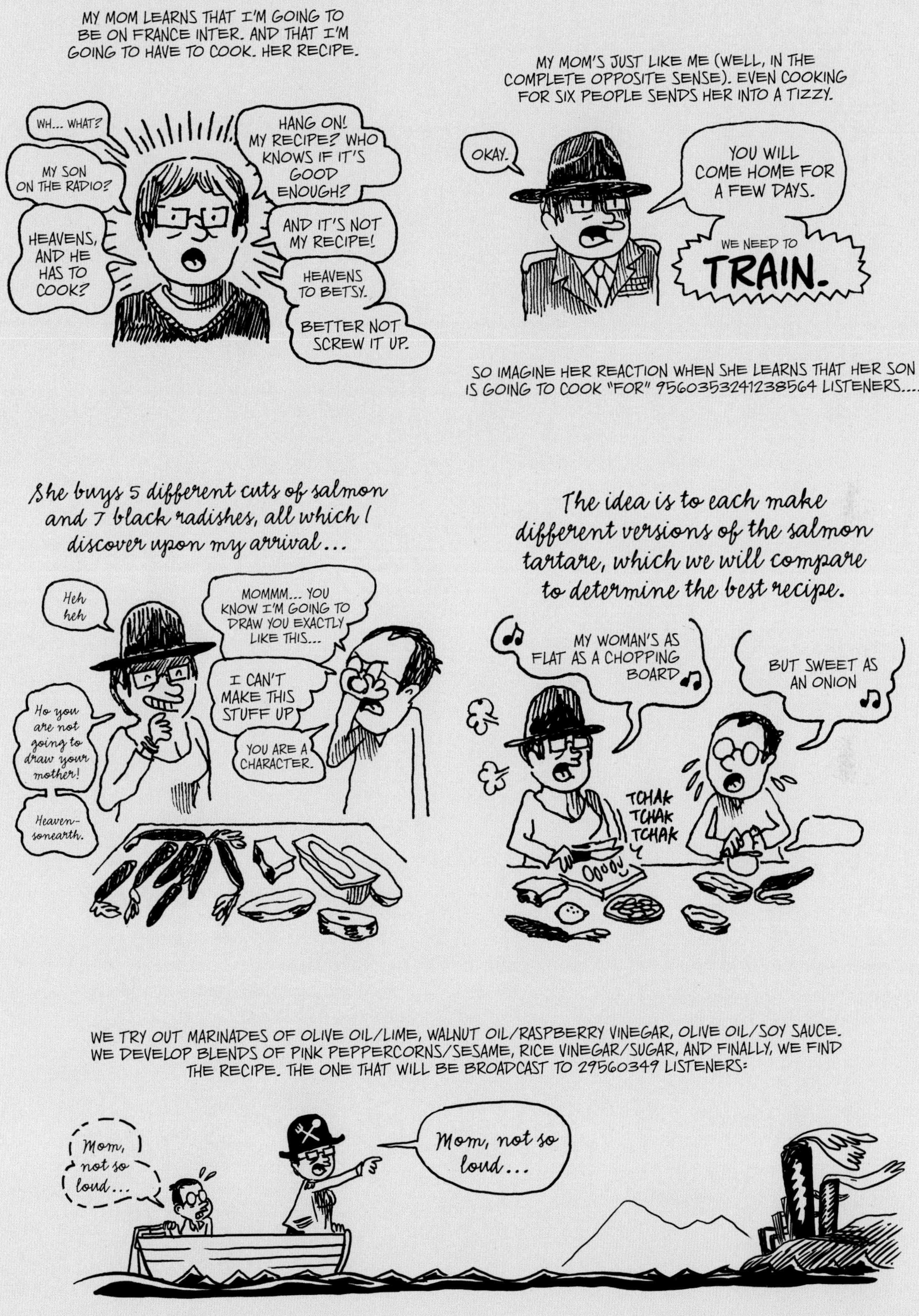

MY MOM LEARNS THAT I'M GOING TO BE ON FRANCE INTER. AND THAT I'M GOING TO HAVE TO COOK. HER RECIPE.
WH... WHAT?
MY SON ON THE RADIO?
HEAVENS, AND HE HAS TO COOK?
HANG ON! MY RECIPE? WHO KNOWS IF IT'S GOOD ENOUGH?
AND IT'S NOT MY RECIPE!
HEAVENS TO BETSY.
BETTER NOT SCREW IT UP.
MY MOM'S JUST LIKE ME (WELL, IN THE COMPLETE OPPOSITE SENSE). EVEN COOKING FOR SIX PEOPLE SENDS HER INTO A TIZZY.
OKAY.
YOU WILL COME HOME FOR A FEW DAYS.
WE NEED TO TRAIN.
SO IMAGINE HER REACTION WHEN SHE LEARNS THAT HER SON IS GOING TO COOK "FOR" 9560353241238564 LISTENERS....
She buys 5 different cuts of salmon and 7 black radishes, all which I discover upon my arrival...
Heh heh
MOMMM... YOU KNOW I'M GOING TO DRAW YOU EXACTLY LIKE THIS...
I CAN'T MAKE THIS STUFF UP
YOU ARE A CHARACTER.
Ho you are not going to draw your mother!
Heaven-sonearth.
The idea is to each make different versions of the salmon tartare, which we will compare to determine the best recipe.
MY WOMAN'S AS FLAT AS A CHOPPING BOARD
BUT SWEET AS AN ONION
TCHAK TCHAK TCHAK
WE TRY OUT MARINADES OF OLIVE OIL/LIME, WALNUT OIL/RASPBERRY VINEGAR, OLIVE OIL/SOY SAUCE. WE DEVELOP BLENDS OF PINK PEPPERCORNS/SESAME, RICE VINEGAR/SUGAR, AND FINALLY, WE FIND THE RECIPE. THE ONE THAT WILL BE BROADCAST TO 29560349 LISTENERS:
Mom, not so loud...
Mom, not so loud...

SALMON TARTARE WITH A BLACK RADISH SALAD

YOU WILL NEED THE FOLLOWING INGREDIENTS (FOR TWO PEOPLE):

OLIVE OIL

WHITE BALSAMIC VINEGAR

JAPANESE RICE VINEGAR

GUÉRANDE SEA SALT

SUGAR

SOY SAUCE

PINK PEPPERCORNS

14 OZ. SALMON FILET

A BLACK RADISH

① CUT THE SALMON INTO SMALL CUBES:

NEXT, IN A LARGE, SHALLOW BOWL, MIX FOUR TABLESPOONS OF OLIVE OIL, TWO TABLESPOONS OF RICE VINEGAR, ONE TABLESPOON OF SUGAR, AND ONE TABLESPOON OF SOY SAUCE. MARINATE THE SALMON IN THIS MIXTURE IN THE FRIDGE FOR AT LEAST ONE HOUR:

(NOT SPECTACULAR TO DRAW, AS YOU CAN SEE.)

② PEEL AND SLICE THE BLACK RADISH WITH A VEGETABLE PEELER (TO MAKE THIN STRIPS):

ARRANGE THE AMOUNT YOU WOULD LIKE ON A PLATE, AND DRIZZLE GENEROUSLY WITH OLIVE OIL AND BALSAMIC VINEGAR.

(ILLUSTRATING THIS RECIPE OFFICIALLY SUCKS.)

③ BEFORE SERVING, SEASON THE BLACK RADISH WITH SALT, AND THEN REMOVE THE SALMON FROM THE FRIDGE. NO NEED TO RESERVE THE MARINADE. ARTFULLY ARRANGE THE SALMON AND THE BLACK RADISH TOGETHER (IT'S POSSIBLE).

PINK PEPPERCORNS FOR DECORATION

AND THAT'S IT.

FUUCK, THE 245698103534 LISTENERS OF FRANCE INTER ARE GOING TO THINK I'M A LOSER.

Thing is, I'm going to have to carry this salmon from Geneva to Paris by train. I'll have to bring a cooler, and the only one available at my parents' house looks like this:

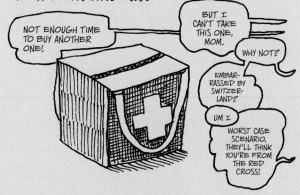

NOT ENOUGH TIME TO BUY ANOTHER ONE!

BUT I CAN'T TAKE THIS ONE, MOM.

WHY NOT?

EMBARRASSED BY SWITZERLAND?

UM I

WORST CASE SCENARIO, THEY'LL THINK YOU'RE FROM THE RED CROSS!

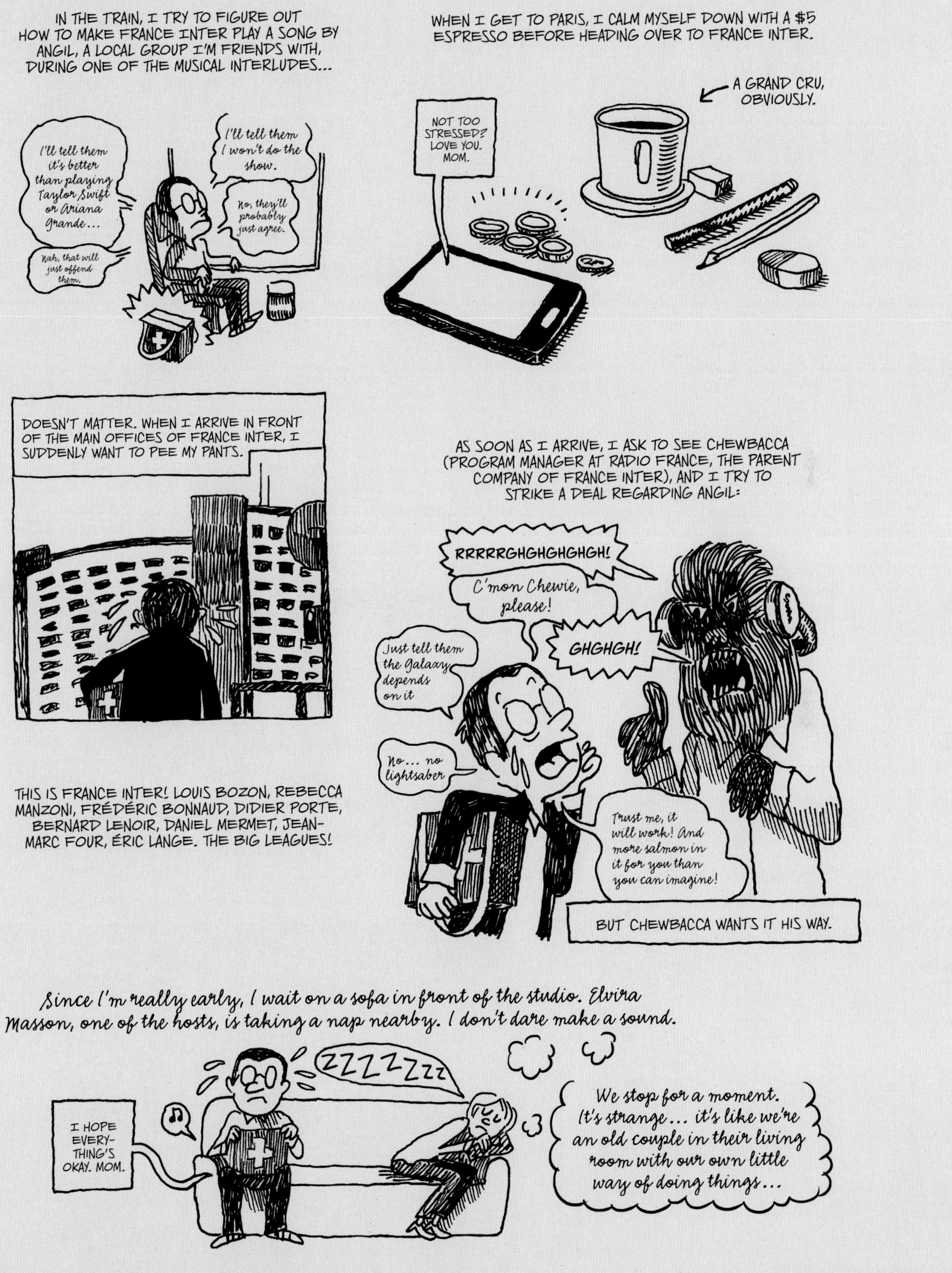

IN THE TRAIN, I TRY TO FIGURE OUT HOW TO MAKE FRANCE INTER PLAY A SONG BY ANGIL, A LOCAL GROUP I'M FRIENDS WITH, DURING ONE OF THE MUSICAL INTERLUDES...
I'll tell them it's better than playing Taylor Swift or Ariana Grande...
Nah, that will just offend them.
I'll tell them I won't do the show.
No, they'll probably just agree.
WHEN I GET TO PARIS, I CALM MYSELF DOWN WITH A $5 ESPRESSO BEFORE HEADING OVER TO FRANCE INTER.
NOT TOO STRESSED? LOVE YOU. MOM.
A GRAND CRU, OBVIOUSLY.
DOESN'T MATTER. WHEN I ARRIVE IN FRONT OF THE MAIN OFFICES OF FRANCE INTER, I SUDDENLY WANT TO PEE MY PANTS.
THIS IS FRANCE INTER! LOUIS BOZON, REBECCA MANZONI, FRÉDÉRIC BONNAUD, DIDIER PORTE, BERNARD LENOIR, DANIEL MERMET, JEAN-MARC FOUR, ÉRIC LANGE. THE BIG LEAGUES!
AS SOON AS I ARRIVE, I ASK TO SEE CHEWBACCA (PROGRAM MANAGER AT RADIO FRANCE, THE PARENT COMPANY OF FRANCE INTER), AND I TRY TO STRIKE A DEAL REGARDING ANGIL:
RRRRRGHGHGHGHGH!
C'mon Chewie, please!
GHGHGH!
Just tell them the Galaxy depends on it
No... no lightsaber
Trust me, it will work! And more salmon in it for you than you can imagine!
BUT CHEWBACCA WANTS IT HIS WAY.
Since I'm really early, I wait on a sofa in front of the studio. Elvira Masson, one of the hosts, is taking a nap nearby. I don't dare make a sound.
ZZZZZzz
I HOPE EVERY-THING'S OKAY. MOM.
We stop for a moment. It's strange... it's like we're an old couple in their living room with our own little way of doing things...

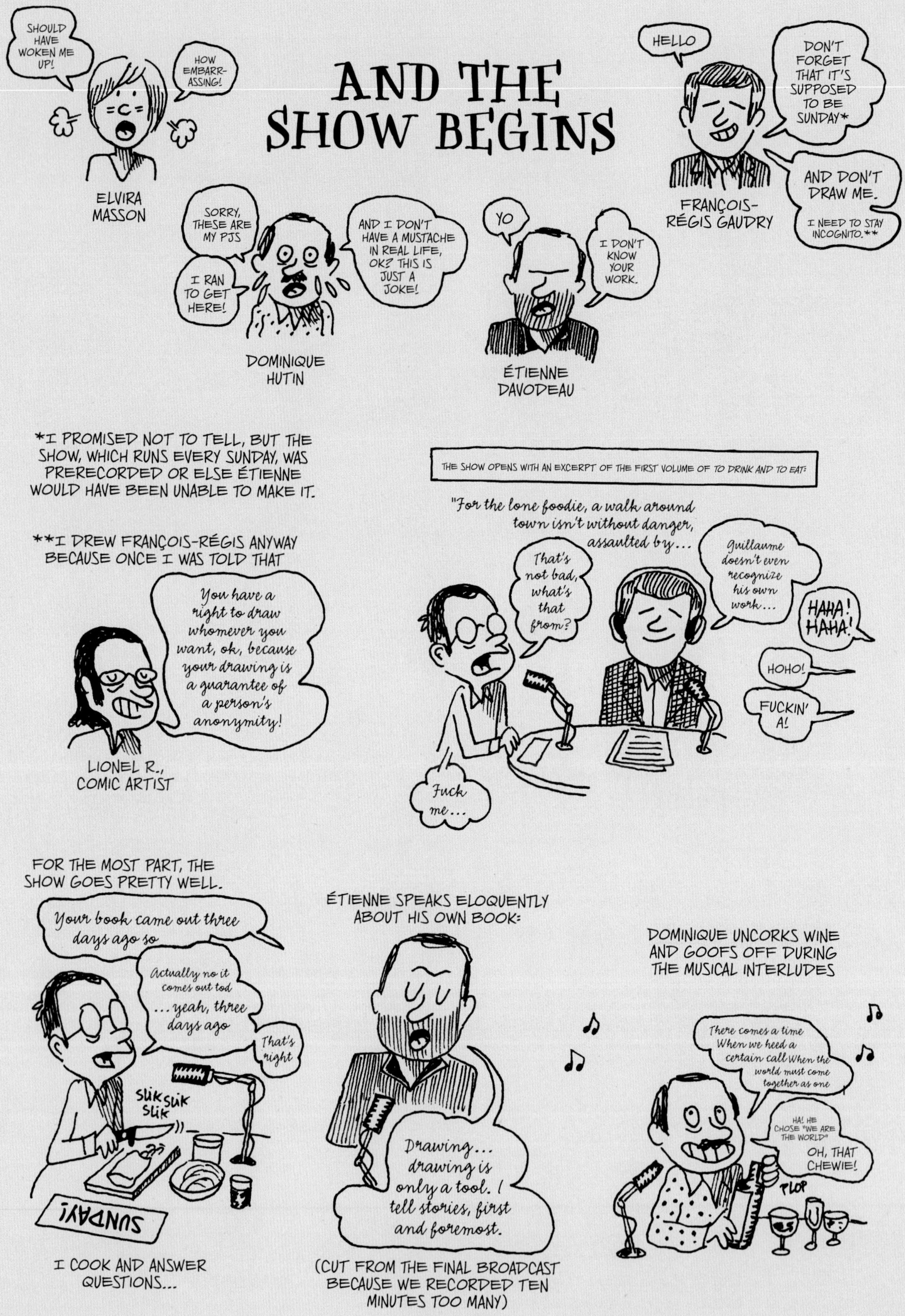

AND THE SHOW BEGINS
SHOULD HAVE WOKEN ME UP!
HOW EMBARR-ASSING!
ELVIRA MASSON
SORRY, THESE ARE MY PJS
I RAN TO GET HERE!
AND I DON'T HAVE A MUSTACHE IN REAL LIFE, OK? THIS IS JUST A JOKE!
DOMINIQUE HUTIN
YO
I DON'T KNOW YOUR WORK.
ÉTIENNE DAVODEAU
HELLO
DON'T FORGET THAT IT'S SUPPOSED TO BE SUNDAY*
AND DON'T DRAW ME.
I NEED TO STAY INCOGNITO.**
FRANÇOIS-RÉGIS GAUDRY
*I PROMISED NOT TO TELL, BUT THE SHOW, WHICH RUNS EVERY SUNDAY, WAS PRERECORDED OR ELSE ÉTIENNE WOULD HAVE BEEN UNABLE TO MAKE IT.
**I DREW FRANÇOIS-RÉGIS ANYWAY BECAUSE ONCE I WAS TOLD THAT
You have a right to draw whomever you want, ok, because your drawing is a guarantee of a person's anonymity!
LIONEL R., COMIC ARTIST
THE SHOW OPENS WITH AN EXCERPT OF THE FIRST VOLUME OF TO DRINK AND TO EAT:
"For the lone foodie, a walk around town isn't without danger, assaulted by...
That's not bad, what's that from?
Guillaume doesn't even recognize his own work...
HAHA! HAHA!
HOHO!
FUCKIN' A!
Fuck me...
FOR THE MOST PART, THE SHOW GOES PRETTY WELL.
Your book came out three days ago so
Actually no it comes out tod
...yeah, three days ago
That's right
SLIK SLIK SLIK
SUNDAY!
I COOK AND ANSWER QUESTIONS...
ÉTIENNE SPEAKS ELOQUENTLY ABOUT HIS OWN BOOK:
Drawing... drawing is only a tool. I tell stories, first and foremost.
(CUT FROM THE FINAL BROADCAST BECAUSE WE RECORDED TEN MINUTES TOO MANY)
DOMINIQUE UNCORKS WINE AND GOOFS OFF DURING THE MUSICAL INTERLUDES
There comes a time When we heed a certain call When the world must come together as one
HA! HE CHOSE "WE ARE THE WORLD"
OH, THAT CHEWIE!
PLOP

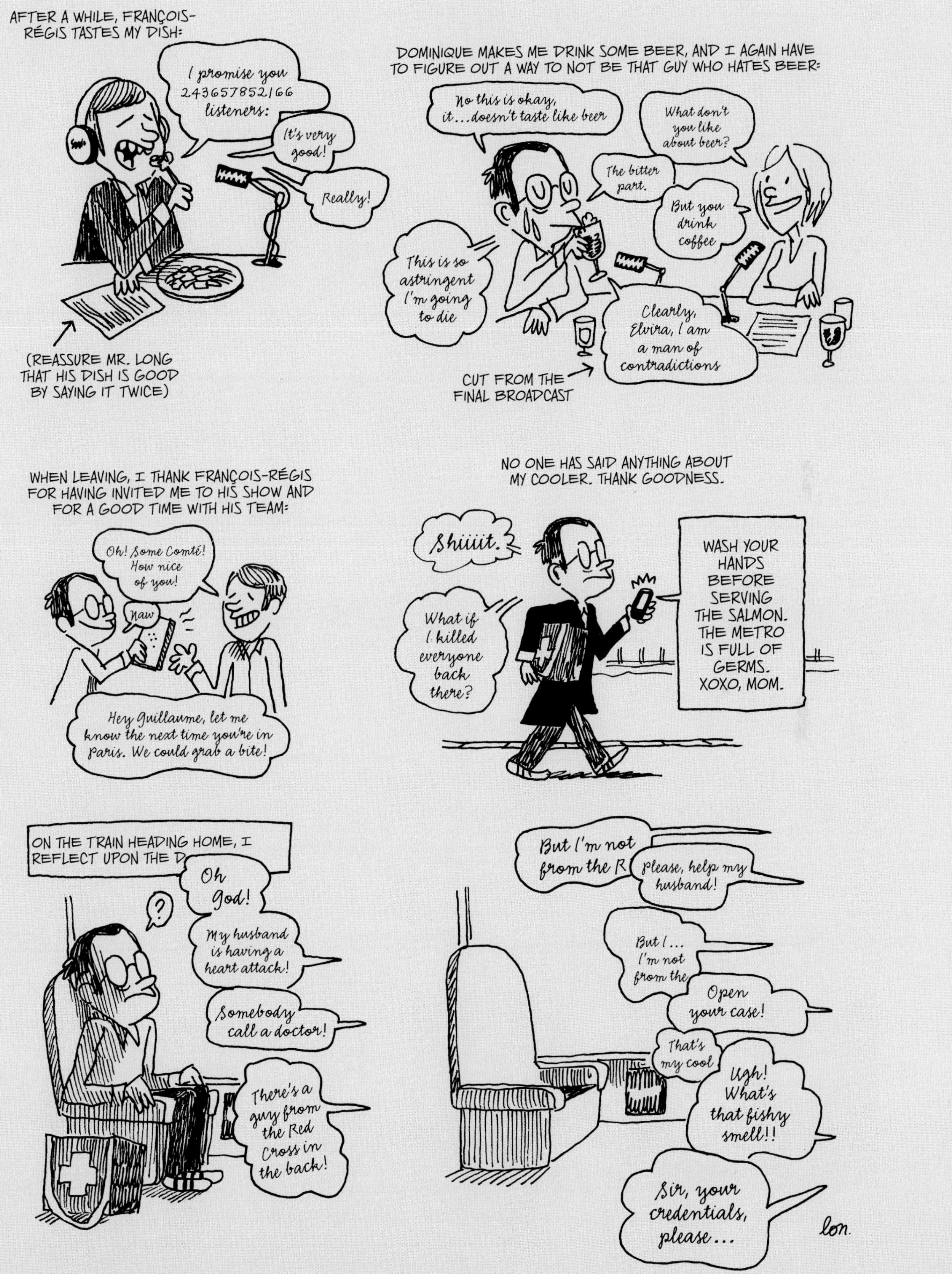
AFTER A WHILE, FRANÇOIS-RÉGIS TASTES MY DISH:
I promise you 2436578521|66 listeners:
It's very good!
Really!
(REASSURE MR. LONG THAT HIS DISH IS GOOD BY SAYING IT TWICE)
DOMINIQUE MAKES ME DRINK SOME BEER, AND I AGAIN HAVE TO FIGURE OUT A WAY TO NOT BE THAT GUY WHO HATES BEER:
No this is okay, it...doesn't taste like beer
What don't you like about beer?
The bitter part.
But you drink coffee
This is so astringent I'm going to die
Clearly, Elvira, I am a man of contradictions
CUT FROM THE FINAL BROADCAST
WHEN LEAVING, I THANK FRANÇOIS-RÉGIS FOR HAVING INVITED ME TO HIS SHOW AND FOR A GOOD TIME WITH HIS TEAM:
Oh! Some Comté! How nice of you!
Naw
Hey Guillaume, let me know the next time you're in Paris. We could grab a bite!
NO ONE HAS SAID ANYTHING ABOUT MY COOLER. THANK GOODNESS.
Shiiiit.
What if I killed everyone back there?
WASH YOUR HANDS BEFORE SERVING THE SALMON. THE METRO IS FULL OF GERMS. XOXO, MOM.
ON THE TRAIN HEADING HOME, I REFLECT UPON THE D
?
Oh God!
My husband is having a heart attack!
Somebody call a doctor!
There's a guy from the Red Cross in the back!
But I'm not from the R
Please, help my husband!
But I... I'm not from the
Open your case!
That's my cool
Ugh! What's that fishy smell!!
Sir, your credentials, please...
lon.

Pépé Roni's Good Advice: a piano whisk

N° 245

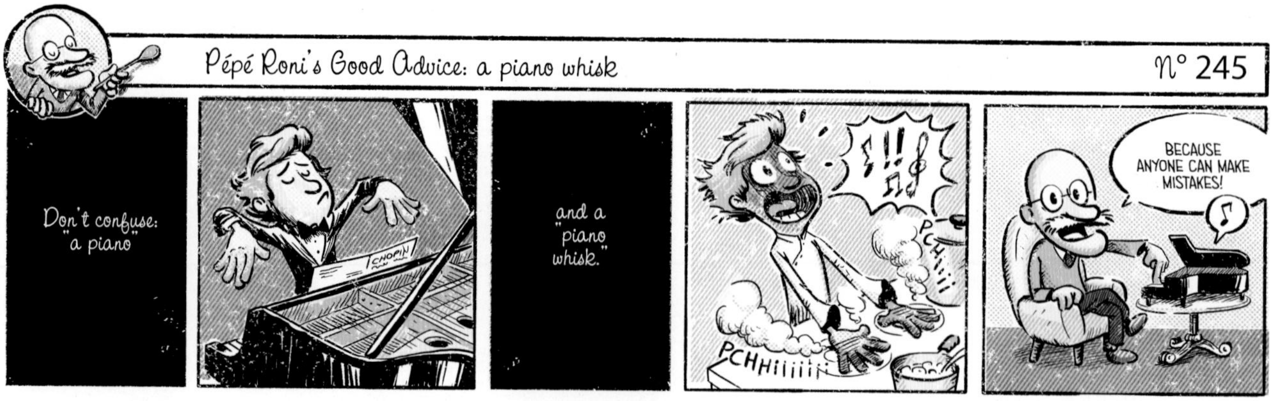

Don't confuse: "a piano"
CHOPIN
and a "piano whisk."
PCHHiiiiii
PCHiiii
BECAUSE ANYONE CAN MAKE MISTAKES!

A piano whisk: A type of whisk with flexible wires used for delicate tasks. especially fluffing batter and beating eggs.

Winter

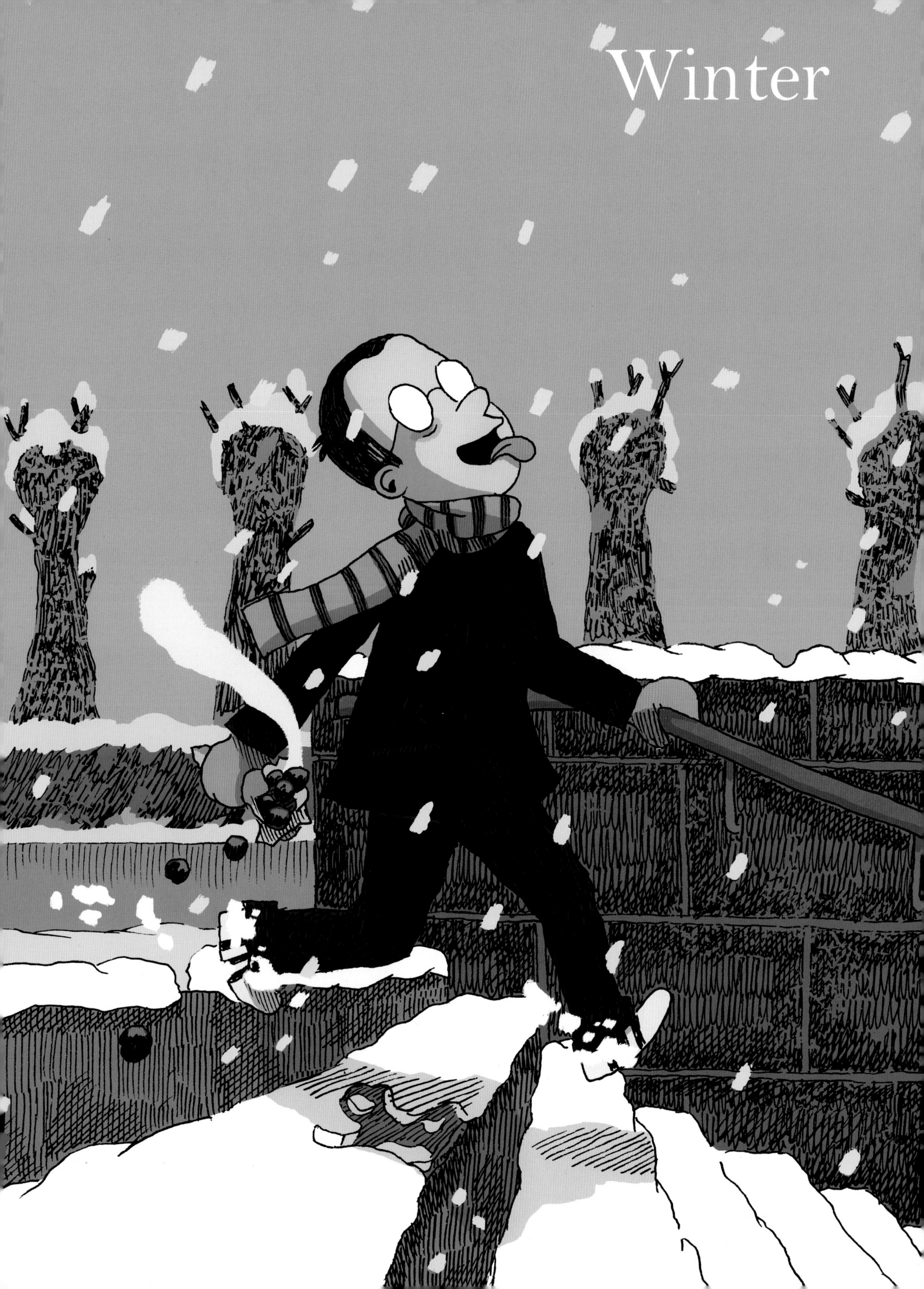

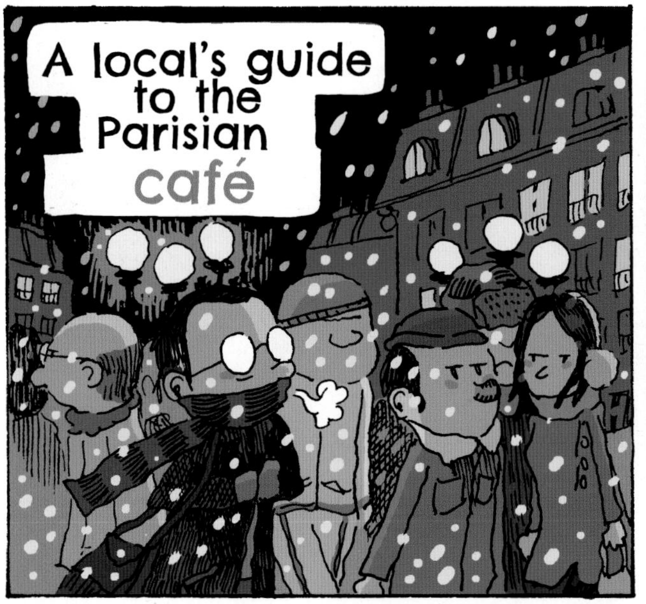
A local's guide to the Parisian café

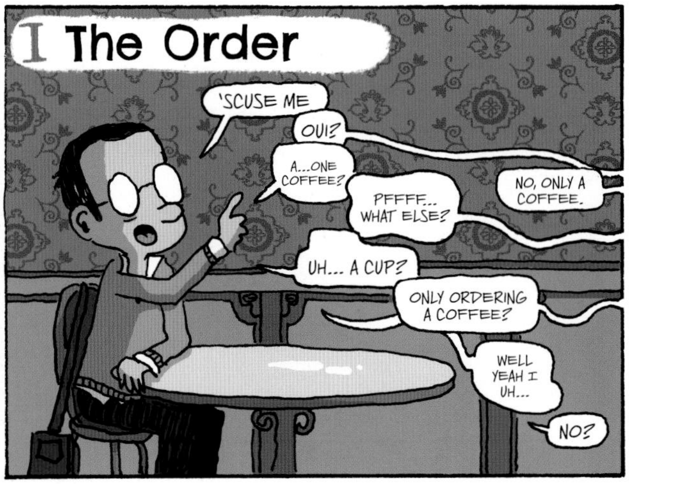
I The Order
'SCUSE ME
OUI?
A...ONE COFFEE?
NO, ONLY A COFFEE.
PFFFF... WHAT ELSE?
UH... A CUP?
ONLY ORDERING A COFFEE?
WELL YEAH I UH...
NO?

Translation: You arrived around noon or 7 P.M. The least you could do is order steak-frites with your coffee. In other words, if the awning outside reads "Café restaurant," ordering "just a coffee" is a little weak.

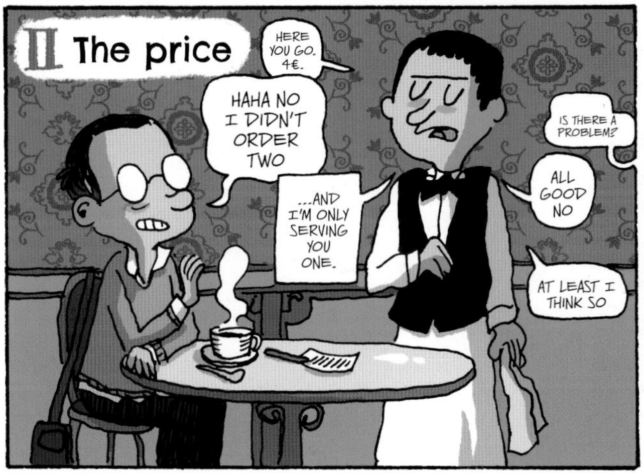
II The price
HERE YOU GO. 4€.
HAHA NO I DIDN'T ORDER TWO
...AND I'M ONLY SERVING YOU ONE.
IS THERE A PROBLEM?
ALL GOOD NO
AT LEAST I THINK SO

Translation: The coffee won't be two times better just because it's twice as expensive. It's just that you're in Paris, in case you hadn't noticed. And there are other diners waiting outside.

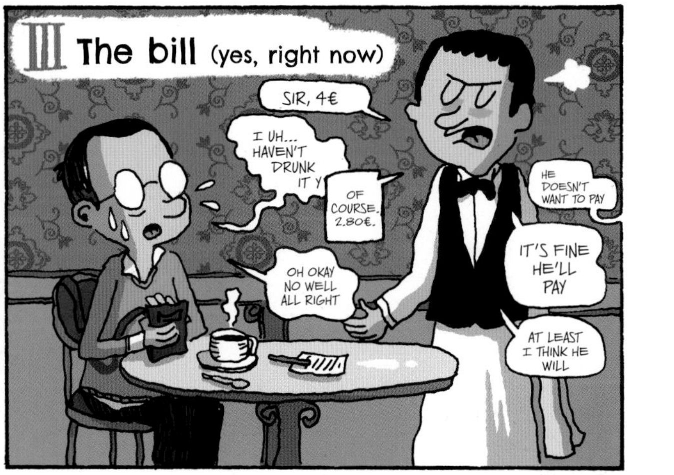
III The bill (yes, right now)
SIR, 4€
I UH... HAVEN'T DRUNK IT Y
OF COURSE. 2.80€.
HE DOESN'T WANT TO PAY
OH OKAY NO WELL ALL RIGHT
IT'S FINE HE'LL PAY
AT LEAST I THINK HE WILL

Translation: Asking you to settle up immediately isn't considered rude. We all know people like you who willfully forget to pay before they leave.

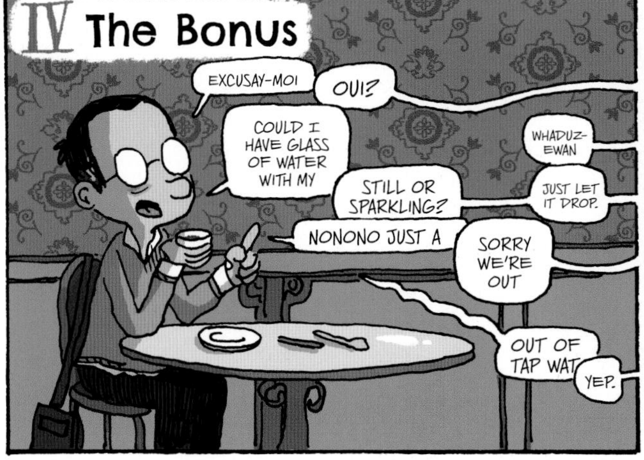
IV The Bonus
EXCUSAY-MOI
OUI?
COULD I HAVE GLASS OF WATER WITH MY
WHADUZ-EWAN
STILL OR SPARKLING?
JUST LET IT DROP.
NONONO JUST A
SORRY WE'RE OUT
OUT OF TAP WAT
YEP.

Translation: Don't count on the boss to pay for your tap water. Do you have any idea how much that stuff costs? And as for the little chocolate square that is typically served with your coffee, you might as well just beg on your knees.

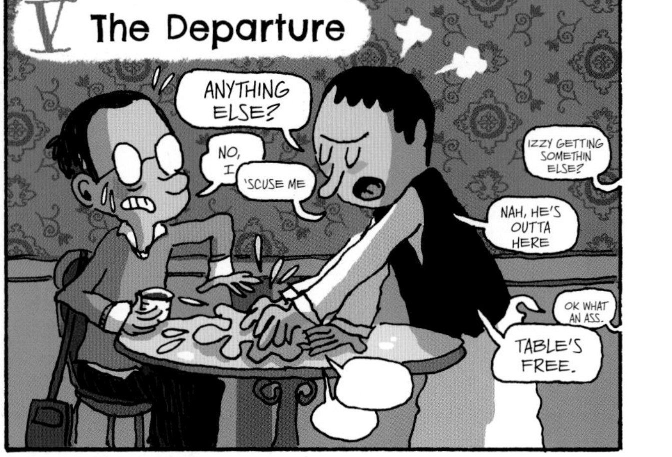
V The Departure
ANYTHING ELSE?
NO, I
'SCUSE ME
IZZY GETTING SOMETHIN ELSE?
NAH, HE'S OUTTA HERE
OK WHAT AN ASS.
TABLE'S FREE.

Translation: It's time for you to go. They need to turn a profit, this time, a bit more efficiently.

lon.

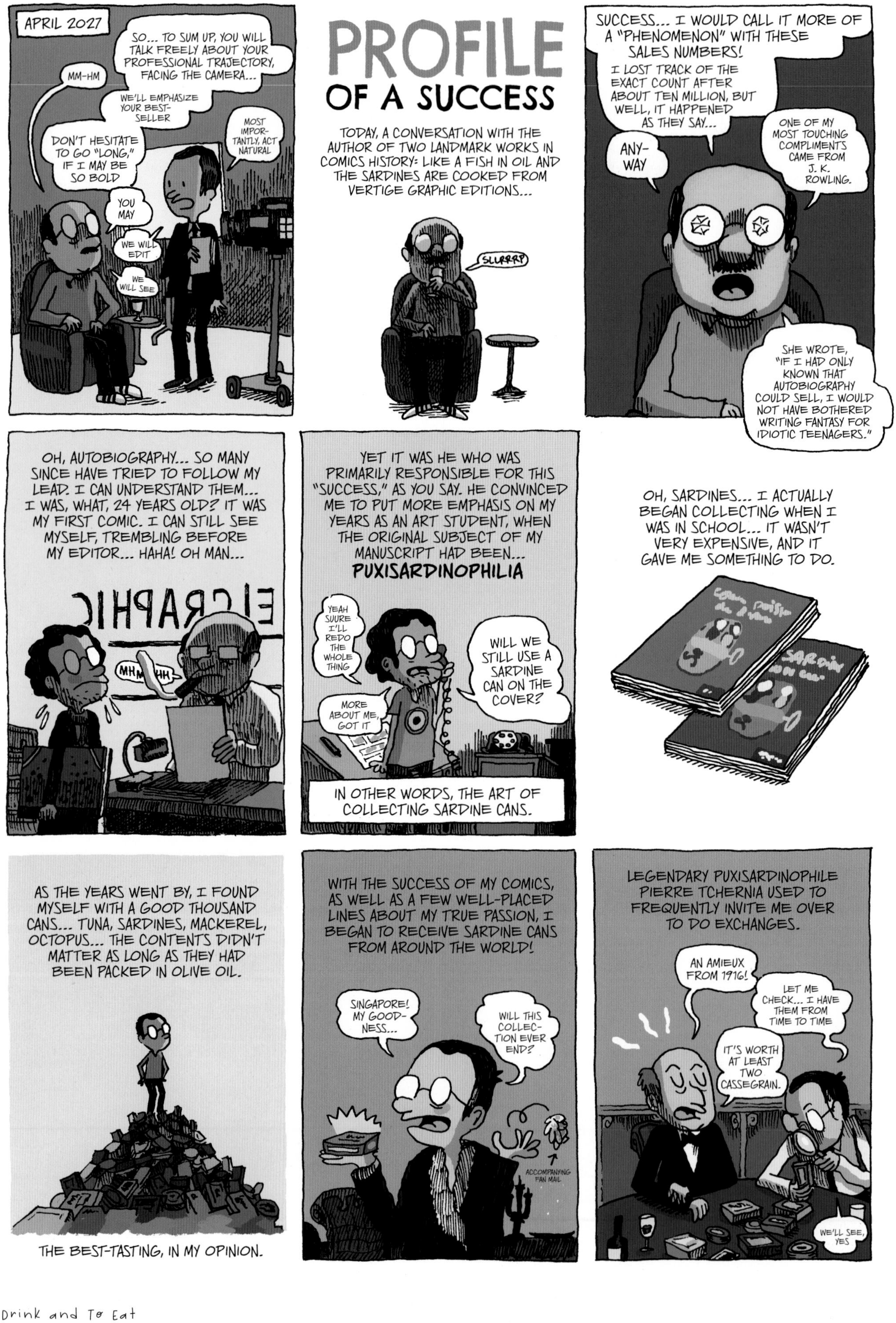
APRIL 2027
SO... TO SUM UP, YOU WILL TALK FREELY ABOUT YOUR PROFESSIONAL TRAJECTORY, FACING THE CAMERA...
MM-HM
WE'LL EMPHASIZE YOUR BEST-SELLER
MOST IMPORTANTLY, ACT NATURAL
DON'T HESITATE TO GO "LONG," IF I MAY BE SO BOLD
YOU MAY
WE WILL EDIT
WE WILL SEE
PROFILE OF A SUCCESS
TODAY, A CONVERSATION WITH THE AUTHOR OF TWO LANDMARK WORKS IN COMICS HISTORY: LIKE A FISH IN OIL AND THE SARDINES ARE COOKED FROM VERTIGE GRAPHIC EDITIONS...
SLURRRP
SUCCESS... I WOULD CALL IT MORE OF A "PHENOMENON" WITH THESE SALES NUMBERS!
I LOST TRACK OF THE EXACT COUNT AFTER ABOUT TEN MILLION, BUT WELL, IT HAPPENED AS THEY SAY...
ANY-WAY
ONE OF MY MOST TOUCHING COMPLIMENTS CAME FROM J. K. ROWLING.
SHE WROTE, "IF I HAD ONLY KNOWN THAT AUTOBIOGRAPHY COULD SELL, I WOULD NOT HAVE BOTHERED WRITING FANTASY FOR IDIOTIC TEENAGERS."
OH, AUTOBIOGRAPHY... SO MANY SINCE HAVE TRIED TO FOLLOW MY LEAD. I CAN UNDERSTAND THEM... I WAS, WHAT, 24 YEARS OLD? IT WAS MY FIRST COMIC. I CAN STILL SEE MYSELF, TREMBLING BEFORE MY EDITOR... HAHA! OH MAN...
MHMHM
YET IT WAS HE WHO WAS PRIMARILY RESPONSIBLE FOR THIS "SUCCESS," AS YOU SAY. HE CONVINCED ME TO PUT MORE EMPHASIS ON MY YEARS AS AN ART STUDENT, WHEN THE ORIGINAL SUBJECT OF MY MANUSCRIPT HAD BEEN... PUXISARDINOPHILIA
YEAH SUURE I'LL REDO THE WHOLE THING
WILL WE STILL USE A SARDINE CAN ON THE COVER?
MORE ABOUT ME, GOT IT
IN OTHER WORDS, THE ART OF COLLECTING SARDINE CANS.
OH, SARDINES... I ACTUALLY BEGAN COLLECTING WHEN I WAS IN SCHOOL... IT WASN'T VERY EXPENSIVE, AND IT GAVE ME SOMETHING TO DO.
AS THE YEARS WENT BY, I FOUND MYSELF WITH A GOOD THOUSAND CANS... TUNA, SARDINES, MACKEREL, OCTOPUS... THE CONTENTS DIDN'T MATTER AS LONG AS THEY HAD BEEN PACKED IN OLIVE OIL.
THE BEST-TASTING, IN MY OPINION.
WITH THE SUCCESS OF MY COMICS, AS WELL AS A FEW WELL-PLACED LINES ABOUT MY TRUE PASSION, I BEGAN TO RECEIVE SARDINE CANS FROM AROUND THE WORLD!
SINGAPORE! MY GOODNESS...
WILL THIS COLLECTION EVER END?
ACCOMPANYING FAN MAIL
LEGENDARY PUXISARDINOPHILE PIERRE TCHERNIA USED TO FREQUENTLY INVITE ME OVER TO DO EXCHANGES.
AN AMIEUX FROM 1916!
LET ME CHECK... I HAVE THEM FROM TIME TO TIME
IT'S WORTH AT LEAST TWO CASSEGRAIN.
WE'LL SEE, YES

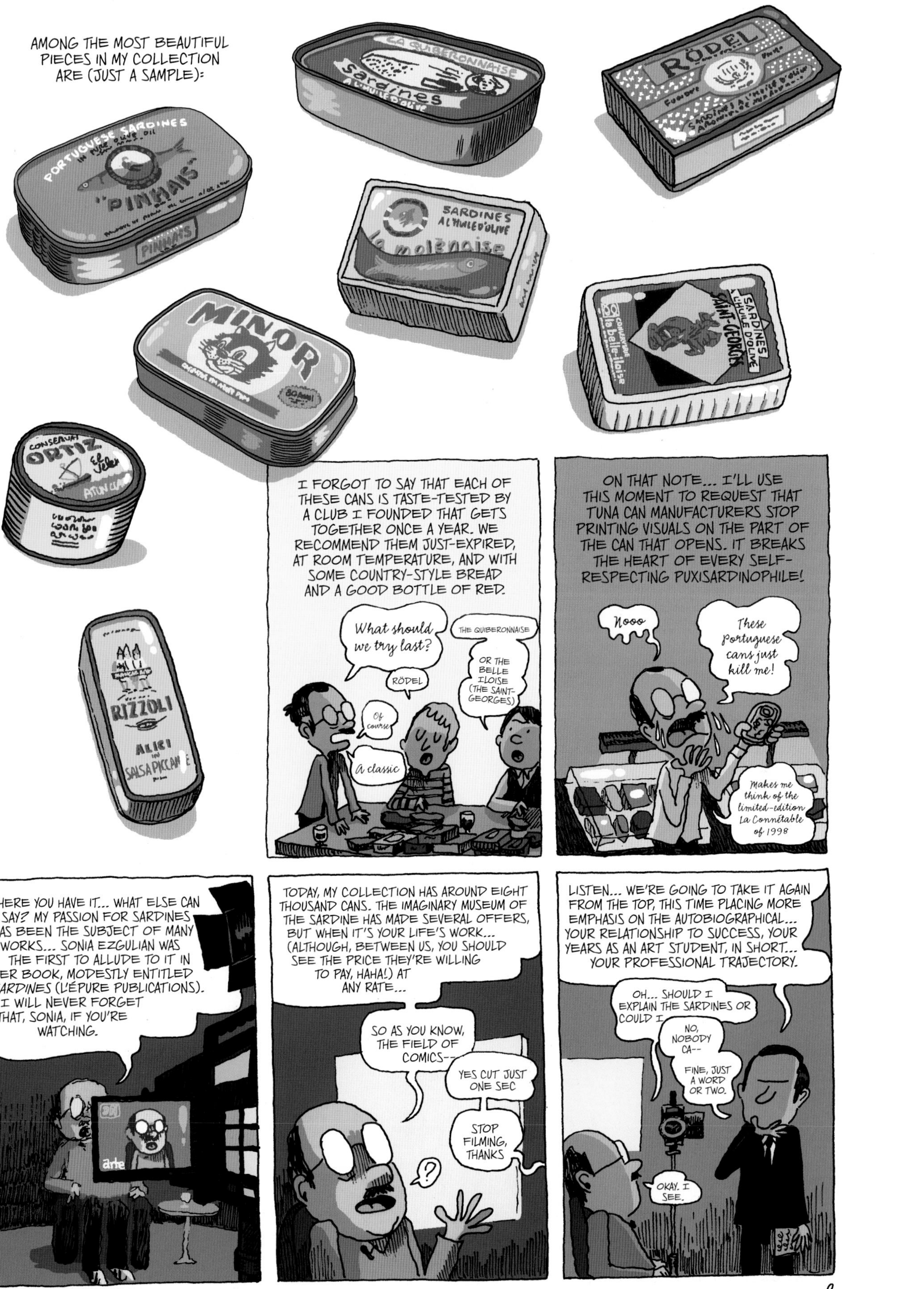
AMONG THE MOST BEAUTIFUL PIECES IN MY COLLECTION ARE (JUST A SAMPLE):
LA QUIBERONNAISE
Sardines À L'HUILE D'OLIVE
RÖDEL
PORTUGUESE SARDINES
"PINHAIS"
PINHAIS
SARDINES À L'HUILE D'OLIVE
La molènaise
MINOR
SARDINES À L'HUILE D'OLIVE
SAINT-GEORGES
la belle-iloise
ORTIZ
El Velero
RIZZOLI
ALICI IN SALSA PICCANTE
I FORGOT TO SAY THAT EACH OF THESE CANS IS TASTE-TESTED BY A CLUB I FOUNDED THAT GETS TOGETHER ONCE A YEAR. WE RECOMMEND THEM JUST-EXPIRED, AT ROOM TEMPERATURE, AND WITH SOME COUNTRY-STYLE BREAD AND A GOOD BOTTLE OF RED.
What should we try last?
THE QUIBERONNAISE
RÖDEL
OR THE BELLE ILOISE (THE SAINT-GEORGES)
Of course
A classic
ON THAT NOTE... I'LL USE THIS MOMENT TO REQUEST THAT TUNA CAN MANUFACTURERS STOP PRINTING VISUALS ON THE PART OF THE CAN THAT OPENS. IT BREAKS THE HEART OF EVERY SELF-RESPECTING PUXISARDINOPHILE!
Nooo
These portuguese cans just kill me!
Makes me think of the limited-edition La Connétable of 1998
THERE YOU HAVE IT... WHAT ELSE CAN I SAY? MY PASSION FOR SARDINES HAS BEEN THE SUBJECT OF MANY WORKS... SONIA EZGULIAN WAS THE FIRST TO ALLUDE TO IT IN HER BOOK, MODESTLY ENTITLED SARDINES (L'ÉPURE PUBLICATIONS). I WILL NEVER FORGET THAT, SONIA, IF YOU'RE WATCHING.
arte
TODAY, MY COLLECTION HAS AROUND EIGHT THOUSAND CANS. THE IMAGINARY MUSEUM OF THE SARDINE HAS MADE SEVERAL OFFERS, BUT WHEN IT'S YOUR LIFE'S WORK... (ALTHOUGH, BETWEEN US, YOU SHOULD SEE THE PRICE THEY'RE WILLING TO PAY, HAHA!) AT ANY RATE...
SO AS YOU KNOW, THE FIELD OF COMICS--
YES CUT JUST ONE SEC
STOP FILMING, THANKS
?
LISTEN... WE'RE GOING TO TAKE IT AGAIN FROM THE TOP, THIS TIME PLACING MORE EMPHASIS ON THE AUTOBIOGRAPHICAL... YOUR RELATIONSHIP TO SUCCESS, YOUR YEARS AS AN ART STUDENT, IN SHORT... YOUR PROFESSIONAL TRAJECTORY.
OH... SHOULD I EXPLAIN THE SARDINES OR COULD I
NO, NOBODY CA--
FINE, JUST A WORD OR TWO.
OKAY. I SEE.
lon.

FOR ONCE, I'D LIKE TO ADDRESS THE YOUNG PEOPLE OUT THERE.

SO... I IMAGINE THAT YOU'RE NOT REALLY INTER-ESTED IN COOKING...

CUZ NOTH-ING'S MORE IMPORTANT THAN A BEAUTIFUL BARBIE©

WHAT COULD BE BETTER THAN A SWEET PS5©?

BUT THAT DOESN'T MEAN THAT COOKING HAS NOTHING TO DO WITH YOU!

I WAS A KID ONCE, I KNOW WHAT I'M TALKING ABOUT!

AND IF THERE WAS ONE THING THAT DROVE ME BAT SHIT CRAZY...

IT'S THAT THE ADULTS (YEAH, MOM, DAD) ALWAYS HAD SOME UNBEATABLE ARGUMENT TO TRICK ME INTO EATING SOMETHING THAT TASTED LIKE ASS-- GROSS!

LIKE SPINACH, FOR EXAMPLE (YES, THIS IS WHAT IT LOOKS LIKE BEFORE IT'S COOKED):

I NEVER HAD ANY GOOD COMEBACKS! SO, SINCE I'M A NICE GUY, I DECIDED I'D HELP YOU GAIN A FEW YEARS OF EXPERIENCE. BECAUSE, AS YOU CAN IMAGINE, I KNOW WHAT I'D SAY TO THEM NOW.

BUT IT NO LONGER MATTERS

I LIKE EVERYTHING, AND NOBODY FORCES ME TO DO ANYTHING

SO HERE YOU GO, KIDDOS...

10 SIMPLE RESPONSES
FOR WHEN SOMEONE ASKS YOU TO CLEAR YOUR PLATE

 *Let's just keep this between us, okay?*

 Tested and approved

1 "Eat your soup. It will help you grow."

THIS ONE'S A CLASSIC, BUT IT HAS NO SCIENTIFIC BASIS. MOST PEOPLE END UP GROWING ONE DAY OR ANOTHER, WHETHER OR NOT THEY'VE EATEN THEIR SOUP.

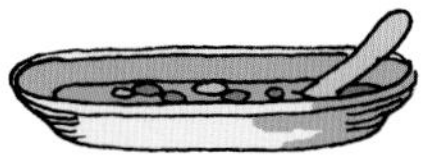

IF YOUR PARENTS ARE SO INTERESTED IN WHAT MAKES YOU GROW, THEY'RE OUT OF LUCK: IT'S ACTUALLY FOODS THAT ARE RICH IN PROTEIN (LIKE HAMBURGERS) OR IN CALCIUM. THIS MEANS YOU CAN ANSWER BY SAYING:

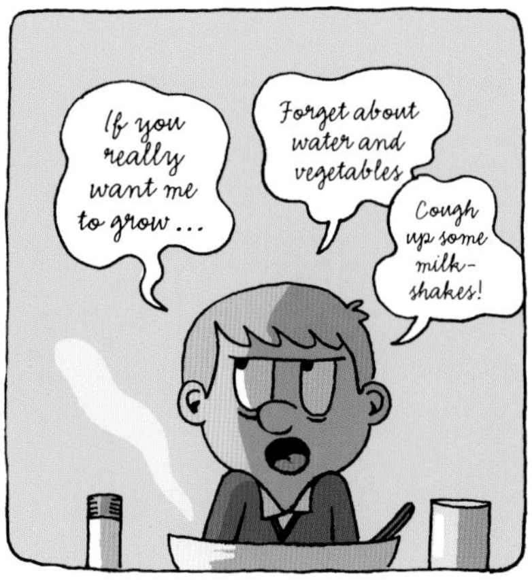
If you really want me to grow ...
Forget about water and vegetables
Cough up some milk-shakes!

2 "You can't leave the table until you've finished your plate."

COME ON... SUPPOSE THAT YOU NEVER FINISHED YOUR PLATE. WHAT WOULD ACTUALLY HAPPEN? WOULD YOU STAY AT THE TABLE FOR THE REST OF YOUR LIFE? OF COURSE NOT. THERE WOULD EVENTUALLY BE SCHOOL, AND THERE'S ALWAYS BEDTIME.

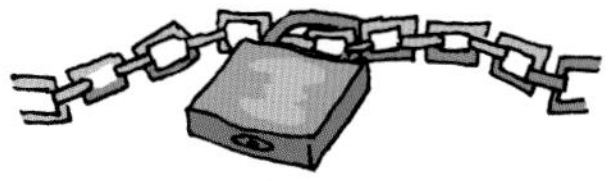

ON THE OTHER HAND, IF YOU WAIT TOO LONG, YOU RISK BEING UPGRADED TO A BIGGER PUNISHMENT OR WORSE: GETTING YOUR SAME PLATE SERVED TO YOU AT THE NEXT MEAL. NOT WORTH IT: STUFF EVERYTHING THAT YOU CAN INTO YOUR MOUTH, AND ANNOUNCE WITH CONFIDENCE:

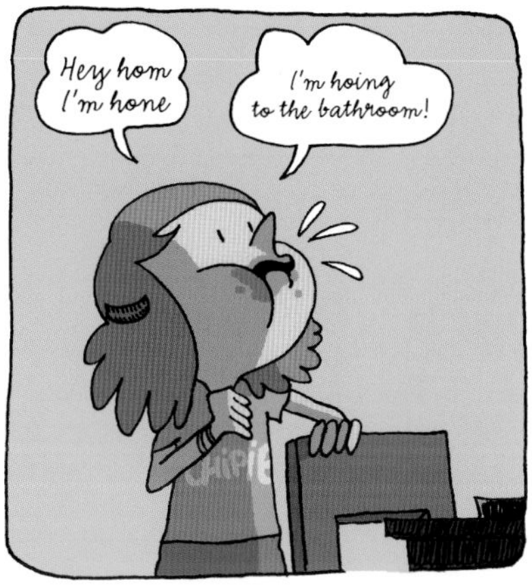
Hey hom I'm hone
I'm hoing to the bathroom!

3 "Your eyes were bigger than your stomach."

HEHE... SOMETIMES, JUST SOMETIMES, FOOD CAN LOOK REALLY GOOD WHEN IT COMES OUT OF THE OVEN, BUT ONCE IT'S ON YOUR PLATE, NOT SO MUCH. IT CAN EVEN BECOME ABSOLUTELY DISGUSTING.

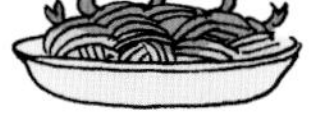

SO, IT WAS A MISTAKE ON YOUR PART... WHAT'S THE BIG DEAL? KEEP IN MIND THAT PRETTY MUCH EVERYONE, EVEN YOUR PARENTS, HAS MOMENTS OF WEAKNESS. DON'T HESITATE TO REMIND THEM OF THIS FROM TIME TO TIME.

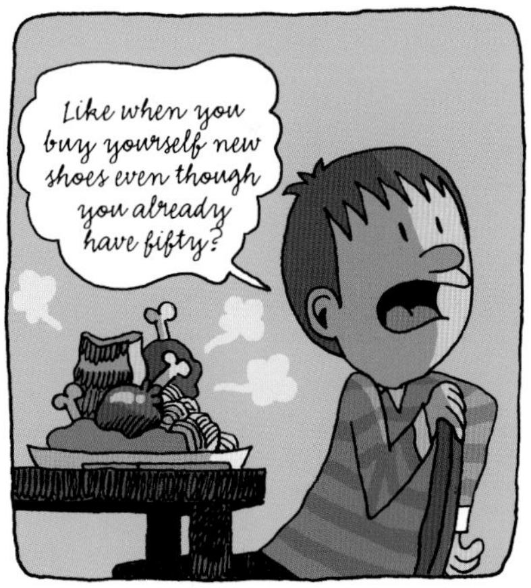
Like when you buy yourself new shoes even though you already have fifty?

4 "Think of all the time I spent cooking this!"

SO WHAT? IS THAT A REASON TO LIKE IT? WHEN YOU'RE PLAYING, IS THERE ALWAYS AN ADULT AROUND TO APPRECIATE YOUR CREATIVITY?

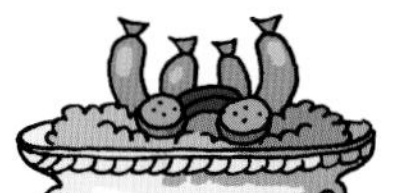

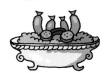

THIS IS JUST EMOTIONAL BLACKMAIL: IF YOU DON'T LIKE A DISH, IT MEANS YOU DON'T LIKE THE PERSON WHO MADE IT. TIME FOR YOU TO BEAT THEM AT THEIR OWN GAME:

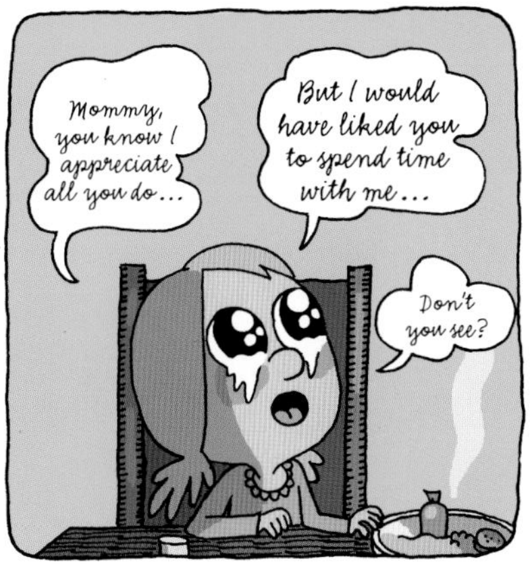
Mommy, you know I appreciate all you do...
But I would have liked you to spend time with me...
Don't you see?

5 "Vegetables taste goooood."

WELL... IT'S NOT UNTRUE, BUT IT'S BECAUSE WHEN YOU'RE A GROWN-UP, YOU BEGIN LIKING THINGS THAT YOU HATED AS A KID, LIKE WINE, POLITICS, AND NURSES (STRANGE BUT TRUE).

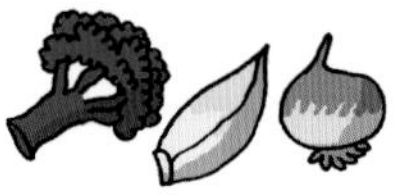

THIS MEANS WHAT IS GOOD IS RELATIVE. TRY TO TURN THE CONVERSATION AROUND TO TASTE (IT'S HARDER TO CHALLENGE HEALTH) AND CONCLUDE WITH THESE MEDIEVAL-INSPIRED MAGIC WORDS FROM HARRY POTTER©:

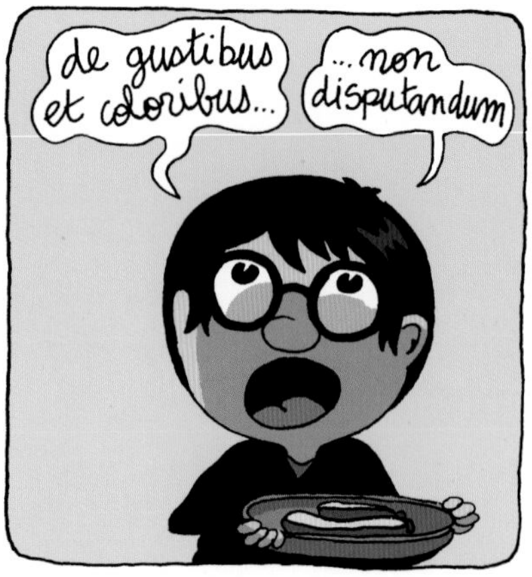
de gustibus et coloribus...
...non disputandum

6 "You will go to bed without dinner."

OKAY... THIS IS THE EASIEST ARGUMENT TO WORK WITH, AS LONG AS YOU SEE IT COMING. IT'S CLEAR THAT THEY'RE TRYING TO INTIMIDATE YOU. I RECOMMEND THAT YOU NEVER GIVE IN, NO MATTER WHAT HAPPENS.

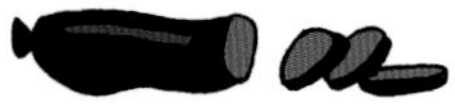

AT BEST, YOUR PARENTS WILL BACK DOWN AND NOT CARRY OUT THEIR THREAT. AT WORST, THEY WILL ACTUALLY SEND YOU TO BED WITHOUT DINNER. HOWEVER, IF YOU GET INTO THE HABIT OF STASHING CANDY AND THE OCCASIONAL CHOCOLATE BAR IN YOUR ROOM, NONE OF THIS WILL REALLY BE A PROBLEM, WILL IT?

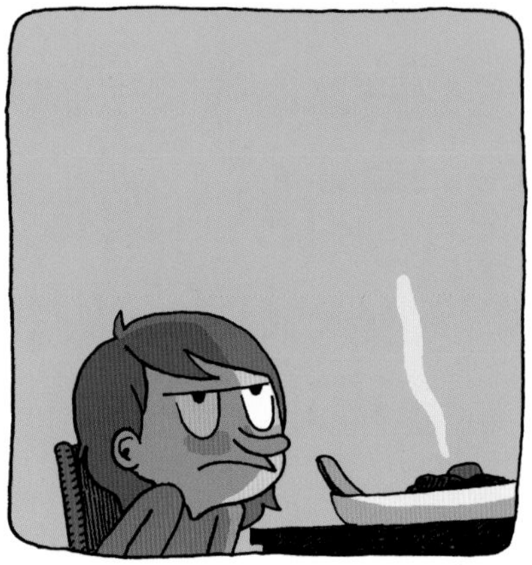

7 "You can only have dessert after you have fruit."

HAHA! THERE'S NOTHING MORE ADULT THAN BEING ASTONISHED THAT SOMEONE WOULD EVER PREFER DESSERT OVER A MUSHY BANANA OR A TINY CAN OF FRUIT COCKTAIL.

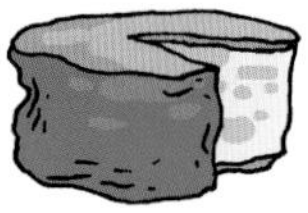

FORTUNATELY, THERE'S A MAGIC WORD THAT IS SURE TO HELP GET YOU OUT OF EATING FRUIT IN THE FUTURE. IT WILL MAYBE EVEN GET YOU A SECOND SLICE OF CAKE! TAKE ON A WORRIED LOOK AND SAY:

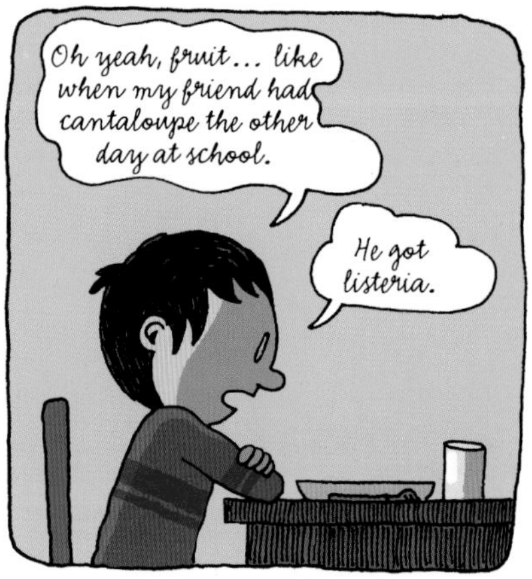
Oh yeah, fruit... like when my friend had cantaloupe the other day at school.
He got listeria.

8 "Taste it before saying you don't like it."

THIS WAS MY MOM'S BIG THING WHEN SHE MADE ME ENDIVE SALAD OR TRIPE (YOU CAN ONLY IMAGINE).

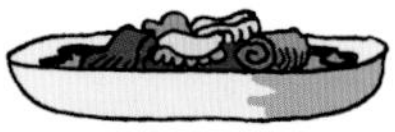

TO BE HONEST... HER STRATEGY WORKED, SEEING THAT I LIKE ALMOST EVERYTHING. BUT JOKES ASIDE, IF I HAD AN IDEA AGAINST THIS ONE, IT WOULD BE TO EXPOSE THE SPEAKER'S OWN CONTRADICTIONS. THIS SURPRISE TACTIC COULD MAKE THE SPEAKER FORGET MOMENTARILY WHAT THEY WANT YOU TO DO, AND YOU CAN TAKE ADVANTAGE OF THEIR SHOCK TO CHANGE THE SUBJECT.

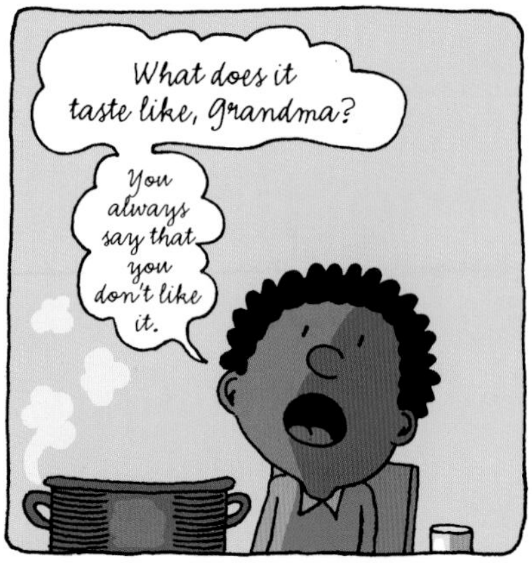
What does it taste like, Grandma?
You always say that you don't like it.

9 "Think of the starving children in Africa."

THIS IS AN OLD TECHNIQUE TO PROVOKE GUILT. GEOGRAPHICALLY, IT'S ALSO NONSENSE. THERE ARE PROBABLY HUNGRY PEOPLE WHERE YOU LIVE RIGHT NOW, AND NOTE THAT MANY POPULATIONS IN AFRICA EAT VERY WELL.

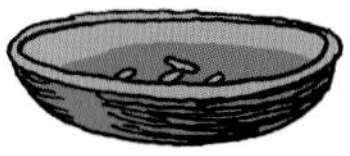

YOU COULD EASILY ANSWER THAT THOSE CHILDREN ARE LUCKY TO NOT BE FORCE-FED THE TUNA NOODLE CASSEROLE THAT IS GROWING COLD IN FRONT OF YOU, BUT YOU HAVE TO ADMIT THAT IT'S NEVER FUN TO HAVE NOTHING TO EAT. SUGGEST AN IDEA THAT WORKS FOR EVERYBODY:

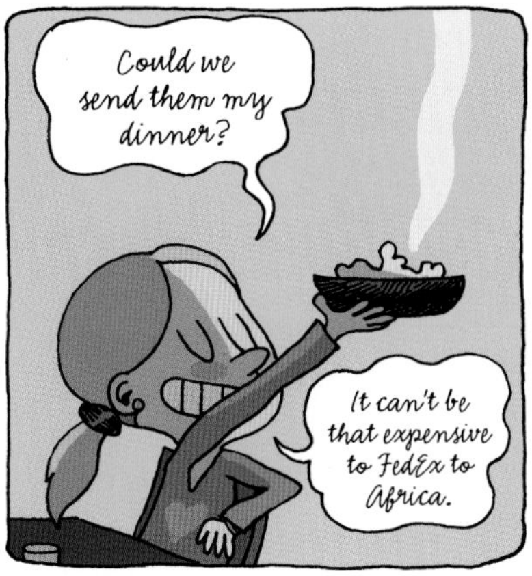
Could we send them my dinner?
It can't be that expensive to FedEx to Africa.

10 "Eat. You never know who will eat you."

ONE THING IS TRUE: NOBODY IS GOING TO EAT YOU (WELL, CHECK AND MAKE SURE YOUR PARENTS DON'T HAVE AN UPCOMING TRIP TO THE ZOO PLANNED).

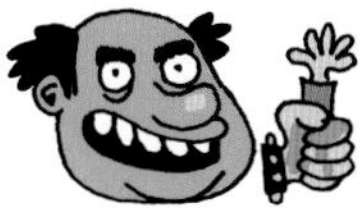

BUT MAKE THEM BELIEVE THAT YOU BOUGHT IT, HOOK, LINE, AND SINKER. TAKE ON A TERRIFIED LOOK (THE SAME KIND OF TERROR BROUGHT ON BY A DISH OF BRUSSELS SPROUTS). OVERPLAY EVERYTHING AND MAKE A HUGE SCENE:

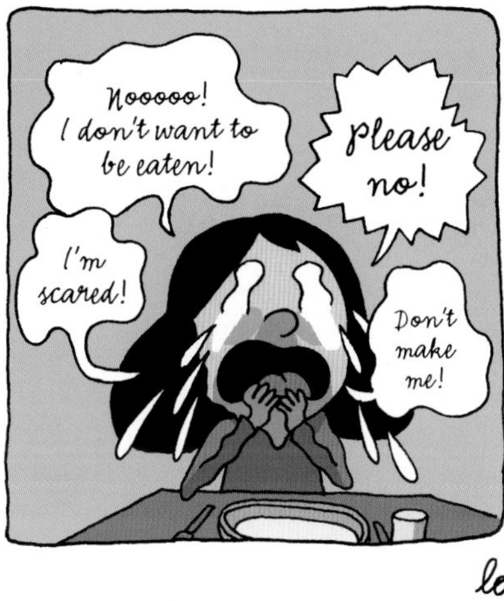
Nooooo! I don't want to be eaten!
Please no!
I'm scared!
Don't make me!
lon.

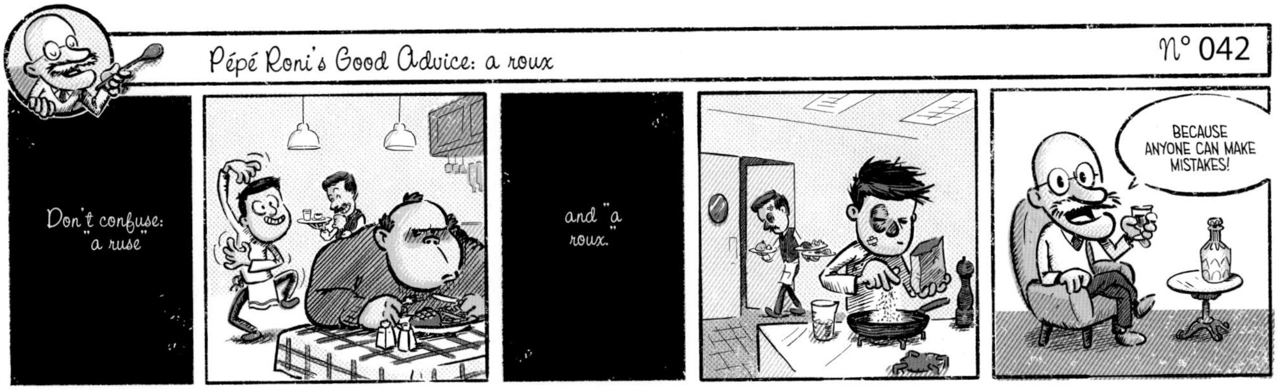
Pépé Roni's Good Advice: a roux
N° 042
Don't confuse: "a ruse"
and "a roux."
BECAUSE ANYONE CAN MAKE MISTAKES!

A roux: A blend of flour and fat cooked together to enrich and thicken sauces.

SEVERAL MONTHS EARLIER, SOMEWHERE OFF THE CHESAPEAKE BAY...

FRANCIS...

YEAH?

I HAVE A BAD FEELING.

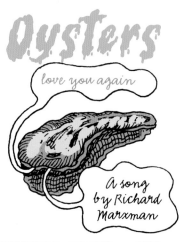

Oysters

love you again

A song by Richard Marxman

SOMETIMES SO SWEET, IN TASTE AND IN TOUCH

JUST LIKE US ALL, HOW GENTLY WE RUSH

BUT SOMETIMES SO HARD THAT EACH WOUND TO THE SOUL

MAKES ME NO LONGER WHOLE, I'M NO LONGER WHOLE

OY-STERS!

I will love you again

OY-STERS!

We are yours 'til the end

I NEVER KNEW LOVE TO COME EASILY

THROUGH PATIENCE AND PAIN HAS LOVE COME TO ME

?

BUT FROM TIME TO TIME, LOVE DOES HEED MY CALL

BOTH FRAGILE AND MIGHTY, HER BEAUTY FOR ALL

FROM EAST OR FROM WEST, A HEART MADE OF STONE

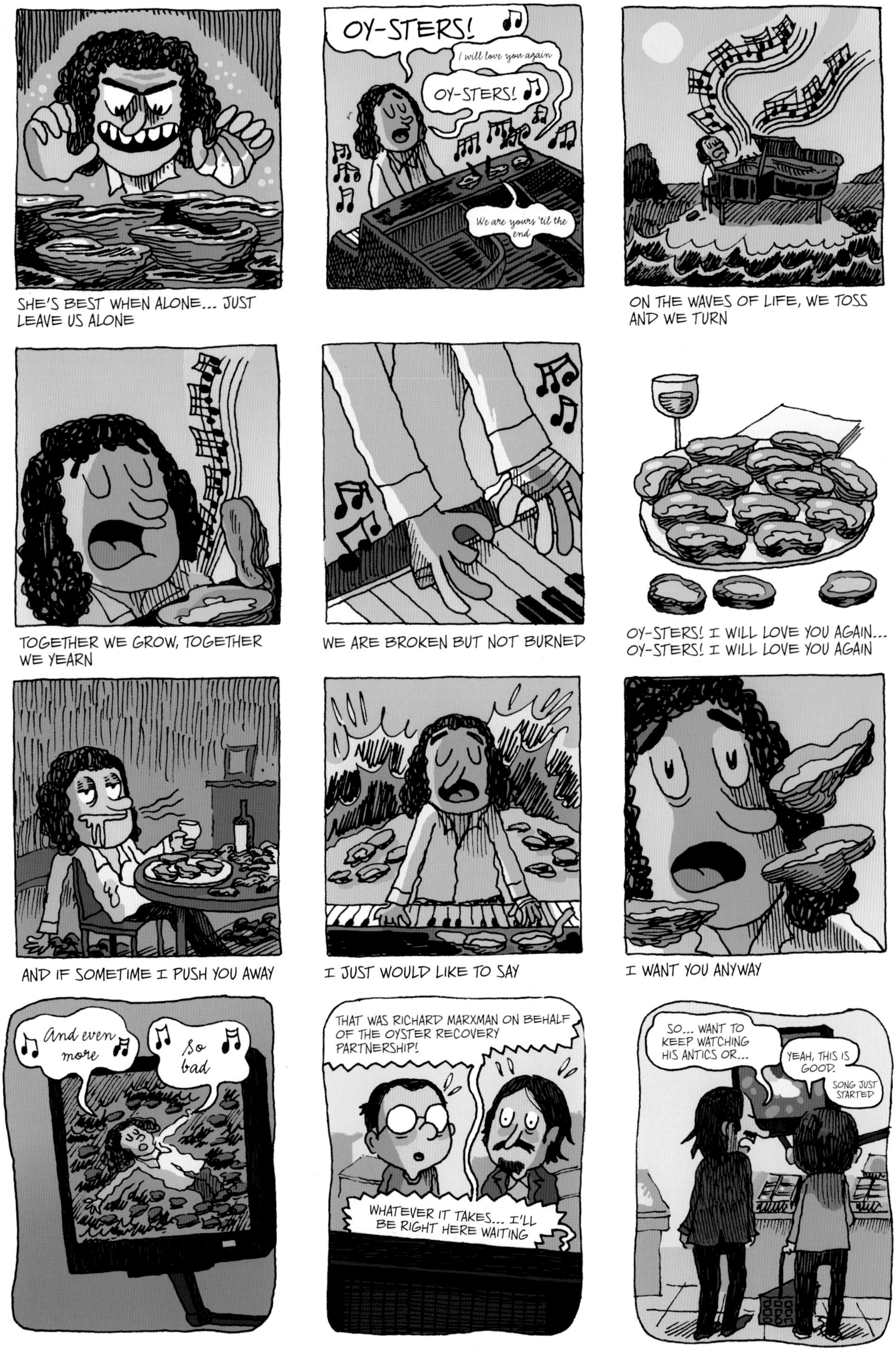
SHE'S BEST WHEN ALONE... JUST LEAVE US ALONE
OY-STERS!
I will love you again
OY-STERS!
We are yours 'til the end
ON THE WAVES OF LIFE, WE TOSS AND WE TURN
TOGETHER WE GROW, TOGETHER WE YEARN
WE ARE BROKEN BUT NOT BURNED
OY-STERS! I WILL LOVE YOU AGAIN... OY-STERS! I WILL LOVE YOU AGAIN
AND IF SOMETIME I PUSH YOU AWAY
I JUST WOULD LIKE TO SAY
I WANT YOU ANYWAY
And even more
So bad
THAT WAS RICHARD MARXMAN ON BEHALF OF THE OYSTER RECOVERY PARTNERSHIP!
WHATEVER IT TAKES... I'LL BE RIGHT HERE WAITING
SO... WANT TO KEEP WATCHING HIS ANTICS OR...
YEAH, THIS IS GOOD.
SONG JUST STARTED

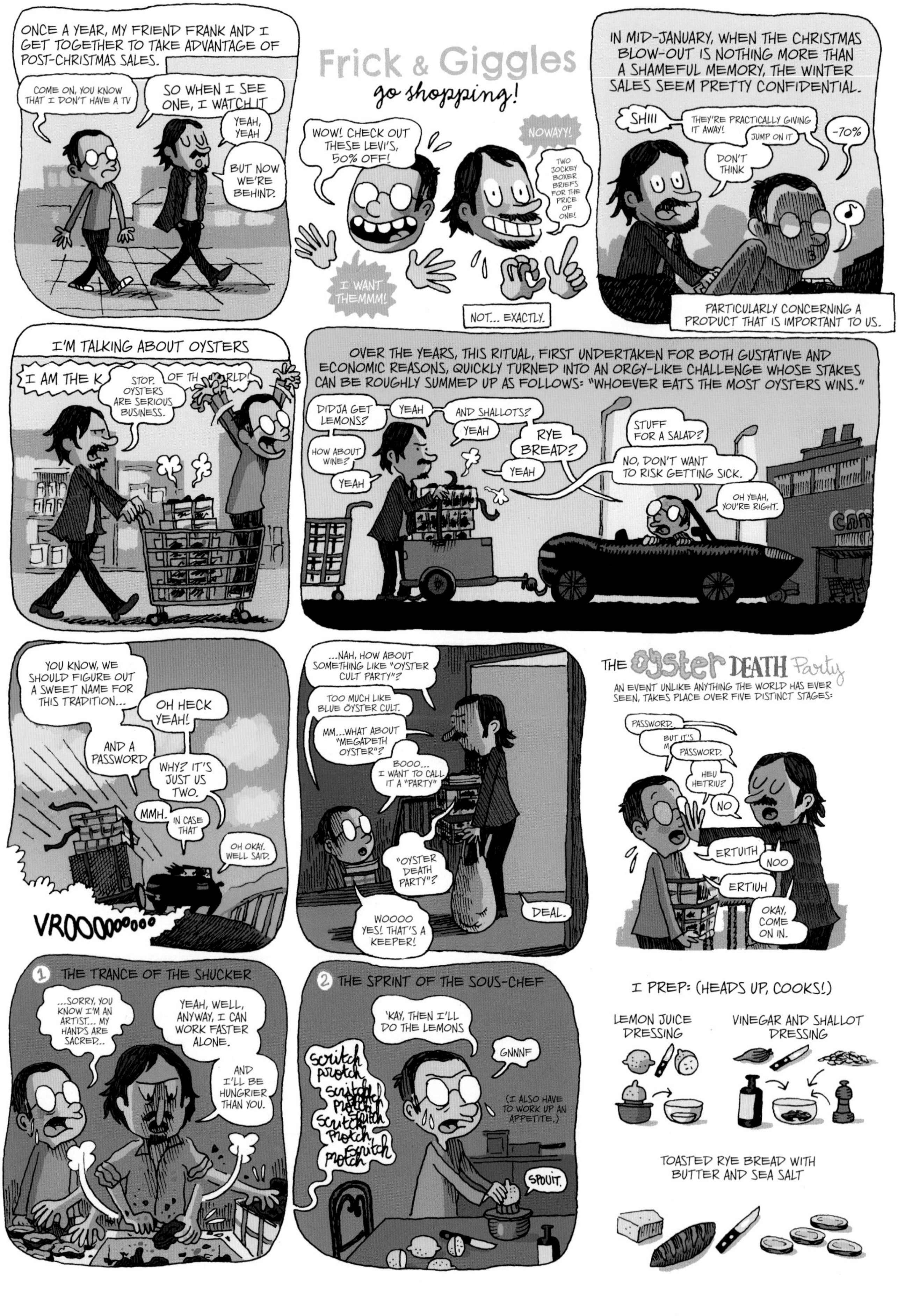

ONCE A YEAR, MY FRIEND FRANK AND I GET TOGETHER TO TAKE ADVANTAGE OF POST-CHRISTMAS SALES.
COME ON, YOU KNOW THAT I DON'T HAVE A TV
SO WHEN I SEE ONE, I WATCH IT
YEAH, YEAH
BUT NOW WE'RE BEHIND.
Frick & Giggles
go shopping!
WOW! CHECK OUT THESE LEVI'S, 50% OFF!
NOWAYY!
TWO JOCKEY BOXER BRIEFS FOR THE PRICE OF ONE!
I WANT THEMMM!
NOT... EXACTLY.
IN MID-JANUARY, WHEN THE CHRISTMAS BLOW-OUT IS NOTHING MORE THAN A SHAMEFUL MEMORY, THE WINTER SALES SEEM PRETTY CONFIDENTIAL.
SHIII
THEY'RE PRACTICALLY GIVING IT AWAY!
JUMP ON IT
-70%
DON'T THINK
PARTICULARLY CONCERNING A PRODUCT THAT IS IMPORTANT TO US.
I'M TALKING ABOUT OYSTERS
I AM THE K
STOP. OYSTERS ARE SERIOUS BUSINESS.
OF TH
OVER THE YEARS, THIS RITUAL, FIRST UNDERTAKEN FOR BOTH GUSTATIVE AND ECONOMIC REASONS, QUICKLY TURNED INTO AN ORGY-LIKE CHALLENGE WHOSE STAKES CAN BE ROUGHLY SUMMED UP AS FOLLOWS: "WHOEVER EATS THE MOST OYSTERS WINS."
DIDJA GET LEMONS?
YEAH
AND SHALLOTS?
YEAH
HOW ABOUT WINE?
YEAH
RYE BREAD?
YEAH
STUFF FOR A SALAD?
NO, DON'T WANT TO RISK GETTING SICK.
OH YEAH, YOU'RE RIGHT.
YOU KNOW, WE SHOULD FIGURE OUT A SWEET NAME FOR THIS TRADITION...
OH HECK YEAH!
AND A PASSWORD
WHY? IT'S JUST US TWO.
MMH.
IN CASE THAT
OH OKAY. WELL SAID.
VROOOOooooo
...NAH, HOW ABOUT SOMETHING LIKE "OYSTER CULT PARTY"?
TOO MUCH LIKE BLUE ÖYSTER CULT.
MM...WHAT ABOUT "MEGADETH OYSTER"?
BOOO... I WANT TO CALL IT A "PARTY"
"OYSTER DEATH PARTY"?
WOOOO YES! THAT'S A KEEPER!
DEAL.
THE Oyster DEATH Party
AN EVENT UNLIKE ANYTHING THE WORLD HAS EVER SEEN, TAKES PLACE OVER FIVE DISTINCT STAGES:
PASSWORD.
BUT IT'S M
PASSWORD.
HEU HETRIU?
NO
ERTUITH
NOO
ERTIUH
OKAY, COME ON IN.
1 THE TRANCE OF THE SHUCKER
...SORRY, YOU KNOW I'M AN ARTIST... MY HANDS ARE SACRED...
YEAH, WELL, ANYWAY, I CAN WORK FASTER ALONE.
AND I'LL BE HUNGRIER THAN YOU.
2 THE SPRINT OF THE SOUS-CHEF
'KAY, THEN I'LL DO THE LEMONS
GNNNF
scritch protch
(I ALSO HAVE TO WORK UP AN APPETITE.)
SPOUIT.
I PREP: (HEADS UP, COOKS!)
LEMON JUICE DRESSING
VINEGAR AND SHALLOT DRESSING
TOASTED RYE BREAD WITH BUTTER AND SEA SALT

③ THE OFFICIAL SCOREBOARD

OYSTER DEATH PARTY
Guillaume | Florian

DRAW STRAIGHT

CHILL, I'M A PROFESSIONAL.

WHY'S MY SPACE SMALLER?

OOOOOH

④ THE PRAYER TO SAINT SONYA "BLACK WIDOW" THOMS *

GIVE ME STRENGTH, LEAD ME NOT INTO TEMPTATION BY THE BREAD, AWAKEN MY PALATE, AND EXPAND MY STOMACH. AMEN.

AMEN.

⑤ THE VOYAGE INTO THE UNKNOWN

WELL... HERE GOES NOTHING!

YEAH! MAY THE BEST MAN WIN!

*552 OYSTERS IN 10 MINUTES, APRIL 2005

I CAN'T BELIEVE THERE ARE PEOPLE WHO DON'T LIKE OYSTERS

SHLRP

MEH. UNDERSTANDABLE, THEY'RE SALTY AND HAVE THE CONSISTENCY OF SNOT

SHLRP

YEAH, BUT WHAT ABOUT THEIR LIGHT NUTTY FINISH?

YOU HAFTA CHEW

HEY, FOR CHRISTMAS, WE MADE OYSTERS WITH FOIE GRAS. YOU PUT A SLICE OF FOIE GRAS ON YOUR OYSTER WITH SOME CHIVES AND SOME PEPPER, AND THEN YOU STICK IT UNDER THE BROILER FOR FIVE MINUTES

MMH.

YOU'D WRECK YOUR STOMACH AFTER EATING FIVE.

TRUE. BUT IT'S SO GOOD.

SHLRP

HOW MANY ARE WE AT?

SHLRP

24 TO 18 I THINK

SHLRP

STILL GOING STRONG?

YEP.

SHLRP

SHLRP

HOW 'BOUT YOU?

WE'RE JUST GETTING STARTED.

THEY SAY THAT IF YOU EAT JUST ONE BAD OYSTER, YOU WILL NEVER EAT OYSTERS AGAIN.

SHLRP

STOP

SHIT WHAT A NIGHTMARE

WANT ANY MORE OF YOUR BREAD?

SHLRP

NO, I'M PACING MYSELF

I THINK I'M STARTING TO SEE THINGS

THAT'S THE POINT

CRAZY TALK

HAHAHAHA

HEHE KRKR

EPILOGUE: SEVERAL MONTHS LATER, STILL IN THE CHESAPEAKE BAY...

PUTTPUTT

THERE! DO YOU HEAR THAT, FRANCIS?

PUTT

OH SHIIIT THE... THE...

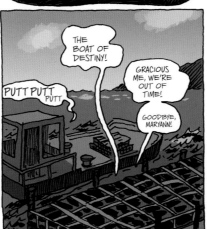

THE BOAT OF DESTINY!

GRACIOUS ME, WE'RE OUT OF TIME!

PUTT PUTT PUTT

GOODBYE, MARYANN!

HAVE YOU HEARD? THEY'VE INVENTED AN EVEN CRUELER WAY TO FINISH US OFF!

OH NO!!

THEY CALL IT AN OYSTER DEATH PARTY!

OH GEEZ!!

NO SURVIVORS.

OH PLEASE LET ME DIE AS AN APPETIZER-- WITH DIGNITY!

PUTT PUTT

lon.

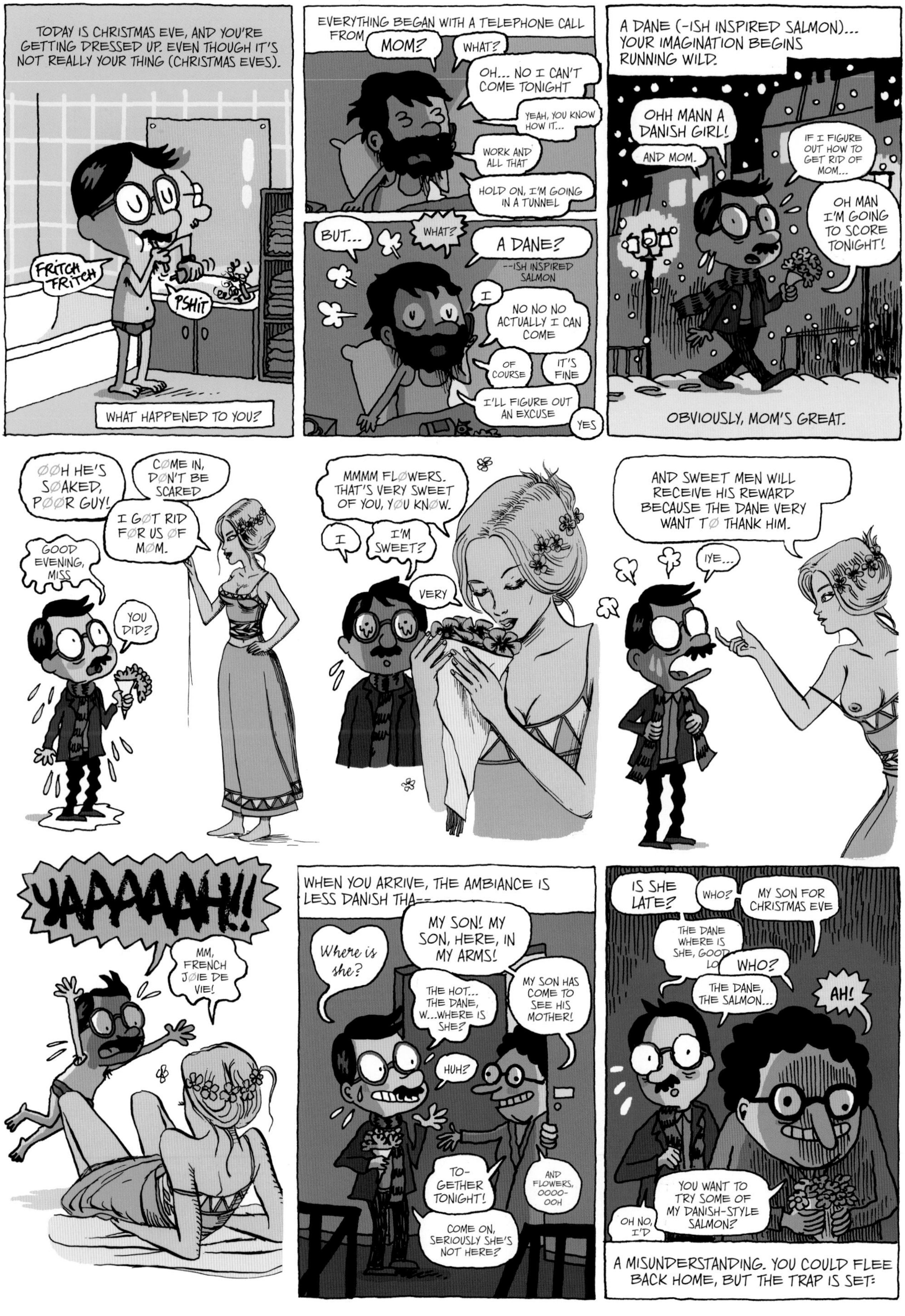
TODAY IS CHRISTMAS EVE, AND YOU'RE GETTING DRESSED UP. EVEN THOUGH IT'S NOT REALLY YOUR THING (CHRISTMAS EVES).
FRITCH FRITCH
PSHIT
WHAT HAPPENED TO YOU?
EVERYTHING BEGAN WITH A TELEPHONE CALL FROM
MOM?
WHAT?
OH... NO I CAN'T COME TONIGHT
YEAH, YOU KNOW HOW IT...
WORK AND ALL THAT
HOLD ON, I'M GOING IN A TUNNEL
BUT...
WHAT?
A DANE?
--ISH INSPIRED SALMON
I
NO NO NO ACTUALLY I CAN COME
OF COURSE
IT'S FINE
I'LL FIGURE OUT AN EXCUSE
YES
A DANE (-ISH INSPIRED SALMON)... YOUR IMAGINATION BEGINS RUNNING WILD.
OHH MANN A DANISH GIRL!
AND MOM.
IF I FIGURE OUT HOW TO GET RID OF MOM...
OH MAN I'M GOING TO SCORE TONIGHT!
OBVIOUSLY, MOM'S GREAT.
ØØH HE'S SØAKED, PØØR GUY!
CØME IN, DØN'T BE SCARED
I GØT RID FØR US ØF MØM.
GOOD EVENING, MISS
YOU DID?
MMMM FLØWERS. THAT'S VERY SWEET OF YOU, YØU KNØW.
I
I'M SWEET?
VERY
AND SWEET MEN WILL RECEIVE HIS REWARD BECAUSE THE DANE VERY WANT TØ THANK HIM.
IYE...
YAAAAAH!!
MM, FRENCH JØIE DE VIE!
WHEN YOU ARRIVE, THE AMBIANCE IS LESS DANISH THA--
MY SON! MY SON, HERE, IN MY ARMS!
Where is she?
THE HOT... THE DANE, W...WHERE IS SHE?
MY SON HAS COME TO SEE HIS MOTHER!
HUH?
TO-GETHER TONIGHT!
AND FLOWERS, OOOO-OOH
COME ON, SERIOUSLY SHE'S NOT HERE?
IS SHE LATE?
WHO?
MY SON FOR CHRISTMAS EVE
THE DANE WHERE IS SHE, GOOD LO
WHO?
THE DANE, THE SALMON...
AH!
YOU WANT TO TRY SOME OF MY DANISH-STYLE SALMON?
OH NO, I'D
A MISUNDERSTANDING. YOU COULD FLEE BACK HOME, BUT THE TRAP IS SET:

MOM BEGINS TO TELL YOU HER RECIPE:

DANISH-STYLE SALMON

IT'S SO EASY, YOU'LL NEVER BELIEVE IT

I FOUND IT WHILE SKIING THE INTERNET

IN A COOKIES OR SOME-THING

EVEN FOR YOU, WHO HATES COOKING

A LITTLE SOME-THING DIF-FERENT

TRY IT

OBVIOUSLY.

YOU'LL NEED (DO YOU WANT SOME PAPER TO WRITE IT DOWN?)

FOR FOUR PEOPLE:

UNSWEETENED GREEK YOGURT OR FROMAGE FRAIS

DILL

SUGAR

CAPERS

A WHITE ONION

A LEMON

10 OZ. SMOKED SALMON

SALT PEPPER

RASPBERRY VINEGAR

4 SLICES OF BREAD

MUSTARD

① IF NECESSARY, FIRST MINCE THE SALMON INTO THIIIIIN SLICES, LIKE FOR A CARPACCIO.

AND THEN ARRANGE THEM ON A SERVING DISH. TOP WITH THE LEMON JUICE, TWO SPRIGS OF DILL, AND A LITTLE PEPPER

② NEXT, COVER YOUR DISH WITH SOME PLASTIC WRAP.

GNii

HUUH

FUCKER

AND THEN YOU LET IT MARINATE IN THE FRIDGE OVERNIGHT... HEY, ARE YOU LISTENING?

SO WHERE WAS I?

FRIDGE

YEAH YEAH

MH

clic
clic
clic

③ WELL... THE NEXT DAY, CHOP UP YOUR WHITE ONION (2/3 CUP). ACTUALLY, MINCE IT, TO BE MORE PRECISE.

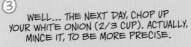

AND THEN SET THE ONIONS ASIDE (BUT NOT LIKE FOR YOUR RETIREMENT!) HEHEHA! I SHOULD SUBMIT THAT TO THAT COOKING WEBSITE THAT HAS JOKES EVERY SUNDAY.

RACHEL RAYNER

LOOK UNDER FAVORITES

THERE

WHERE

NO, NEVER HEARD OF IT

OH. THAT. YEAH, THIS LOOKS AWFUL

clic

④ NEXT, MAKE THE SAUCE IN A PRETTY BOWL. MIX 2 TABLESPOONS OF MUSTARD, 4 TABLESPOONS OF SUGAR, 2 TABLESPOONS OF CAPERS, AND 2 TABLESPOONS OF RASPBERRY VINEGAR, AND FINALLY ABOUT 2 OZ. GREEK YOGURT, THINNED OUT WITH A LITTLE MILK OR WATER.

ADD SOME SALT AND PEPPER, AND THEN MIX UNTIL IT'S SMOOTH. ADD IN THE ONIONS AND MIX AGAIN.

⑤ WHEN IT'S TIME TO EAT, TOAST THE BREAD.

SERVE THE SALMON WITH THE SAUCE AND THE TOAST, AND THAT'S ALL THERE IS TO IT!

ISN'T IT GOOD?

M-HM

IT'S GOOD TO SPEND CHRIST-MAS EVE WITH YOUR MOM.

MH

BUT YOU COULD ALSO FIND YOUR-SELF A NICE GIR—

SHH, I'M WATCHING

AT YOUR AGE...

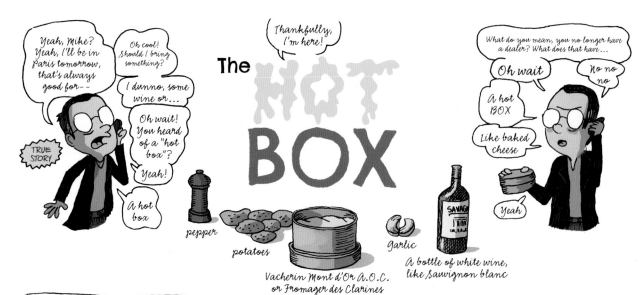

The HOT BOX

Yeah, Mike? Yeah, I'll be in Paris tomorrow, that's always good for--

TRUE STORY

Oh cool! Should I bring something?

I dunno, some wine or...

Oh wait! You heard of a "hot box"?

Yeah!

A hot box

Thankfully, I'm here!

pepper

potatoes

Vacherin Mont d'Or A.O.C. or Fromager des Clarines

garlic

A bottle of white wine, like Sauvignon blanc

What do you mean, you no longer have a dealer? What does that have...

Oh wait

A hot BOX

Like baked cheese

No no no

Yeah

Mont d'Or is much more than just a cheese that stinks. It's a legend passed down from generation to generation:

Do you have any Grey Poupon? / NOOO

MONDOR!!!

Mont d'Or is a gastronome's cheap secret...that is, when you buy it in the region of Franche-Comté, France.

7€ / 7€

FAUCHON "Mont d'or" / BADOZ le mont d'or

A recipe copied by the Swiss, but not completely.

I'M NOT HEAT-ING; I'M WARMING

HOW ELSE SHOULD WE SPIN THIS?

You can eat Mont d'Or a bunch of different ways or even just straight up. But I prefer it baked in the oven and served with potatoes and a salad.

① Soak the box of Mont d'Or in cold water for a few minutes, or cover it in aluminum foil,

And heat some water for the potatoes while your oven preheats to 425°F.

② Slice up a garlic clove (or two, if your Mont d'Or is family-sized)

Dig out a hole of about ¾ inches in diameter in the center of your cheese, and pour some wine in.

③ Cut slits into the surface of the cheese with a knife, and slide your garlic pieces inside. Season with pepper.

And bake in the oven for 20 to 30 minutes, depending on the size of your cheese.

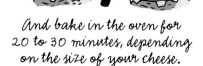

④ Boil your potatoes. If, since step 2, you were wondering what to do with the cheese that you dug out, well, make some toast and have a snack!

Cook's privilege!

⑤ You can stir the cheese while it's cooking to make it creamier, and broil it for the last two minutes before serving with a bunch of heart-healthy charcuterie and the white wine you opened in step 2!

NEED SOME MISO.

leon.

FOIE GRAS 24

"THE FOLLOWING TAKES PLACE BETWEEN 10 A.M. AND 11 A.M. THE FOLLOWING DAY ON THE DAY BEFORE CHRISTMAS. THE EVENTS ARE REPORTED IN REAL TIME."

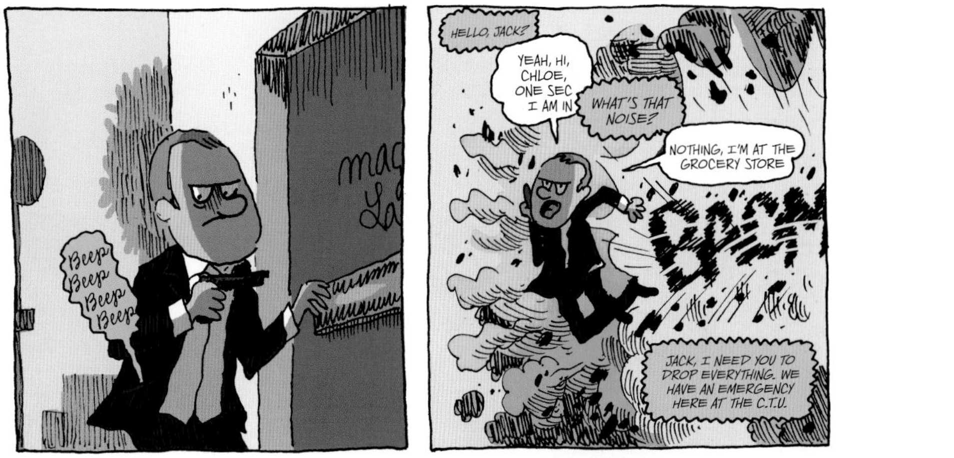
Beep Beep Beep Beep
HELLO, JACK?
YEAH, HI, CHLOE, ONE SEC I AM IN
WHAT'S THAT NOISE?
NOTHING, I'M AT THE GROCERY STORE
JACK, I NEED YOU TO DROP EVERYTHING. WE HAVE AN EMERGENCY HERE AT THE C.T.U.

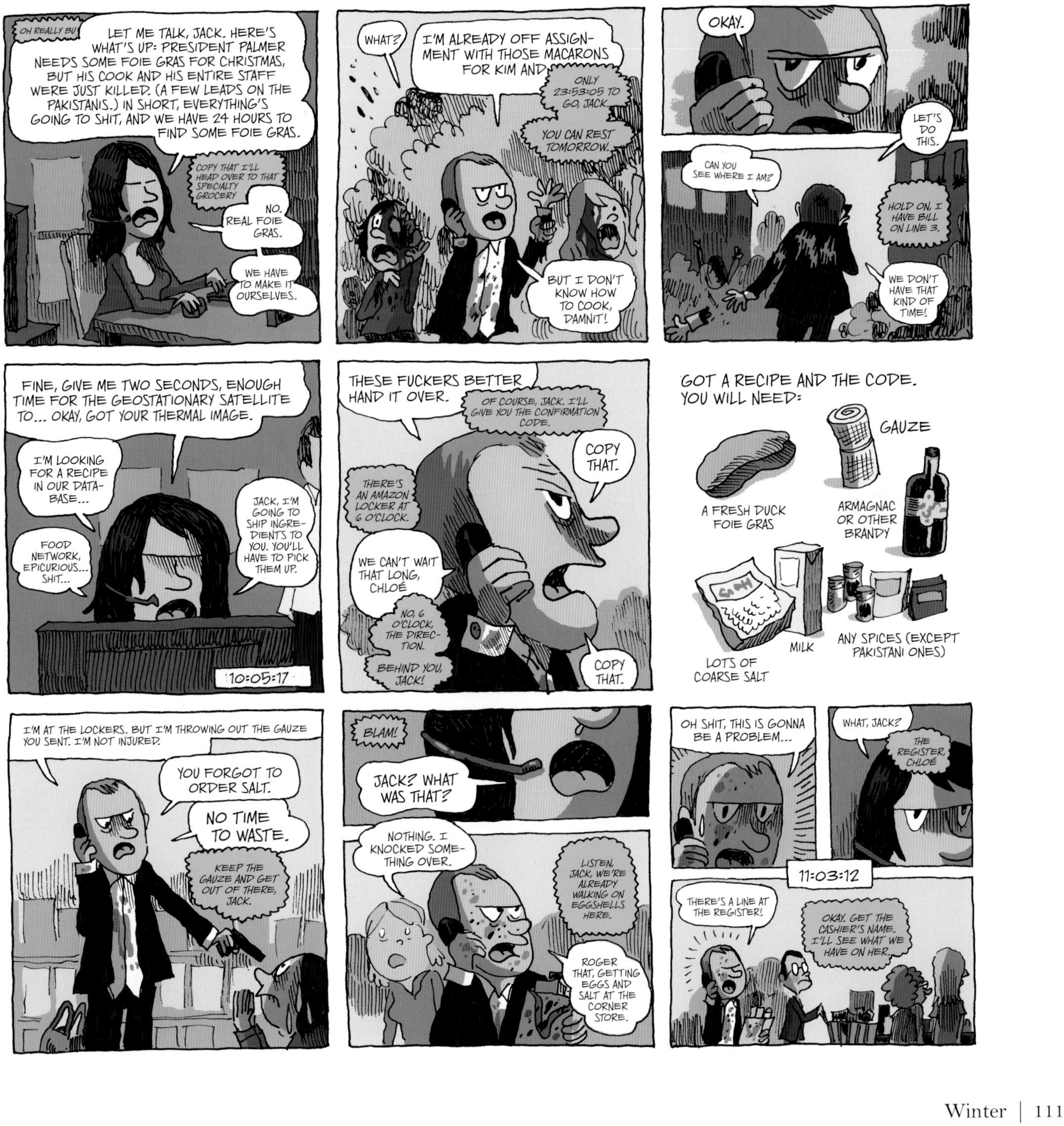
OH REALLY BU
LET ME TALK, JACK. HERE'S WHAT'S UP: PRESIDENT PALMER NEEDS SOME FOIE GRAS FOR CHRISTMAS, BUT HIS COOK AND HIS ENTIRE STAFF WERE JUST KILLED. (A FEW LEADS ON THE PAKISTANIS.) IN SHORT, EVERYTHING'S GOING TO SHIT, AND WE HAVE 24 HOURS TO FIND SOME FOIE GRAS.
COPY THAT I'LL HEAD OVER TO THAT SPECIALTY GROCERY
NO. REAL FOIE GRAS.
WE HAVE TO MAKE IT OURSELVES.
WHAT?
I'M ALREADY OFF ASSIGNMENT WITH THOSE MACARONS FOR KIM AND
ONLY 23:53:05 TO GO, JACK.
YOU CAN REST TOMORROW.
BUT I DON'T KNOW HOW TO COOK, DAMNIT!
OKAY.
LET'S DO THIS.
CAN YOU SEE WHERE I AM?
HOLD ON, I HAVE BILL ON LINE 3.
WE DON'T HAVE THAT KIND OF TIME!
FINE, GIVE ME TWO SECONDS, ENOUGH TIME FOR THE GEOSTATIONARY SATELLITE TO... OKAY, GOT YOUR THERMAL IMAGE.
I'M LOOKING FOR A RECIPE IN OUR DATABASE...
FOOD NETWORK, EPICURIOUS... SHIT...
JACK, I'M GOING TO SHIP INGREDIENTS TO YOU. YOU'LL HAVE TO PICK THEM UP.
10:05:17
THESE FUCKERS BETTER HAND IT OVER.
OF COURSE, JACK. I'LL GIVE YOU THE CONFIRMATION CODE.
COPY THAT.
THERE'S AN AMAZON LOCKER AT 6 O'CLOCK.
WE CAN'T WAIT THAT LONG, CHLOÉ.
NO, 6 O'CLOCK, THE DIRECTION.
BEHIND YOU, JACK!
COPY THAT.
GOT A RECIPE AND THE CODE. YOU WILL NEED:
GAUZE
A FRESH DUCK FOIE GRAS
ARMAGNAC OR OTHER BRANDY
LOTS OF COARSE SALT
MILK
ANY SPICES (EXCEPT PAKISTANI ONES)
I'M AT THE LOCKERS. BUT I'M THROWING OUT THE GAUZE YOU SENT. I'M NOT INJURED.
YOU FORGOT TO ORDER SALT.
NO TIME TO WASTE.
KEEP THE GAUZE AND GET OUT OF THERE, JACK.
BLAM!
JACK? WHAT WAS THAT?
NOTHING. I KNOCKED SOMETHING OVER.
LISTEN, JACK, WE'RE ALREADY WALKING ON EGGSHELLS HERE.
ROGER THAT, GETTING EGGS AND SALT AT THE CORNER STORE.
OH SHIT, THIS IS GONNA BE A PROBLEM...
WHAT, JACK?
THE REGISTER, CHLOÉ
11:03:12
THERE'S A LINE AT THE REGISTER!
OKAY. GET THE CASHIER'S NAME. I'LL SEE WHAT WE HAVE ON HER.

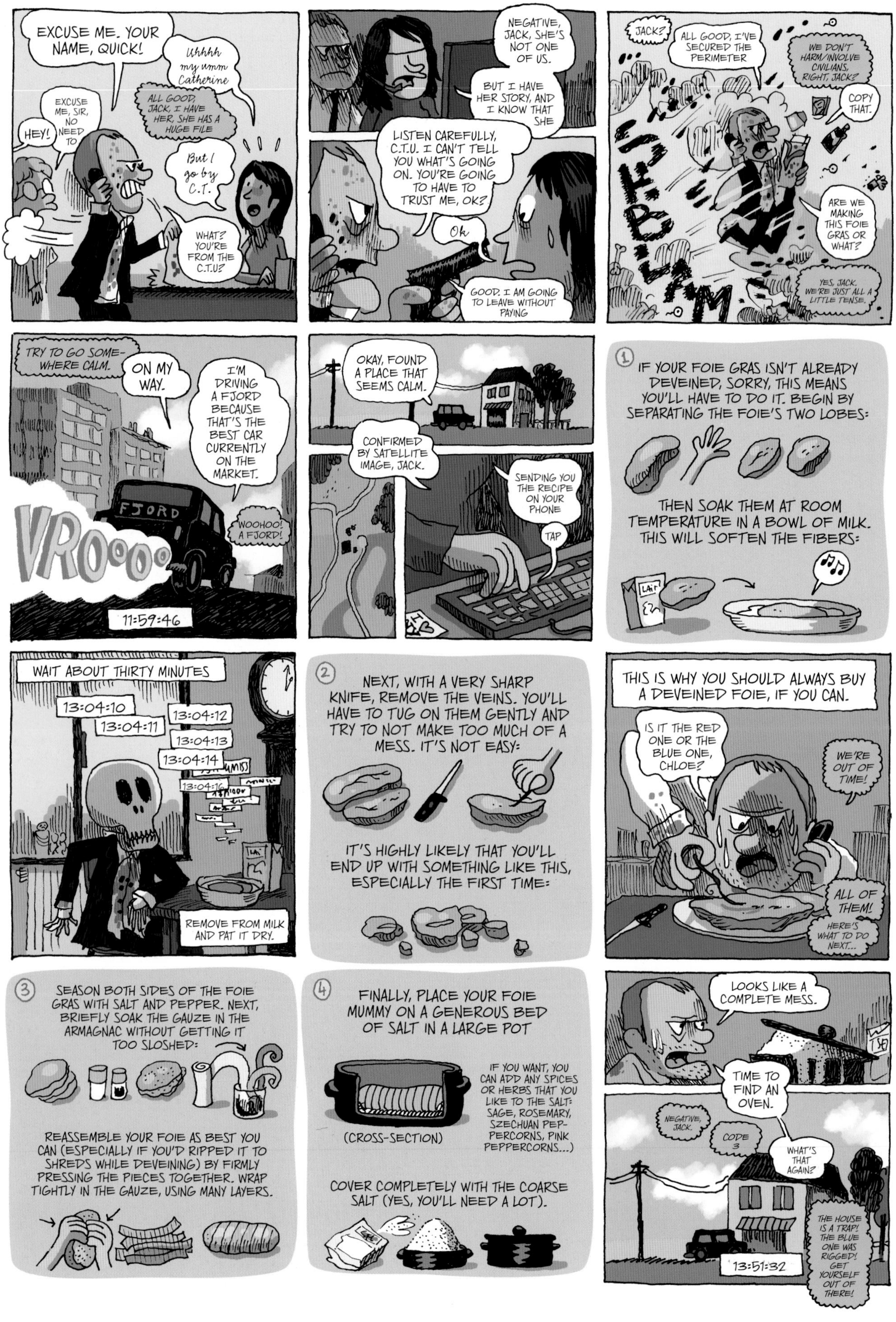
EXCUSE ME. YOUR NAME, QUICK!
Uhhhh my umm Catherine
EXCUSE ME, SIR, NO NEED TO
HEY!
ALL GOOD, JACK, I HAVE HER, SHE HAS A HUGE FILE
But I go by C.T.
WHAT? YOU'RE FROM THE C.T.U?
NEGATIVE, JACK, SHE'S NOT ONE OF US.
BUT I HAVE HER STORY, AND I KNOW THAT SHE
LISTEN CAREFULLY, C.T.U. I CAN'T TELL YOU WHAT'S GOING ON. YOU'RE GOING TO HAVE TO TRUST ME, OK?
Ok
GOOD. I AM GOING TO LEAVE WITHOUT PAYING
JACK?
ALL GOOD, I'VE SECURED THE PERIMETER
WE DON'T HARM/INVOLVE CIVILIANS, RIGHT, JACK?
COPY THAT.
SHBLAM
ARE WE MAKING THIS FOIE GRAS OR WHAT?
YES, JACK. WE'RE JUST ALL A LITTLE TENSE.
TRY TO GO SOMEWHERE CALM.
ON MY WAY.
I'M DRIVING A FJORD BECAUSE THAT'S THE BEST CAR CURRENTLY ON THE MARKET.
FJORD
VROoooo
WOOHOO! A FJORD!
11:59:46
OKAY, FOUND A PLACE THAT SEEMS CALM.
CONFIRMED BY SATELLITE IMAGE, JACK.
SENDING YOU THE RECIPE ON YOUR PHONE
TAP
1 IF YOUR FOIE GRAS ISN'T ALREADY DEVEINED, SORRY, THIS MEANS YOU'LL HAVE TO DO IT. BEGIN BY SEPARATING THE FOIE'S TWO LOBES:
THEN SOAK THEM AT ROOM TEMPERATURE IN A BOWL OF MILK. THIS WILL SOFTEN THE FIBERS:
LAIT
WAIT ABOUT THIRTY MINUTES
13:04:10
13:04:11
13:04:12
13:04:13
13:04:14
13:04:16
REMOVE FROM MILK AND PAT IT DRY.
2 NEXT, WITH A VERY SHARP KNIFE, REMOVE THE VEINS. YOU'LL HAVE TO TUG ON THEM GENTLY AND TRY TO NOT MAKE TOO MUCH OF A MESS. IT'S NOT EASY:
IT'S HIGHLY LIKELY THAT YOU'LL END UP WITH SOMETHING LIKE THIS, ESPECIALLY THE FIRST TIME:
THIS IS WHY YOU SHOULD ALWAYS BUY A DEVEINED FOIE, IF YOU CAN.
IS IT THE RED ONE OR THE BLUE ONE, CHLOE?
WE'RE OUT OF TIME!
ALL OF THEM!
HERE'S WHAT TO DO NEXT...
3 SEASON BOTH SIDES OF THE FOIE GRAS WITH SALT AND PEPPER. NEXT, BRIEFLY SOAK THE GAUZE IN THE ARMAGNAC WITHOUT GETTING IT TOO SLOSHED:
REASSEMBLE YOUR FOIE AS BEST YOU CAN (ESPECIALLY IF YOU'D RIPPED IT TO SHREDS WHILE DEVEINING) BY FIRMLY PRESSING THE PIECES TOGETHER. WRAP TIGHTLY IN THE GAUZE, USING MANY LAYERS.
4 FINALLY, PLACE YOUR FOIE MUMMY ON A GENEROUS BED OF SALT IN A LARGE POT
IF YOU WANT, YOU CAN ADD ANY SPICES OR HERBS THAT YOU LIKE TO THE SALT: SAGE, ROSEMARY, SZECHUAN PEPPERCORNS, PINK PEPPERCORNS...)
(CROSS-SECTION)
COVER COMPLETELY WITH THE COARSE SALT (YES, YOU'LL NEED A LOT).
LOOKS LIKE A COMPLETE MESS.
TIME TO FIND AN OVEN.
NEGATIVE, JACK.
CODE 3
WHAT'S THAT AGAIN?
THE HOUSE IS A TRAP! THE BLUE ONE WAS RIGGED! GET YOURSELF OUT OF THERE!
13:51:32

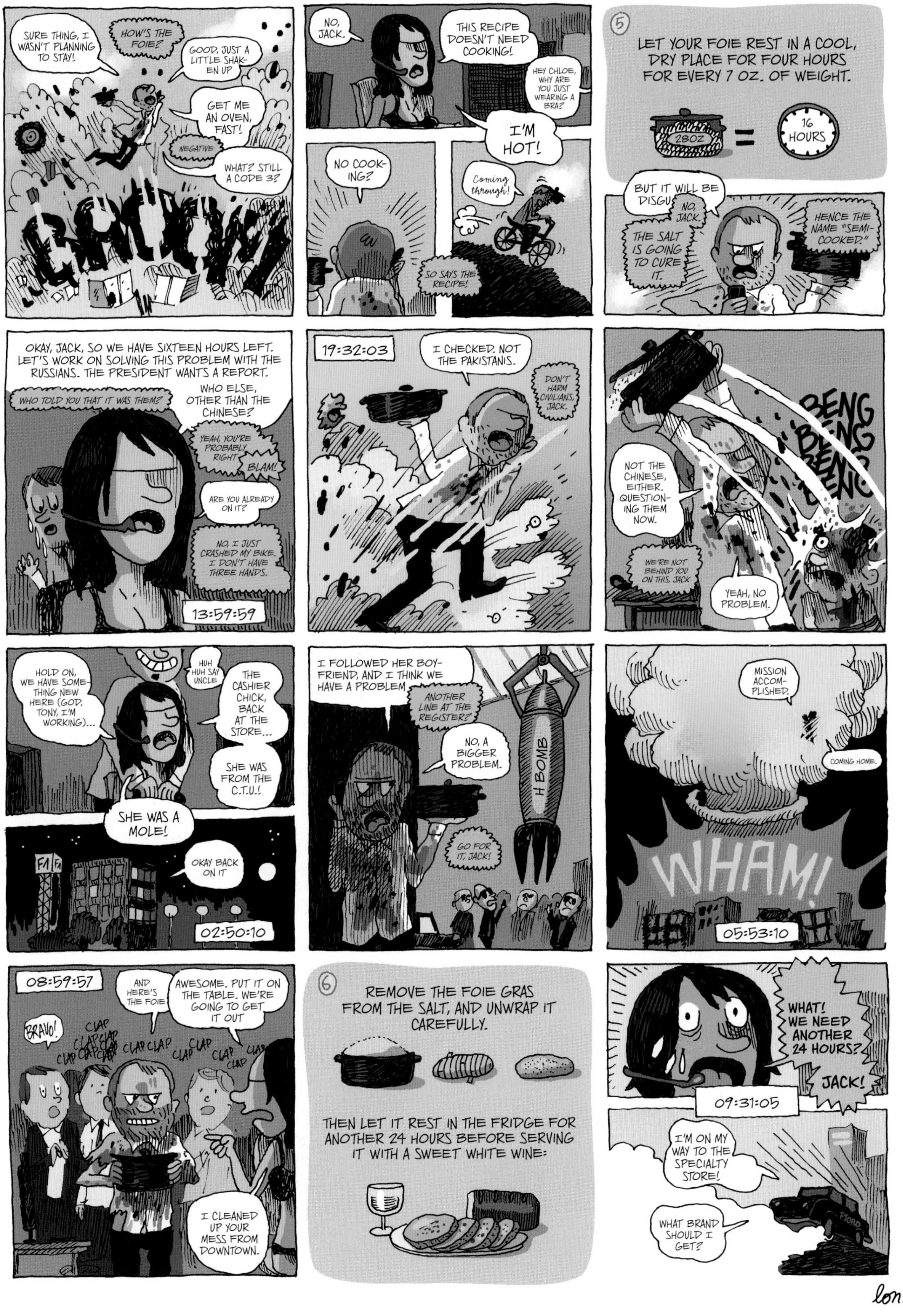
SURE THING, I WASN'T PLANNING TO STAY!
HOW'S THE FOIE?
GOOD, JUST A LITTLE SHAKEN UP
GET ME AN OVEN, FAST!
NEGATIVE
WHAT? STILL A CODE 3?
NO, JACK.
THIS RECIPE DOESN'T NEED COOKING!
HEY CHLOE, WHY ARE YOU JUST WEARING A BRA?
I'M HOT!
NO COOKING?
SO SAYS THE RECIPE!
Coming through!
5
LET YOUR FOIE REST IN A COOL, DRY PLACE FOR FOUR HOURS FOR EVERY 7 OZ. OF WEIGHT.
28OZ
=
16 HOURS
BUT IT WILL BE DISGU
NO, JACK.
THE SALT IS GOING TO CURE IT.
HENCE THE NAME "SEMI-COOKED."
OKAY, JACK, SO WE HAVE SIXTEEN HOURS LEFT. LET'S WORK ON SOLVING THIS PROBLEM WITH THE RUSSIANS. THE PRESIDENT WANTS A REPORT.
WHO TOLD YOU THAT IT WAS THEM?
WHO ELSE, OTHER THAN THE CHINESE?
YEAH, YOU'RE PROBABLY RIGHT
BLAM!
ARE YOU ALREADY ON IT?
NO, I JUST CRASHED MY BIKE. I DON'T HAVE THREE HANDS.
13:59:59
19:32:03
I CHECKED. NOT THE PAKISTANIS.
DON'T HARM CIVILIANS, JACK.
BENG BENG BENG BENG
NOT THE CHINESE, EITHER. QUESTIONING THEM NOW.
WE'RE NOT BEHIND YOU ON THIS, JACK
YEAH, NO PROBLEM.
HOLD ON, WE HAVE SOMETHING NEW HERE (GOD, TONY, I'M WORKING)...
HUH HUH SAY UNCLE
THE CASHIER CHICK, BACK AT THE STORE...
SHE WAS FROM THE C.T.U.!
SHE WAS A MOLE!
OKAY BACK ON IT
02:50:10
I FOLLOWED HER BOYFRIEND, AND I THINK WE HAVE A PROBLEM
ANOTHER LINE AT THE REGISTER?
NO, A BIGGER PROBLEM.
H BOMB
GO FOR IT, JACK!
MISSION ACCOMPLISHED.
COMING HOME.
WHAM!
05:53:10
08:59:57
AND HERE'S THE FOIE
AWESOME. PUT IT ON THE TABLE. WE'RE GOING TO GET IT OUT
BRAVO!
CLAP CLAP CLAP CLAP CLAP CLAP CLAP CLAP CLAP CLAP CLAP CLAP
I CLEANED UP YOUR MESS FROM DOWNTOWN.
6
REMOVE THE FOIE GRAS FROM THE SALT, AND UNWRAP IT CAREFULLY.
THEN LET IT REST IN THE FRIDGE FOR ANOTHER 24 HOURS BEFORE SERVING IT WITH A SWEET WHITE WINE:
WHAT! WE NEED ANOTHER 24 HOURS?
JACK!
09:31:05
I'M ON MY WAY TO THE SPECIALTY STORE!
WHAT BRAND SHOULD I GET?
lon.

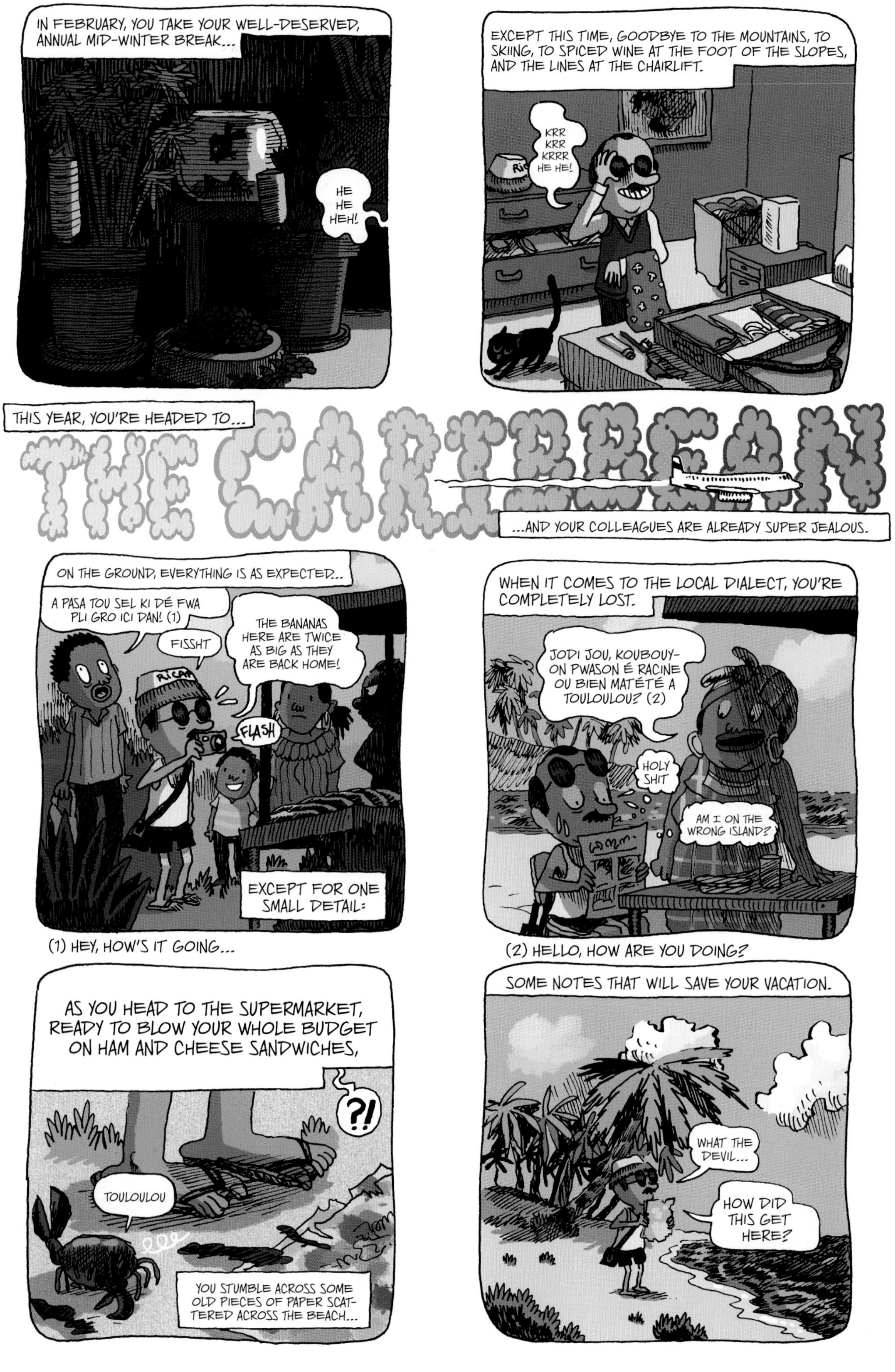
IN FEBRUARY, YOU TAKE YOUR WELL-DESERVED, ANNUAL MID-WINTER BREAK...
HE HE HEH!
EXCEPT THIS TIME, GOODBYE TO THE MOUNTAINS, TO SKIING, TO SPICED WINE AT THE FOOT OF THE SLOPES, AND THE LINES AT THE CHAIRLIFT.
KRR KRR KRRR HE HE!
THIS YEAR, YOU'RE HEADED TO...
THE CARIBBEAN
...AND YOUR COLLEAGUES ARE ALREADY SUPER JEALOUS.
ON THE GROUND, EVERYTHING IS AS EXPECTED...
A PASA TOU SEL KI DÉ FWA PLI GRO ICI DAN! (1)
FISSHT
THE BANANAS HERE ARE TWICE AS BIG AS THEY ARE BACK HOME!
FLASH
EXCEPT FOR ONE SMALL DETAIL:
(1) HEY, HOW'S IT GOING...
WHEN IT COMES TO THE LOCAL DIALECT, YOU'RE COMPLETELY LOST.
JODI JOU, KOUBOUY-ON PWASON É RACINE OU BIEN MATÉTÉ A TOULOULOU? (2)
HOLY SHIT
AM I ON THE WRONG ISLAND?
(2) HELLO, HOW ARE YOU DOING?
AS YOU HEAD TO THE SUPERMARKET, READY TO BLOW YOUR WHOLE BUDGET ON HAM AND CHEESE SANDWICHES,
?!
TOULOULOU
YOU STUMBLE ACROSS SOME OLD PIECES OF PAPER SCATTERED ACROSS THE BEACH...
SOME NOTES THAT WILL SAVE YOUR VACATION.
WHAT THE DEVIL...
HOW DID THIS GET HERE?

July 17th, 187[illegible]: Today is the 785th day on the island. The gangrene has gained ground, and I fear I will have to undergo a new amputation. I do not think any boats will pass by from here on out, as it is the rainy season and with it, my hopes vanish as quickly as the rum punch goes down.

Marie-Aimée: a new nurse who arrived this morning at the clinic converses with me in a charming manner. She taught me how to recognize some of the local cuisine that I describe below, so that one day this list may be of service to other ~~[illegible]~~ exploring this beautiful country.

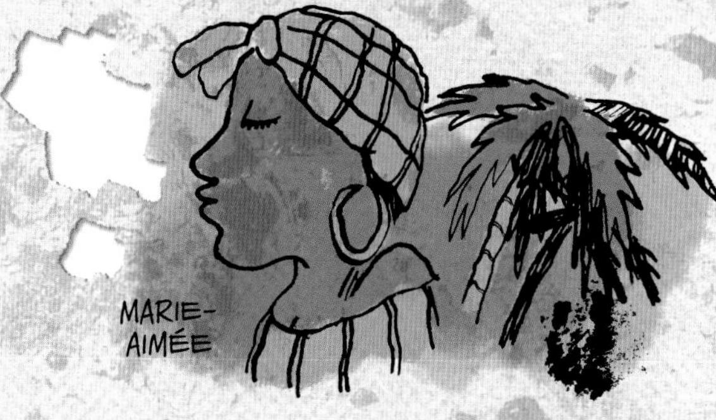
MARIE-AIMÉE

SELECTED GUIDE
TO FRENCH CARIBBEAN FOOD FOR THE MODERN ADVENTURER

BY PROFESSOR ALEXIS HARLAINE 1831-?

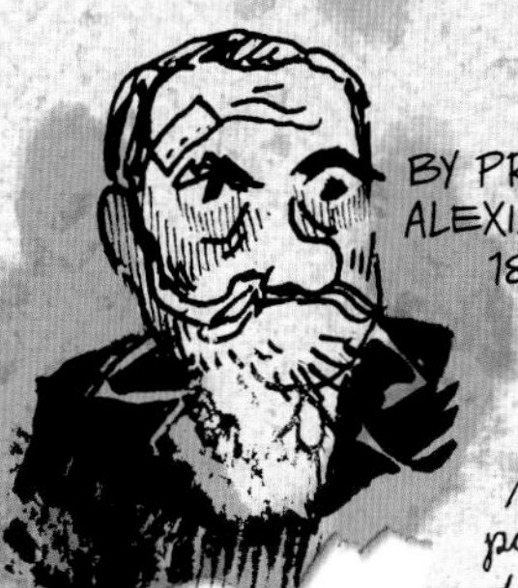

Self-portrait, day 185

(in alphabetical order)

Blaff

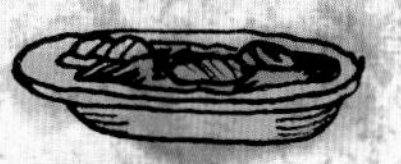

A stock made of fish or crawfish

Bélélé

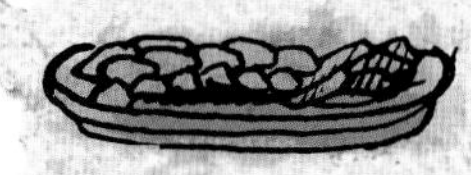

A curious name for a dish of tripe and "ti-nain" that requires several hours of preparation and cooking

Bois-Bandé

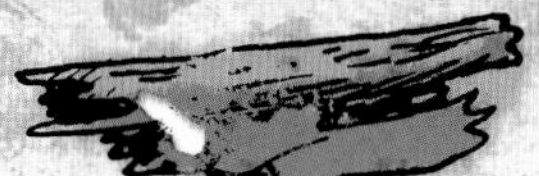

Tree bark that is served with rum. Marie-Aimée seemed to blush when talking about the qualities of this bark

Boquite

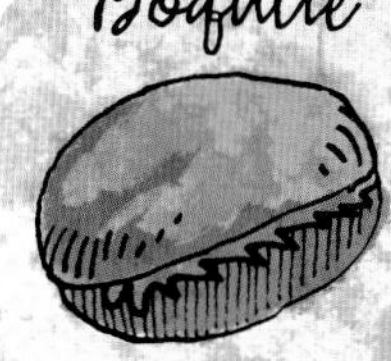

Savory fritters served with a variety of garnishes (on the mainland, the young Turkish vagabonds call it "rebab").

Calalou

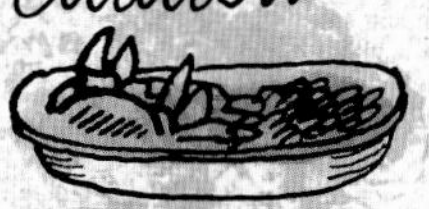

Shown here with crab, a dish served at Easter made with "madère" leaves

Chatrou

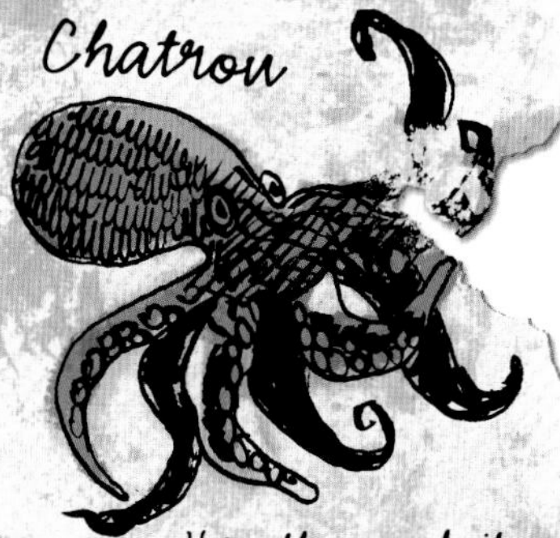

Here, they cook it in its own juices! (Drawing of an octopus)

Chadek

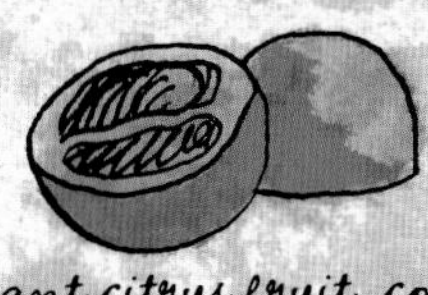

Giant citrus fruit, cousin of the grapefruit

Chaudeau

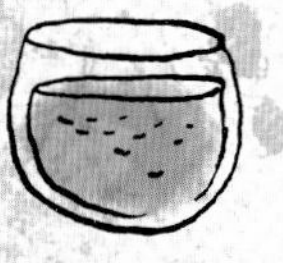

Dessert made with milk, eggs, and spices, served on special occasions

Chiquetaille de morue

Desalted cod, grilled with an onion-lemon sauce

Christophines or "chayottes"

Fruit that tastes like zucchini or cucumber

C.R.S.

A "ti punch" cocktail made of lemon ("citron," in French), rum, and sugar. For men (or for boosting the morale of the mainland police)

Variation: décollage: without lemon or sugar. The locals drink it before working the fields

Colombo (of young goat)

Traditional dish whose name comes from the spice used in the cooking

Corossol

Giant fruit whose velvety flesh resembles cooked cod

Dombrés

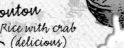

Dough balls served with a specific dish (often "ouassous" [reference 1], red beans, and shrimp)

Doucelettes

Rectangular sweets made from coconut milk. I get the children to leave my room by throwing them some as far as I can.

It also works with Floup©, a dessert kind of like a Freeze Pop

→

Also with quénettes. I made them run, the little rascals, with this acidic fruit that they love!

Giraumon (winter squash)

Gombos (≠ gambas)

Sticky vegetable from the cucumber family, usually eaten in a salad.

Lambi

A huge shellfish cooked in its own juices (the locals pound this poor creature of God in order to tenderize it).

Madère or taro

Root with black, irritating skin, a kind of manioc. I sculpted one into a friend that I talk to from time to time. His name is Wilson.

Matété ou matoutou

Rice with crab (delicious)

Féroce

A dish prepared from avocado, manioc flour, cod, and chili pepper

Touloulou

Red earth crab that cries "touloulou" as it runs away when you approach

Pisquettes

Small fish marinated in garlic and lemon juice and prepared in balls

Souskaï

A spicy salad of unripe fruit (mango, avocado…)

Ti-nains

Strange insult to people of smaller stature, also referring to green bananas that are eaten as legumes

Reference 1: ouassous (crawfish)

Tourments d'amour

A cake filled with a variety of jams, coconut, banana, or guava

lon.

SELECT GIFT GUIDE FOR FOODIES

Oh!

A chaffing dish for mulled wine!

Can this also work for soup?

A BIALETTI ESPRESSO MAKER: A DURABLE PIECE, MUCH PRETTIER THAN A NESPRESSO©, THAT, UNLIKE THAT CONTRAPTION, MAKES VERY GOOD COFFEE.

MINUSCULES EXTASES BY D. GROZDANOVITCH (NIL PUBLICATIONS): A LITTLE BOOK FULL OF VERY WELL-WRITTEN SHORT STORIES (IN FRENCH) THAT WILL MAKE YOUR MOUTH WATER.

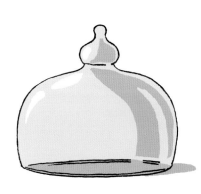

A GLASS DOME: FOR COVERING CAKES, PIES, OR AN ASSORTMENT OF CUCURBITACEAE

THE SPLENDID TABLE: RECIPES FROM EMILIA-ROMAGNA, THE HEARTLAND OF NORTHERN ITALIAN FOOD BY LYNNE ROSSETTO KASPER (WILLIAM MORROW COOKBOOKS). A THOROUGH, GO-TO KITCHEN STAPLE, EVEN TWENTY-FIVE YEARS AFTER ITS PUBLICATION.

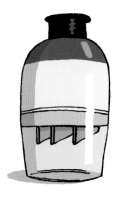

A SLAP SHOP©-STYLE CHOPPER: OKAY, SO IT CHOPS UP VEGETABLES EVERY WHICH WAY, BUT IT'S LIGHTENING FAST, AND IT MAKES YOU FEEL LIKE YOU'RE ON A GAME SHOW IN YOUR OWN KITCHEN.

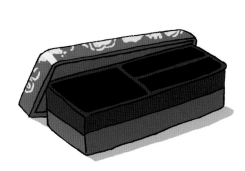

A BENTO BOX: IT'S HIP, IT'S CUTE, AND SOMETIMES EVEN PRETTY. GREAT FOR ORGANIZING YOUR LUNCH (PB&J NOT INCLUDED).

A FISH SCALER: PRACTICAL FOR WHEN YOU FORGET TO ASK YOUR FISH-MONGER TO DO THE DIRTY WORK FOR YOU, WHICH HE NOTICED BUT DID NOT MENTION AS YOU WERE LEAVING.

A SCALE: INDISPENSABLE IN THE KITCHEN

Makes an excellent gift

CANNED GOODS FROM CANNED JUNK. BECAUSE HAVING SOME CANNED ARMADILLO ON THE HALF SHELL OR CREAMED POSSUM IS PRETTY FUNNY AND A SURE CONVERSATION STARTER!

A TEMPERED GLASS CUTTING BOARD: MULTIPURPOSE, THIS BOARD IS GOOD FOR CUTTING STUFF (OBVIOUSLY). IT CAN ALSO BE USED AS A TRIVET FOR HOT PANS OR FOR DISPLAYING TABLE DECORATIONS.

A MORTAR AND PESTLE: IN WOOD OR STONE (BUT YOU PAY MORE FOR THE LATTER). USEFUL BUT NOT SOMETHING YOU CAN'T LIVE WITHOUT.

A MICROPLANE© GRATER: FOR ZESTING AND GRATING PRETTY MUCH EVERYTHING, INCLUDING YOUR FINGERS. I'D HAVE A HARD TIME GIVING MINE UP.

A NUTMEG MILL: A KITCHEN TOOL THAT I DON'T USE MUCH BUT THAT BRINGS ME JOY EACH TIME I REMEMBER HOW SHITTY IT IS TO GRATE NUTMEG BY HAND.

A SHARP KNIFE: I KNOW IT SOUNDS STUPID, BUT A BEAUTIFUL NEW KNIFE IS ALWAYS GREAT, EVEN WHEN YOU ALREADY HAVE A DRAWERFUL OF UNSHARPENED OTHERS.

A SPICE AND HERB INFUSER: GOOD FOR NOT LOSING THE BAY LEAF IN YOUR RATATOUILLE OR THE CLOVES IN A POT-AU-FEU. PLUS, IT LOOKS LIKE A CLOWN'S NOSE (WASH THOROUGHLY BEFORE AND AFTER USING).

1001
SAVEURS

1001 FOODS YOU MUST TASTE BEFORE YOU DIE (UNIVERSE PUBLISHING): A HUGE BOOK THAT PROVOKES THE NEED TO VERIFY EVERYTHING YOU'VE ALREADY EATEN AND EVERYTHING THAT YOU HAVE YET TO TRY. IDEAL FOR THE BATHROOM, FOR READING AND REREADING.

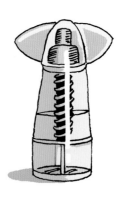

A GARLIC MILL: BECAUSE YOU CAN NO LONGER FIND ONE ANYWHERE, YET IT IS EXCELLENT FOR SHAVING GARLIC, PARMESAN, CHOCOLATE, ETC.

A PINEAPPLE SLICER: I DIDN'T BELIEVE THAT IT WOULD WORK, BUT IT SLICES AND PEELS PINEAPPLES WITHOUT TOO MUCH WASTE. NO MORE EXCUSES FOR BUYING MUSHY PINEAPPLE IN CANS.

A TAGINE POT: STEER CLEAR OF THE ORNAMENTAL KNICK-KNACKS. GET ONE THAT'S ENAMELED EARTHENWARE: EVEN IT DOESN'T COST AN ARM AND A LEG.

A STAUB© DUTCH OVEN: IT'S A LITTLE EXPENSIVE, BUT WHATEVER. YOUR CHILDREN WILL GIVE IT TO THEIR CHILDREN, AND IT MAKES YOU WANT TO COOK.

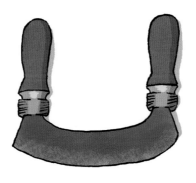

A WINE DECANTER: FOR AERATING, DECANTING, EVEN SERVING. CLASSY FOR CHEAP.

A DOUBLE BLADE MEZZALUNA OR CRESCENT CHOPPER: IT REMINDS ME OF MY CHILDHOOD AND WAS ONE OF THE FIRST KITCHEN TOOLS I BOUGHT FOR MY OWN KITCHEN. I DON'T USE IT MUCH, BUT IT HANGS ON MY WALL AND BRINGS BACK GOOD MEMORIES.

la cuisine japonaise

JAPANESE CUISINE: THE TRADITIONS, TECHNIQUES, INGREDIENTS, AND RECIPES BY E. KAZUKO (SOUTHWATER PUBLISHING). A THOROUGH INTRODUCTION TO JAPANESE COOKING AND CULTURE.

A DIGITAL THERMOMETER: WHEN I DIDN'T HAVE ONE, I GOT ALONG JUST FINE, BUT NOW I USE IT WITH EVERYTHING EXCEPT GRILLED CHEESE SANDWICHES.

EN CUISINE AVEC
ALAIN PASSARD

IN THE KITCHEN WITH ALAIN PASSARD (CHRONICLE BOOKS): BACKSTAGE WITH A MASTER CHEF, DRAWN BY CHRISTOPHE BLAIN... ONE OF MY FAVORITE COMICS OF 2011.

AN ASSORTMENT OF CANNED SARDINES FROM LA BELLE-ILOISE: WHETHER OR NOT YOU'RE AN AVOWED PUXISARDIONPHILE, THESE SARDINES ARE GOOD QUALITY AND REASONABLY PRICED.

Makes an excellent gift

A COPPER SAUCEPAN: BECAUSE COOKING WITH ONE IS PRACTICAL, BECAUSE COPPER EVENLY DISTRIBUTES HEAT, BECAUSE IT'S BEAUTIFUL.

de BUYER

A MANUAL EXTRACTOR FROM DE BUYER: DIFFERENT THAN A CLASSIC CORER, THIS ONE HAS A DETACHABLE HOOK THAT KEEPS YOU FROM CUTTING ALL THE WAY THROUGH YOUR FOOD. COMES WITH A BUILT-IN RULER.

HIDDEN ANIMAL TEACUPS BY IMM LIVING: GREAT IDEA TO HIDE ANIMALS IN PORCELAIN CUPS, WITH A BEAUTIFUL EFFECT ON YOUR GUESTS.

THE BROKEASS GOURMET COOKBOOK BY GABI MOSKOWITZ: BECAUSE SHE ALSO HAS A BLOG AND TEACHES YOU HOW TO LIVE WELL FOR CHEAP.

YU-ZEN WASHI TEA CANISTERS BY KOTODO: 90 DIFFERENT DESIGNS AND 16 DIFFERENT SIZES MEANS YOU CAN STORE YOUR TEA PROPERLY, FOR ONCE.

AN APPLE PEELER: I ALWAYS THOUGHT THAT THIS GADGET WAS JUST A CHEAP TRICK. BUT NOW I OWN ONE, AND IT WORKS REALLY WELL, ESPECIALLY WHEN THE APPLES ARE AROUND THE SAME SIZE.

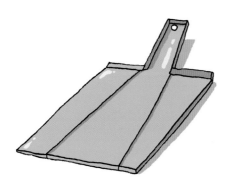

A FLEXIBLE CUTTING BOARD: PRETTY UGLY BUT VERY PRACTICAL FOR COLLECTING JUICES FROM A ROAST OR WHEN DUMPING DICED ONIONS INTO A CONTAINER WITHOUT GETTING THEM EVERYWHERE.

LILYBIRD SOY SAUCE CONTAINER BY ALESSI: THIS OBJECT IS RATHER EXPENSIVE, EASY TO LIVE WITHOUT, AND COMPLETELY ADORABLE. THEREFORE, PERFECT FOR SHOWING OFF ON YOUR TABLE.

AN EGG CRACKER: BECAUSE HAVING TO CHIP THE SHELL OFF YOUR HARD-BOILED EGG WITH A SPOON JUST SPOILS BRUNCH.

lon.

Carbonara Inspection Office

ᦁ membership card ᦁ

Name............. *Brayden*

Last Name........ *Smith*

Date of birth..... *February 3 1991*

Signature *SMKAUS*

Membership No: 1238 456 8421

Table of Recipes

Appetizers

Entrees

Desserts

Index

L

leeks, 51
Lego, 65
lemon, 51, 106, 109
lightsaber, 72

M

mandonline*, 60
monkfish, 50-51
mont d'or, 110

N

nutmeg, 72, 118

O

onion, 14, 17, 18, 76, 79, 84-85, 109
oysters, 104-107

P-Q

pancetta, 19, 79, 81
parmesan, 15, 21, 45, 81
parsley (flat), 21
pasta, 7, 76-82
peas, 17
pecorino, 45, 81
pesto, 45
piano whisk, 94
pine nuts, 45
potatoes, 27, 110
puxisardinophilia, 98-99
Queen Elizabeth*, 59

R

rabbit, 19

refrigerator, 43, 79
reindeer, 38
restaurant, 25, 29, 30, 32, 34-36, 38
rice, 20, 51
ricotta, 53
risotto, 14-15, 85
rollmops, 27, 38
rosemary, 43, 112
roux*, 103

S

sage, 19, 43, 112
salmon, 27, 29, 36, 38, 89-90, 109
salsify, 21
sardines, 38, 98-99, 119
shallots, 51, 74, 84-85, 106
shrimp, 27, 28, 29
skimming*, 40
spaghetti squash, 71-82
spider*, 86
spinach, 18, 20, 100
Sweden (gastronomy of), 27-29, 32, 34, 38
sweet cream, 27
soy sauce, 90

T-Z

tête de moine*, 68
thyme, 43, 74
tomato, 53
trout, 43-44
walnuts, 84-85

*Pépé Roni's Good Advice

Acknowledgements

First, thank you to the readers of my blog and of the previous volume, as well as the bookstores that support my work. You make me want to continue.

Next, to Nicolas, Olivier, Caroline, Muriel, Sandrine, and Thierry at Gallimard. You're like a family, and I'm honored to work with you.

That means a lot.

Thanks also to the team at Monde.fr, who has put up with me for a long time now.

Kolik Publishers knows how to receive. Josefin and Fabian are delightful, and I will never forget Kristiina. Régis and Jean-Yves almost made me like beer for real. Elvira, Dominique, and François-Régis are excellent hosts. Catherine knows how to take good pictures but also write like a teenager. Floriana is Italian, obviously. Arlène knows the French Caribbean like the back of her hand and doesn't have an accent. Florian knows how to open an oyster and more. Florian (the other one) continually brings his precious contributions to my work. Céline is still here for sorting things out in moments of panic. My parents are the best.

Talented authors generously contributed their original stories to my blog: Anne Montel and Loïc Clément, Daniel Blancou, Dorothée de Monfreid, Frederik Peeters, Gally, Gilles Rochier, Guillaume Plantevin, Greg Shaw, Hervé Bourhis, Lison Bernet, Leslie Plée, Louis-Bertrand Devaud, Martin Vidberg, Mathias Martin, Nancy Peña, Pochep, Terreur Graphique, Thibaut Soulcié, Un et deux.

I wish I could make all of you a good cup of a coffee right now; we still can't find a garlic mill anywhere.

Thank you.

About the Author

Guillaume Long was born in 1977 in Geneva, the land of chocolate and cheese. From an early age, he was passionate about cooking and observed his mother in the kitchen. (Though that did not mean his first attempt at bread was well-received.) Long graduated from the fine arts of Saint-Etienne in visual communication in 2002 and won the Töpffer Prize for his comic *The Sardines Are Cooked.* Since 2009, this fine gourmet is a happy man married to humor, cooking, and comics. Long runs the gastronomic blog hosted by LeMonde.fr cleverly entitled *To Drink and To Eat.*